After the Eagles Landed

After the Eagles Landed

The Yemenites of Israel

Herbert S. Lewis

Westview Press
BOULDER, SAN FRANCISCO, & LONDON

This Westview softcover edition is printed on acid-free paper and bound in library-quality, coated covers that carry the highest rating of the National Association of State Textbook Administrators, in consultation with the Association of American Publishers and the Book Manufacturers' Institute.

Copyright © 1989 by Westview Press, Inc.

Published in 1989 in the United States of America by Westview Press, Inc., 5500 Central Avenue, Boulder, Colorado 80301, and in the United Kingdom by Westview Press, Inc., 13 Brunswick Centre, London WC1N 1AF, England

Library of Congress Cataloging-in-Publication Data
Lewis, Herbert S.
   After the eagles landed : the Yemenites of Israel / Herbert S. Lewis.
      p.   cm.
   Includes bibliographical references.
   ISBN 0-8133-7803-6
   1. Jews, Yemenite—Israel. 2. Jews—Yemen. 3. Immigrants—Israel. 4. Israel—Ethnic relations. 5. Yemen—Ethnic relations.
I. Title.
DS113.8.Y4L49   1989
305.8'92405332—dc20   89-24877
                                                                          CIP

Printed and bound in the United States of America

⊙ The paper used in this publication meets the requirements of the American National Standard for Permanence of Paper for Printed Library Materials Z39.48-1984.

10   9   8   7   6   5   4   3   2   1

For Marcia, Tammy, Paula, and Josh

"You have seen what I did to the Egyptians,
and how I bore you on wings of eagles
and brought you to myself."

Exodus, 19:4

Contents

Preface

I initially prepared this book for publication in 1985, but unfortunately, the firm that was to publish it went out of business. While submitting the manuscript for publication elsewhere, I continued to gather more material, following developments in the lives of the people of Kiryat Eliahu. Above all, I spent three months there during the summer of 1987, inquiring into the careers, marriages, and attitudes of the first generation of those born in Israel. It was not possible for me to rewrite the whole book to accommodate the new material. Instead, I have added a Postscript discussing recent changes, as well as additional footnotes and occasional references to newer information in the text itself. I hope that this will not prove confusing to the reader.

The city that I call Kiryat Eliahu was chosen as the site for this research after an extensive survey. I sought a heterogeneous community since I had intended to investigate such topics as cultural change and continuity, the similarities and differences in adaptation to Israel of two or more ethnic groups, and questions of integration and inter-ethnic relations. I purposely avoided such homogeneous places as the cooperative agricultural villages (*moshavim*), the virtually all-Yemenite town of Rosh Ha'Ayin, and development towns like Netivot or Ma'alot, whose inhabitants are overwhelmingly of Moroccan origin. Kiryat Eliahu suited my needs very well, for its people are derived in almost equal numbers from Europe, on the one hand, and Africa and Asia on the other. There are substantial numbers of people from Morocco, Poland, Romania, Yemen, Egypt, Turkey, Iraq, and the Soviet Union.

Kiryat Eliahu is located near a major industrial center and a large city, so its people have a variety of opportunities available to them for work, recreation, and education. This suited the requirements of my research because I wanted to avoid a setting with few options and restricted choices. But, as a city of 23,000, it was not as daunting or as difficult to study as a section of Tel Aviv or the larger cities such as Netanya or Petah Tikva. Furthermore, it looked like a pleasant place to live for two years with my wife and three children, then aged thirteen, ten, and six.

My intention was to study ethnicity among the Jews of this city, based on their countries of origin. I was interested in ethnicity in all of its aspects: social, cultural, political, and ideological, and I hoped to study a number of different groups in order to compare their reactions, adaptations, and the significance of ethnicity among them. Above all, I thought I would compare Yemenites and Moroccan Jews. In the event, while I did learn a great deal about the members of the Moroccan community, I found myself more and more deeply involved with the Yemenites, and this book reflects that part of my research.

A certain amount of my time was devoted to learning about the city and all of its peoples, and this was done through such means as: checking records from the municipality, the schools, the social welfare office, the government rental agency (Ami-Gur), the chief rabbis, etc.; interviewing teachers, public health nurses, social workers, municipal officials; accompanying workers from the rental agency on their rounds, visiting families; observing the work of the community center; and simply living in this small city for two years with my family, walking the streets, using its shops and services, going to school events and generally observing, talking to people, and participating in a wide variety of activities. I attended political functions such as party rallies for the 1977 election and the celebration of the upgrading of Kiryat Eliahu's political status from a "local council" to a "municipality." I observed festivals and ceremonials (Purim, Shavuot, and Lag b'Omer; Independence Day and the Day of Remembrance, for example) and went to concerts, movies, and plays. And I attended the synagogue services of many of the city's numerous ethnic communities.

After almost two years of research, in contrast to my usual modus operandi, I ventured to administer a questionnaire to the tenth and eleventh grade students of the two high schools. Some limited use is made of the results in Chapter 7. In my follow-up research in June–August 1987 I carried out many open-ended interviews with young couples and conducted an extensive survey of the education, residence, occupations, marriages, and attitudes of people between the ages of twenty and forty.

Early in our stay I was fortunate to gain entree to the Yemenite community, above all through my meeting and subsequent close friendship with Eli Mlihi, a social worker on the staff of the community center. Although a newcomer to the city himself, Eli lived in the Yemenite section of town, worshipped in its synagogues, and rapidly came to know his neighbors. He generously took me along on his work, his worship, and his friendships. My networks grew rapidly and I was soon able to visit, hang around, interview, and participate in many activities, especially in the synagogues and at the events associated with the sabbath and with weddings. I became very familiar with the Yemenite community (of about 1,200 people) and many of them got to know me as well. Although I spent a great deal of time in synagogues and celebrations in the company of men, I had many contacts and discussions with middle-aged and younger women as well. Much interviewing was done in homes, in family contexts, and women were often as outspoken as the men.

Through the Yemenites of Kiryat Eliahu, and through Eli and Shoshana Mlihi, I was able to meet Yemenite Jews in other parts of Israel. They were kind enough to refer me to others or to take me with them sometimes on their visits to relatives living elsewhere. Over the years I have made friends with Yemenites all over the country who have introduced me to their families and invited me to their synagogues, their homes, and their celebrations, spoken to me about their communities, given me the benefit of their professional experience, as teachers, social workers, etc. And Ovadiah Ben-Shalom, guiding spirit and chairman of a leading Yemenite cultural organization, has always encouraged my participation in that group's many events. In this way I have extended my own network and range of experience even more widely.

Finally, in this day of "reflexive anthropology" some words about my own background may be in order. In contrast to most anthropologists who have done fieldwork in Israel, I did not begin specializing in this area. Although I started following events and developments in Israel since before it was Israel (in 1945, when I was eleven years old), my research took me first to the West Indies (1955, 1956) and then to Ethiopia (1958-60, 1965-66), where I studied other peoples and other problems in very different settings. In 1969 my family and I lived in Jerusalem for a year while I taught anthropology and African Studies at the Hebrew University, improved my knowledge of the Hebrew language, and began surveying Israeli communities and planning my research.

Although I am Jewish by background, I was not raised in the orthodox religious tradition. To some extent I had to learn to participate in the Yemenite Jewish religious activities as I would have had to learn to participate in any strange cultural setting. (Of course, the Oromo of Ethiopia never expected me to participate in their religious worship, whereas it was appropriate and even pleasing to me, as well as useful, to join these fellow Jews in their services.) I participated in ritual events, but I never tried to learn enough to become really skilled to the point, for instance, of reading my own Torah portion in the Yemenite manner. (Moshe Shokeid offers an interesting account of his dilemmas as a non-religious native-born Israeli doing research among orthodox Moroccan Jews. See "Involvement Rather than Spectacle in Fieldwork," in Shlomo Deshen and Moshe Shokeid, *The Predicament of Homecoming*. Ithaca: Cornell University Press, 1974.) For me, some members of the older generation could be almost as "exotic" as older Oromo in Ethiopia, and trying to understand them required the same attempt to suspend my ethnocentrism as trying to understand Oromo. With the younger generation, those educated in Israel, there was the necessity to guard against the ethnocentrism that leads one to "naturally" assume that people who dress like oneself and work in offices and drive cars, who are, in short, "middle class," are "just like me." This may not be the case. It takes an effort to see beyond the similarities and be aware of the subtle differences.

While I do not necessarily share all of the beliefs and values of the people I present here, and might disagree on political issues with many of them, the respect that I have for them—for their history and traditions, their values, their accomplishments—will be clear. Indeed, at least one reviewer of the manuscript seems to have been troubled by my evident appreciation. Perhaps I run the risk of seeming to be guilty of boosterism and endorsing the positive "stereotypes" of the Yemenites in Israel. As the reader will discover, I believe that this "stereotype" is based on perceptions that are not out of line with reality and I think that I have the material to support this contention. Two other critics were troubled by my claim that the Yemenites, members of an "oriental" community, have been successfully upwardly mobile in a rather short time. They prefer to see Israel as a land of structured inequality where such a thing is impossible. To them the work also seems like a piece of boosterism, this time on behalf of Israel. I hope that readers who hold this position will consider the evidence that is presented below and perhaps modify their views accordingly.

Herbert S. Lewis

Acknowledgments

This study originated in research carried out in the Israeli city called here Kiryat Eliahu from September 1975 through June 1977. But the work neither began nor ended on those dates. I had been concerned with Israel and its peoples for many years before my family and I moved into this community, and since then I have visited Israel and Kiryat Eliahu almost every year, trying to keep up with continuing developments. I spent three more months in the community in 1987, gathering material on changes and on the cohort that came of age after 1977. The list of people I must thank and whose contributions I must acknowledge is, therefore, a very long one. It includes, in addition to the normal list of colleagues, friends, and informants, many people met casually over the years in various places who have given me ideas, information, criticism, or contacts. I shall try to thank as many of these as I can, but I fear that some will escape my best efforts at recall.

My list begins with several people who showed me Israeli communities they knew and shared their knowledge with me. These include Ya'acov Avitsuk, teacher and folklorist of Kiryat Malakhi, and Frances Salzberg, social work teacher, then of Ashkelon. David Solomoniko introduced me to several communities within his jurisdiction as social scientist for the Settlement Department of the Jewish Agency. It was Professor Dov Noy who directed me to these people in 1969-70.

Dr. Mishael Maswari Caspi of the University of California, Santa Cruz, helped introduce me to the Yemenites of Kiryat Eliahu. It was a treat and an education to walk with him through the Yemenite neighborhood and observe his enthusiasm and his knowledge of and love for his people.

To Eli Mlihi, once of Tel Aviv, now living in Ḥadera, I owe more than I can possibly convey. He gave, unstintingly, assistance, guidance, friendship, and the benefit of his observations, ideas, and insights for two years and on each subsequent occasion when we have been together. The friendship and hospitality of Eli and Shoshana Mlihi and their

children, and the Aryeh family of Geulei Teyman, were a vital part
of my family's life in Israel for those two years and have been since.

In the academic world I have many debts. I must thank: Harvey
Goldberg, Moshe Shokeid, Shlomo Deshen, Henry Rosenfeld, Phyllis
Palgi, Alex Weingrod, Judah Matras, Hagit Matras, Yael Katzir, Vivian
Klaff, Emanuel Marx, Sammy Smooha, Vered Kraus, Yossi Shavit,
Amir Ben-Porat, Lisa Gilad, Jack Habib, Judith Alter, Joanna G. Harris,
Don Handelman, Eliezer Ben-Rafael, Laurence Loeb, Erik Cohen, Elihu
Katz, Awraham Zloczower, Yosef Tobi, Yoel Horowitz, Arnold Lewis,
Shlomo Swirski, Gavrush Nechushtan, Dorothy Willner, Walter Zenner,
Miriam Dembo, Haim Hazan, Jeff Halper, Percy Cohen, Yehuda Nini,
S. D. Goitein, Yehuda Ratzaby; and John A. Armstrong, Michael V. Fox,
Gilad Morahg, and Jack Kugelmass of the University of Wisconsin. They
all offered ideas and advice of one sort or another. They cannot, of
course, be held accountable for any of the errors which may appear in
the book, especially since some of them will certainly disagree with key
portions of it.

There are several members of the Yemenite community beyond Kiryat
Eliahu whose help I would also like to acknowledge. Ovadiah Ben-
Shalom of the *Aguda* (Association for Society and Culture in Israel)
was always very helpful and anxious that the culture and heritage of his
people be understood and propagated. I had worthwhile discussions with
Rabbi Ratson Arusi, Yisrael Vahab, and Ephraim Ya'acov. Shalom Ben-
Zekhariah of Netanya and Meir and Batya Malakhi of Jerusalem offered
friendship and information. Nissim B. Gamlieli of Ramle, Bezalel Tabib
of Arad, and Mazal Shama of Givat Koah all opened their homes and
gave support.

The research for the book was made possible by a grant from
the National Science Foundation, while the University of Wisconsin
Graduate School provided support for a summer and a semester,
for additional research and writing. The Fulbright Scholar Program
supported three more months of research during the summer of 1987,
and three foundations helped provide a partial subvention for publication.
They are: Dolores Kohl Education Foundation (Dolores Kohl Solovy,
President); the Jerusalem Center for Anthropological Studies (Edgar
E. Siskin, President); and the Wisconsin Society for Jewish Learning
(Lisa Hiller, Executive Director). Many thanks to them, as well as to
Professor John Nitti of the University of Wisconsin, who very generously
gave much needed advice on the preparation of the manuscript for

publication. Peter Kracht and Lynn Arts of Westview Press and John O'Neill of the University of Wisconsin have also been very helpful in the production of the book.

Professor Conrad Arensberg's lectures at Columbia University in the mid-1950's first suggested this topic to me, alerted me to the persistence of culture, and encouraged me to doubt the conventional wisdom of the time. I also want to thank my fellow graduate students and friends of those days—and still today: Sidney Greenfield, Morton Klass, and Arnold Strickon. Arnie Strickon has not only contributed through years of discussion and shared teaching on ethnicity, but he also carefully read the first draft of the book and made many suggestions for significant changes and additions.

Unfortunately, the *many* people of Kiryat Eliahu to whom I owe an enormous debt must remain nameless here. To name them would divulge the identity of the actual city, in contravention of a principal canon of Israeli community studies. The actual list would have to include people of all ethnic backgrounds, including the mayor, the head of the tax department of the municipality, teachers, nurses, social workers, and the team at Ami-Gur. I hope all will understand the necessity for anonymity. Above all, of course, there are the members of the Yemenite community, who admitted my family and me into their midst with kindness, good humor, understanding, and patience. I hope that they will not be displeased with the results of the study and will forgive any errors or differences of interpretation. I will be happy if they feel that I have understood and conveyed a part of the reality of their lives and if they can recognize themselves in this portrait.

Finally, I must acknowledge my debt to my wife and children. Tammy, Paula, and Josh participated in the life of the city, in the schools and youth movements and social groups. I must thank them for their observations and insights as well as for their support and good humor. And to Marcia, who has always been a willing partner, able to uproot herself and the family, to make a new life—whether in Evanston or Madison, Jimma or Ambo, Jerusalem or Kiryat Eliahu—words cannot express my appreciation. Not only has she endured all this moving, she has also read and criticized almost all my writing. This, surely, is beyond the call of duty.

H. S. L.

1

Introduction

To an extent which few outsiders appreciate, Israel's Jewish population contains within it a remarkable diversity of peoples, derived from more than sixty countries and six continents. Although both supporters and detractors of the State of Israel usually represent it as a "Western" nation, more than half of its Jewish population originated in Asia and Africa, with major elements having come from Morocco, Iraq, Yemen, Egypt, Libya, Turkey, Tunisia, and Iran. Perhaps no immigrant society other than the United States has quite the extent and variety of ethnic complexity that Israel has. Indeed there are a number of ways in which the situation of Jewish ethnicity in Israel and that of European ethnicity in the United States resemble each other and make for interesting comparison.

Especially prominent in Israel's ethnic medley are the Jews from Yemen who, though they comprise only about 5 percent of the Jewish population, have occupied a special position in the social, economic, and artistic life of the Jewish community for a century. To some extent they are physically recognizable, and one may still occasionally see old men and women wearing distinctive dress and, for men, the side-curls (*pe'ot*) which very orthodox Jewish men wear. But it is their behavior and their cultural and artistic traditions which have really distinguished them and given them prominence far beyond their numbers. This population, and especially one community of Yemenite Jews, is the focus of our concern in this book.

The book portrays aspects of the life of a community of over 1,200 Jews who were either born in Yemen, or who were, in 1975-77, the young sons and daughters of immigrants from Yemen. In the first instance it is an ethnography, or community study, which will attempt to convey some sense of the history, the social life, the activities, and the values and ideals of a particular group of people. The Yemenites are a remarkable people whose contributions and particularities have made them highly visible, and I hope to represent a picture of their current lives in a way which has not been done in the literature previously. Despite the importance of Yemenites in the public mind, relatively few Israelis are aware of the actualities of Yemenite life. The popular literature still depicts Yemenites either as quaint immigrants or as hapless, poverty-ridden victims of Ashkenazi (European Jewish) discrimination. Neither of these views approaches an adequate picture of current realities. The scholarly social science literature, which contains some excellent and important work dealing with life in Yemen, has, with very few exceptions,[1] little to offer with respect to Yemenite Jewish life and culture since the mid-1950s.

More generally, the book has implications for the important and currently debated topic of ethnic integration in Israel. When, after the mass immigration of the 1950s, which tripled Israel's Jewish population, the extent of the ethnic diversity was recognized, it was hoped and assumed that, with education and modernization and the passage of a generation (the "generation of the desert") all of these ethnic groups could be integrated and united on a basis of equality. Israel's leaders looked for a true integration of the various ethnic communities and spoke of *mizug galuyot*, the "fusion of the exiles," drawing upon traditional Jewish terms.

This expectation was very well expressed by David Ben-Gurion:

> Within the State the differences between various kinds of Jews will be obliterated in the course of time, the communities and tribes will sooner or later fuse into one national and cultural unity. Common education, the Hebrew language, universal service in the Israel Defense forces, the establishment of a common minimum standard of living, the entry of workers from various countries and communities into a single labour federation, mixed marriages between the various tribes, common political action in non-communal parties, and so on, will produce a new type of Jew with the favourable qualities and characteristics of all the tribes of Israel.[2]

As the first generation drew to a close in the 1970s, however, there was increasing disappointment and some disillusionment as the evidence of a persisting social and economic gap between ethnic groups could not be ignored. This gap (*pa'ar*, as it is known in Israel) involves differentials in income, educational attainment, occupational status, and political influence. In general, Israelis of European and American origin are found on the higher end of the scale on all of these measures, while those Israelis from Asia and North Africa are at the lower end.[3]

Some sociologists continue to believe that it is still only a matter of time before the ethnically based gap is closed, that full integration and equality can be achieved, and that assimilation will be accomplished through intermarriage.[4] Others, however, see in the continuing inequality evidence of either major structural or political-economic flaws in the state,[5] or of ignorance, arrogance, and discrimination on the part of the largely European-derived establishment.[6] An older view, one no longer popular in academic circles though undoubtedly still widely believed among the public, sought reasons for this inequality in the characteristics of the original populations. The Europeans and Americans came from societies characterized as "modern," whereas those from African and Asian countries came from "traditional" societies, and thus were bound to have problems during the transition or "resocialization" period. At least they would undergo a trauma, a "crisis of immigration" that would in many cases impede their adjustment to Israeli society.[7] For a while the concepts of "culture of poverty"[8] and "cultural disadvantage" were popular as explanations of the failure of children of Asian and African background to equal their European and American counterparts in school and work performance.[9]

While it is not my intention to enter the argument about the ethnic gap directly, this book deals with a people from Asia, from the Arabian Peninsula, who would be considered by most observers as part of "the Other Israel" or "the Second Israel" because of their origins and because of the assumed relative standing of their ethnic group on the scale of success. I shall try to give an accurate and realistic picture of their lives, of their relationships with others, and of their attitudes. In contrast to much of the literature of the past decade this account will not be negative in tone. It will find neither Israeli society nor the Yemenites themselves wanting. Neither a culture of poverty, cultural deprivation, nor persistent discrimination or a political economy of exploitation and inequality will be evident from this account of the Yemenite community of Kiryat Eliahu.[10]

Theories of Ethnicity and the Case of the Yemenites

At a more general level, this study is meant as a contribution to the growing literature on ethnicity in the world today. The phenomenon of ethnicity has become a major concern of social scientists during the past decade. Although once thought to be condemned to an early (and according to some, justly deserved) demise, ethnicity—behavior and sentiment based upon membership in ethnic categories and groups—has proven itself to be a most persistent and significant phenomenon in the modern world. Some scholars go so far as to claim that modernization, far from wiping out ethnicity, frequently strengthens ethnic identities and heightens interethnic tensions.[11] Ethnicity is a worldwide phenomenon, has many different manifestations, and lies close to the center of major sociopolitical concerns. These include the integration and integrity of states; freedom and self-determination; and equality, group honor, and self-respect. Although there are some who consider the scholarly and political concern with ethnicity to be just a fad, if not a pernicious political or romantic tendency, ethnicity has become a central topic, but one about which there is a great deal of fundamental disagreement.

Among the basic controversies regarding ethnicity there are several which are particularly relevant to the subject of this book. These disputes concern the origins, the future, and the nature or dimensions of ethnicity, above all in immigrant societies. Immigrant societies are those that, like the United States, Argentina, and Israel, have been formed by immigrant groups from many different ethnic backgrounds.

The Origins of Ethnic Groups
and Ethnic Attitudes

Until recently the unquestioned assumption underlying the study of ethnic groups in the United States and Israel was that those ethnic categories or groups which are called "the Italians," "the Irish," and "the Jews," in the United States, and "the Yemenites," "the Moroccans," and "the Iraqis," in Israel, were formed abroad and brought to their respective new countries by the immigrants. In other words, it was assumed that the groups and their characteristics originated in the countries of origin and simply continued in the new country, at least until the forces of acculturation and assimilation diluted them and led to their eventual absorption.

This way of looking at ethnic groups has been criticized recently on the grounds that the ethnic group in reality only receives its identity, its awareness of being an ethnic group, and its characteristics, as a result of the settlement in the new land. According to W. L. Yancey and his colleagues, ethnic groups as we know them are created by the structural, political, and economic realities of the new situation. "The assumption of a common heritage as the essential aspect of ethnicity is erroneous. Ethnicity may have relatively little to do with Europe, Asia, or Africa, but much more to do with the exigencies of survival and the structure of opportunity in this country [the United States]. In short, the so-called 'foreign heritage' of ethnic groups is taking shape in this country."[12] Shlomo Swirski and Sara Katzir have taken a similar approach to "Oriental" Jewish ethnicity in Israel, arguing that a new ethnic group is being created by conditions in Israel.[13]

In the Israeli context those who see merit in this approach might point to the well-known complaint, "In Morocco I was called a Jew; here I am called a Moroccan." (The name of any other country and ethnic group may be substituted with similar effect. American and English Jews note the humorous irony that in Israel they have become "Anglo-Saxons.") Or perhaps they will be called "Sephardi" (meaning "one from Spain") or "Oriental," and thus new identifications and affiliations may be created in time.

The Yemenite Jews, however, had a very clear-cut identity in Yemen, and a very strong sense of their history.[14] Nevertheless, some social scientists in Israel have suggested that the traits which are often said to typify Yemenites, such as their industriousness, their cheerfulness and acceptance of menial labor, and their frugality, are adaptations to conditions in Israel rather than an inheritance from Yemen. This is a question we shall have to address in the course of the book.

The Nature of Ethnicity

It was long held by scholars and many political leaders that ethnicity was a transitory phenomenon and one doomed to extinction. For some the death of ethnicity would be the result of modernization, political democracy, mass education, and the melting pot. Those writers of a Marxist bent have always expected ethnic and national differences to be superseded by those of class. But as Nathan Glazer and Daniel Patrick Moynihan point out, both the "liberal expectancy" and the "radical expectancy" of the weakening and fading away of ethnicity have proven to be more than just premature; they are probably quite wrong as well.[15] The "end of ethnicity" ideology has been demonstrated to be an inadequate predictor of reality in the world of the 1980s.

The apparent growth of ethnicity and its study have not been greeted with equanimity, however, and there is, in the scholarly literature, a good deal of hostility to the idea of the significance of ethnicity, as well as to the phenomenon itself. Some sociologists still insist that the so-called revival of ethnicity in the United States is merely symbolic and that it is still on its way out.[16] Immanuel Wallerstein represents the Marxist view as he argues that the reality behind ethnicity is, in fact, class conflict. Once the class differences disappear, he contends, "status-group antagonisms" will also disappear.[17] Orlando Patterson, Howard Stein and Robert Hill, and Stephen Steinberg have all written books attacking both those who practice ethnic politics and those who study it uncritically or supportively.[18] Elaine Burgess and Joseph Rothschild both discuss the roots of antiethnic attitudes and the reasons social scientists have avoided the subject.[19]

More common than an attitude of hostility, however, is an approach which accepts ethnicity as a fact of modern life but wishes to restrict its depth and significance. This is commonly called the "instrumentalist," "circumstantialist," or "situationalist" perspective. This point of view accepts the usefulness of ethnicity in forming interest groups to compete for economic and political advantage with other such groups. Those who hold to it regard ethnic categories primarily as fluid and flexible, often recent formations with little historical depth, organized to meet particular circumstances in order to further the interests of those who respond to the same symbols and appeals. For them ethnicity is seen as a shallow phenomenon, without deep roots, sentiment, or consciousness. Leaders and others play upon symbols but above all on the self-interest of potential followers.

There is another perspective, however, which sees ethnic identification and differentiation as a more normal and natural part of social life in modern society, and one that will probably not disappear, even in the absence of structured inequality. It is a point of view implicit, at least, in the writings of Clifford Geertz, Andrew Greeley, and Harold Isaacs.[20] From this perspective ethnicity may exist because, like kinship and family, it is one locus of learning, sharing, sentiment, identification, and significant social relations. Rather than merely convenient bases for instrumental organization held together by common interest, as is the case in occupational and class associations, ethnicity *may* be among the primary bases of social affiliation and association.

In 1963 Clifford Geertz spoke of the ethnic tie as "one that stems from the givens . . . of social existence: immediate contiguity and kin connections mainly, but beyond them the givenness that stems from being born into a particular religious community, speaking a particular language, or even a dialect of a language, and following particular social practices. These congruities of blood, speech, custom, and so on, are seen to have ineffable, and at times overpowering, coerciveness in and of themselves."[21] Perhaps Geertz was too sweeping and overly general in his claims for the coerciveness of these phenomena, but I believe that we have much to lose by seeing the ethnic tie as *only* an instrument for economic and political manipulation, serving either the oppressed or the oppressors.

In complex modern states the ethnic tie may—indeed often does— involve common custom, social practice, sentiment, a sense of belonging, identification and identity, and even a sort of moral or spiritual imperative in the relationship. As Judith Nagata points out, "the idea that ethnic identity is inherited and carried by such primary groups as the family, and its associations with domesticity, socialization, and the most private and intimate of activities such as eating, sleeping, and mating, may reinforce the imperativeness of the ethnic status."[22] And as Daniel Bell says, "Ethnicity has become more salient [than class] because it can combine an interest with an affective tie."[23]

All ethnicity is by definition reactive. It exists only when there are two or more groups within a state and when there can be a "we"/"they" distinction. But this relationship need not be one of hostility, discrimination, superiority and inferiority for ethnicity to be maintained. There can be positive elements of attraction, common understandings, sentiment, shared values, pride in a tradition, religious beliefs, and enjoyment which serve to bind the members of an ethnic category together in a variety of ways. Shlomo Deshen's discussion of what he calls "cultural ethnicity" among Tunisian Jews in Israel is a good example of one type of nonconfrontational, nonpoliticized ethnicity.[24] Elsewhere I have presented the case for the continuing significance of ethnicity among rural and small town Wisconsinites of European origin, where no evident inequality is present.[25] There can be positive and apolitical reasons for ethnic continuity as well as negative, political ones. It is pointless and self-defeating to insist that ethnicity is only a creature of circumstances, awakened to do battle on behalf of the economic and political interests of a group. As James McKay has argued, it makes sense to recognize *both* the instrumental and political aspects *and* the more affective, subjective, expressive, culturally and socially based elements of ethnicity.[26] Above all, it is a serious mistake to consider ethnicity no more than an epiphenomenon of political or economic interest, as significant as ethnopolitics may be. As we shall see in the case that follows, the Yemenite Jews of Israel show a particular commitment to the positive value of their history and traditions, and in general seem to genuinely enjoy, even cherish, their participation in their distinctive social and cultural activities.

Ethnicity and Cultural Content

If ethnopolitics is the most readily accepted and grasped aspect of ethnicity, the one that seems least acceptable and least understood is that of culture. The idea that members of the same state or society may differ from each other along ethnic lines with respect to their values, attitudes, ideas, behavior, or "style"[27] is resisted alike by Marxists, social anthropologists interested in symbolism, and sociologists who believe that to speak of cultural differences is to "blame the victim."[28] Even anthropologists to whom the concept of culture is so important have shied away from the subject, especially since 1969 when Fredrik Barth seemed to give social scientists a mandate to ignore the problem.[29]

In the last section I argued that ethnicity may involve bonds of sentiment and emotion among the members of an ethnic category. Now I shall suggest that ethnicity *may* also entail the sharing, to greater or lesser degrees, of "culture," that is, shared understandings, expectations, values, and patterns for behavior.[30]

Despite many vicissitudes throughout the past eighty years, culture remains a key concept for American anthropology. Anthropologists maintain that the transmission of ways of being, perceiving, and behaving are a *sine qua non* of human existence. Geertz has written that humans only become human, and individual, under the guidance of culture, and that individuals must grow up being taught the specific codes, the recipes for behavior, of particular times and places.[31] And these "standards for perceiving, predicting, judging, and acting"[32] must be transmitted, and learned, in social groups. This much is undeniable; we base our studies on the expectation that there are such patterns, such codes, in any society. Our task is not normally to prove that culture plays a role in any human group, but to describe and interpret these codes as accurately and meaningfully as possible. And yet we encounter uneasiness, if not outright resistance, when we suggest that, in a complex multiethnic state, significant cultural differences may exist between ethnic groups.

It has long been recognized that in dealing with complex modern societies with regional, status, occupational, and ethnic differences we encounter serious problems of variation, and generalization becomes very difficult. We must recognize that the sources of socialization are many and include, in addition to the usual primary ones of parents, siblings, near kin, and peer groups, additional important inputs from teachers, classmates, fellow workers, army buddies, and the mass media. Throughout a person's life he or she is exposed to influences from occupational groups, class or status groups, community, and region. That we are dealing with a complex reality, composed of cross-cutting factors which produce dynamic and variable (and often unpredictable) outcomes should be evident. But it is important to recognize that for many complex societies a vital part of the pattern of variation, of the processes of socialization, may be the ethnic element. Fellow ethnics may comprise an important part of the "significant others" involved in socialization and in ongoing social relations. [33]

When parents, kinsfolk, peers, and neighbors transmit values and attitudes to others, they may be transmitting ethnically specific codes, in addition, perhaps, to elements derived from the state, region, and class. Those who transmit these ethnically derived tendencies may not be aware that they are doing so. Indeed, if they live in ethnically homogeneous enclaves they may not be aware that their behavior and values are different from others in the wider population. [34] Since these variations are often manifest primarily in what A. L. Epstein calls "intimate culture" rather than "public culture," they are best seen in the "backstage" areas, at home, and in ethnically specific places of worship which outsiders rarely penetrate. [35] Those who know members of other ethnic categories only from public places, from school, work, and the marketplace, may not be aware of just how different they are from each other. [36]

The cultural element of ethnicity may be particularly strong *if* fellow ethnics live in a geographical clustering and have a demographic base large enough to permit endogamy and the maintenance of ethnically specific institutions. The importance of ethnicity may be heightened also if it is combined with shared socioeconomic status in what Milton Gordon called *ethclass*. [37]

In what I have said about the possible importance of the cultural element of ethnicity I do *not* mean to imply that individuals respond automatically to a simple set of rules for behavior. I envision a far more flexible, open-ended, choice-filled, undetermined, and variable situation in which individuals decide, make choices, as they perceive their situations and their interests. These perceptions are viewed in the light of circumstances and in terms of the various sentiments and principles they have learned throughout their lives, from all the various sources to which they have been exposed. (Royce stresses the *choice* of what she calls "styles" in ethnicity. Alan Howard, in his study of a Hawaiian-American community speaks of "cultural paradigms" and associated "lifestyles.")[38] They also make their choices in terms of the perceptions they have of the reactions of their fellows.[39] In a complex society the "others" to whom one refers when making decisions come from a number of possible sources. Fellow ethnics may be only one of these, and their influence may vary from quite weak, or nonexistent, to very powerful indeed. In the case of Israel's Yemenites the influence of these fellow ethnics, and of some elements of the distinctive culture they share, is quite significant.

In the rest of this book we shall be considering one ethnic group, the Jews from Yemen who now live in Israel. Our primary focus is on the Yemenite community of a small city, but many of the things which are true for this group also hold for others throughout the country. This is a case where ethnicity plays a powerful role in the lives of the people who identify themselves as "Yemenites" (*Teymanim* in Hebrew). We shall consider the role of ethnicity with respect to identity and self-image, social relations, practices and institutions, values and attitudes, and the conscious maintenance of their traditions.

Notes

1. Yael Katzir, "The Effects of Resettlement on the Status and Role of Yemeni Jewish Women: The Case of Ramat Oranim, Israel" (doctoral dissertation, University of California, Berkeley, 1976); Norman Berdichevsky, "The Impact of Urbanization on the Social Geography of Reḥovot" (doctoral dissertation, University of Wisconsin, Madison, 1974); Norman Berdichevsky, "The Persistence of the Yemeni Quarter in an Israeli Town," *Ethnicity* 4:287-309, 1977. Lisa Gilad's *Ginger and Salt: Yemeni Jewish Women in an Israeli Town*, focussing on inter-generational change among women, has just appeared. (Boulder, Colorado: Westview, 1989) And Phyllis Palgi has published papers dealing with problems of psychological adjustment among Yemenite immigrants and their children. These include: "Mental Health, Traditional Beliefs, and the Moral Order among Yemenite Jews in Israel," in L. Romanucci-Ross,

D. E. Moerman, and L. Tancredi, eds., *The Anthropology of Medicine: From Culture to Method* (New York: Praeger, 1982) and "Discontinuity in the Female Role Within the Traditional Family in Modern Society: A Case of Infantcide," in E. J. Anthony and C. Koupernik, eds., *The Child in His Family* (New York: John Wiley, 1973).

2. Quoted in J. Isaac, "Israel: A New Melting Pot?" in W. D. Borrie, ed., *Cultural Integration of Immigrants* (Paris: UNESCO, 1959), p. 266.

3. See Sammy Smooha and Yochanan Peres, "The Dynamics of Ethnic Inequalities: The Case of Israel," *Social Dynamics* 1:63-79,1975; Michael Inbar and Chaim Adler, *Ethnic Integration in Israel* (New Brunswick, N. J.: Transaction Books, 1977); Avraham Shama and Mark Iris, *Immigration Without Integration: Third World Jews in Israel* (Cambridge, Mass.:Schenkman, 1977); Sammy Smooha, *Israel: Pluralism and Conflict* (Berkeley: University of California Press, 1978); Judith Bernstein and Aaron Antonovsky, "The Integration of Ethnic Groups in Israel," *Jewish Journal of Sociology* 23:5-23, 1981. Sammy Smooha recently produced a very useful survey and bibliography, selectively annotated, of the literature on Jewish ethnicity in Israeli society. Sammy Smooha, *Social Research on Jewish Ethnicity in Israel* (Haifa: Haifa University Press, 1987).

4. See Judah Matras, "Sociology and Its Own Society: Israel" (Departmental Working Paper 82-3, Department of Sociology and Anthropology, Carlton University, Ottawa, 1982), pp. 34-35.

5. See Shlomo Swirski and Sara Katzir, *Orientals and Ashkenazim in Israel: An Emerging Dependency Relationship* (Haifa: Research and Critique Series, 1978); Deborah Bernstein, "Immigrant Transit Camps: The Formation of Dependent Relations in Israeli Society," *Ethnic and Racial Studies* 4:26-43, 1981; Shlomo Swirski, *Not Disadvantaged, But Disenfranchised: Oriental and Ashkenazim in Israel* (Haifa: Research and Critique Series, 1981) [Hebrew]; Deborah Bernstein and Shlomo Swirski, "The Rapid Economic Development of Israel and the Emergence of the Ethnic Division of Labour," *British Journal of Sociology* 33:65-85, 1982.

6. See Sammy Smooha, *Israel: Pluralism and Conflict*; Arnold Lewis, *Power, Poverty and Education* (Ramat Gan: Turtledove, 1979); Ephraim Yuchtman-Yaar and Moshe Semyenov, "Ethnic Inequality in Israeli Schools and Sports: An Expectation-States Approach," *American Journal of Sociology* 85:576-590, 1979; George R. Tamarin, "Three Decades of Ethnic Coexistence in Israel," *Plural Societies* 2:3-46, 1980.

7. On this social psychological view, see Joseph Ben-David, "Ethnic Differences or Social Change?" in C. Frankenstein, ed., *Between Past and Future* (Jerusalem: Henrietta Szold Foundation, 1953); S. N. Eisenstadt, "The Process of Absorption of Immigrants in Israel," in *Between Past and Future*; S. N. Eisenstadt, *The Absorption of Immigrants* (London: Routledge & Kegan Paul, 1954); Rivka W. Ben-Yosef, "Desocialization and Resocialization: The

Adjustment Process of Immigrants," *International Migration Review* 2:27-45, 1968; Aharon F. Kleinberger, *Society, Schools and Progress in Israel* (Oxford: Pergamon Press, 1969).

8. See Oscar Lewis, "The Culture of Poverty," *Scientific American* 215(4):19-25, 1966.

9. For criticisms of this perspective, see Arnold Lewis, *Power, Poverty and Education*, and Shlomo Swirski, *Not Disadvantaged, But Disenfranchised.*

10. As Chapter 3 makes clear, discrimination and exploitation *did* mark the relations between many of the prestate immigrants from Yemen and the wider Jewish community. This has been much less the case, however, for those who came after 1948, as did the Yemenites of Kiryat Eliahu.

11. See Nathan Glazer and Daniel P. Moynihan, eds., *Ethnicity: Theory and Experience* (Cambridge, Mass.: Harvard University Press, 1975), p. 8; Elaine Burgess, "The Resurgence of Ethnicity: Myth or Reality?" *Ethnic and Racial Studies* 1:278-279, 1978; Mary Fainsod Katzenstein, *Ethnicity and Inequality: The Shiv Sena Party and Preferential Policies in Bombay* (Ithaca, N. Y.: Cornell University Press, 1979), pp. 19, 212.

12. W. L. Yancey, E. P. Ericksen, and R. N. Juliani, "Emergent Ethnicity: A Review and Reformulation," *American Sociological Review* 41:400.

13. Shlomo Swirski and Sara Katzir, "Orientals and Ashkenazim in Israel."

14. See Yael Katzir, "Preservation of Jewish Ethnic Identity in Yemen: Segregation and Intregration as Boundary Maintenance Mechanisms," *Comparative Studies in Society and History* 24:264-279, 1982.

15. Glazer and Moynihan, eds., *Ethnicity: Theory and Experience*, pp. 6-7.

16. See Herbert J. Gans, "Symbolic Ethnicity: The Future of Ethnic Groups and Cultures in America," *Ethnic and Racial Studies* 2:1-20, 1979.

17. Immanuel Wallerstein, "Social Conflict in Post-Independence Black Africa: The Concepts of Race and Status-Group Reconsidered," in E. Q. Campbell, ed., *Racial Tensions and National Identity* (Nashville: Vanderbilt University Press, 1972), p. 15.

18. Orlando Patterson, *Ethnic Chauvinism* (Briarcliff Manor, N. Y.: Stein & Day, 1977); Howard F. Stein and Robert F. Hill, *The Ethnic Imperative: Examining the New White Ethnic Movement* (University Park, Pa.: Pennsylvania State University Press, 1977); Stephen Steinberg, *The Ethnic Myth: Race, Ethnicity, and Class in America* (New York: Atheneum, 1981).

19. Elaine Burgess, "The Resurgence of Ethnicity;" Joseph Rothschild, *Ethnopolitics: A Conceptual Framework* (New York: Columbia University Press, 1981).

20. Clifford Geertz, "The Integrative Revolution," in *Old Societies and New States* (New York: The Free Press, 1963); Andrew M. Greeley, *That Most Distressful Nation: The Taming of the American Irish* (Chicago: Quadrangle, 1972); Harold R. Isaacs, "Basic Group Identity: The Idols of the Tribe," in

Nathan Glazer and Daniel P. Moynihan, *Ethnicity: Theory and Experience* (Cambridge, Mass.: Harvard University Press, 1975).

21. Geertz, "The Integrative Revolution," p. 109.

22. Judith Nagata, *Malaysian Mosaic* (Vancouver: University of British Columbia Press, 1979), p. 190.

23. Daniel Bell, "Ethnicity and Social Change," in Nathan Glazer and Daniel P. Moynihan, eds., *Ethnicity: Theory and Experience* (Cambridge, Mass.: Harvard University Press, 1975), p. 169.

24. Shlomo A. Deshen, "Political Ethnicity and Cultural Ethnicity in Israel During the 1960s," in Abner Cohen, ed., *Urban Ethnicity* (London: Tavistock, 1974). These points have been underlined and expanded upon in the work of George DeVos. See, e.g., George DeVos and Lola Romanucci-Ross, eds., *Ethnic Identity* (Chicago: University of Chicago Press, 1983), esp. pp. 363-389; and Chang Soo Lee and George DeVos, *Koreans in Japan* (Berkeley: University of California Press, 1981), esp. pp. 354-383.

25. Herbert S. Lewis, "European Ethnicity in Wisconsin: An Exploratory Formulation," *Ethnicity* 5:174-188, 1978. See also Arnold Strickon and Robert A. Ibarra, "The Changing Dynamics of Ethnicity: Norwegians and Tobacco in Wisconsin," *Ethnic and Racial Studies* 6:174-197, 1983.

26. James McKay, "An Exploratory Synthesis of Primordial and Mobilizationist Approaches to Ethnic Phenomena," *Ethnic and Racial Studies* 5:412-413, 1982.

27. Anya Peterson Royce, *Ethnic Identity: Strategies of Diversity* (Bloomington: Indiana University Press, 1982), pp. 27-28.

28. See, for example, William Ryan, *Blaming the Victim* (New York: Vintage, 1976).

29. In an influential statement on ethnicity and ethnic boundaries, Barth pointed out that boundaries could exist between ethnic groups even though the cultural content enclosed within each of the groups might change over time, or despite relatively little "objective" cultural differentiation between groups. Cultural differences, therefore, do not necessarily define ethnic groups, according to Barth. See Fredrik Barth, *Ethnic Groups and Boundaries* (Boston: Little, Brown, 1969), pp. 9-16. He did not, however, suggest that cultural differences did not exist or were not of interest to the student of society. Nevertheless this source is often cited as validating the proposition that culture is irrelevant to ethnicity and can be ignored. Harvey Goldberg has effectively criticized the dismissal of culture from ethnicity in the Israeli context. See "Historical and Cultural Dimensions of Ethnic Phenomena in Israel," in Alex Weingrod, ed., *Studies in Israeli Ethnicity: After the Ingathering* (New York: Gordon and Breach, 1985).

30. It should be clear that I am not speaking here primarily of "custom," as important as this might sometimes be, but of a deeper and more general set of understandings and guides to behavior. I agree, more or less, with Naomi Rosh

White that we may usefully distinguish between "culture as institutions" and "culture as value orientations" for this purpose. (See N. R. White, "Ethnicity, Culture and Cultural Pluralism," *Ethnic and Racial Studies* 1:141-143, 1978.)

31. Clifford Geertz, "The Impact of the Concept of Culture on the Concept of Man," in E. Hammel and W. Simmons, eds., *Man Makes Sense* (Boston: Little, Brown, 1970).

32. Ward H. Goodenough, *Cooperation in Change* (New York: Russell Sage Foundation, 1963), p. 259.

33. In their study of the St. Paul Jewish community, Dashefsky and Shapiro write, "Jewish identification is in large part a function of interaction with significant others in primary-group and other reference-group situations. The activities, expectations, and more subtle influences of these others are indispensable to the development of Jewish, or any other, group identification." (See Arnold Dashefsky and Howard Shapiro, *Ethnic Identification Among American Jews*, [Lexington, Mass.: D. C. Heath, 1974] p. 3.)

34. Naomi Rosh White writes, "These value orientations need not be part of the self-conscious awareness of societal members. In this respect, a culture is comparable to Kuhn's notion of a paradigm whose dominant assumptions may not be known or recognized until they are challenged or made known in some way, as through cross-cultural research." (See White, "Ethnicity, Culture and Cultural Pluralism," p. 142.)

35. A. L. Epstein, *Ethos and Identity: Three Studies in Ethnicity* (London: Tavistock, 1978), p. 112.

36. Cf. Dafna N. Izraeli, "Ethnicity and Industrial Relations: An Israeli Factory Case Study," *Ethnic and Racial Studies* 2:84, 1979.

37. Milton M. Gordon, *Assimilation in American Life: The Role of Race, Religion, and National Origins* (New York: Oxford University Press, 1964), p. 51.

38. Royce, *Ethnic Identity*, p. 28. See Alan Howard, *Ain't No Big Thing: Coping Strategies in a Hawaiian-American Community* (Honolulu: University of Hawaii Press, 1974). More generally, compare Sally Falk Moore, "Epilogue: Uncertainties in Situations, Indeterminacies in Culture," in Sally Falk Moore and Barbara G. Myerhoff, eds., *Symbol and Politics in Communal Ideology* (Ithaca, N. Y.: Cornell University Press, 1975).

39. Fine and Kleinman offer a similar perspective in their attempt to rethink "subculture." They speak of "socialization into a subsociety in which the individual makes explicit choices among the alternative cultural models available. Culture can be employed strategically and should not be conceptualized as a conditioned response. Usage of culture requires motivation and, in particular, identification with those who use the cultural items." Their view of "subculture" has a good deal in common with what I see as true of the cultural element in ethnicity as well: "Subculture has been conceived of as a set of understandings, behaviors, and artifacts used by particular groups and

diffused through interlocking group networks. Such a conception (1) explains how cultural elements can be widespread in a population, (2) explains the existence of local variations in cultural content through interactional negotiation in group settings . . ." Gary A. Fine and Sherryl Kleinman, "Rethinking Subculture: An Interactionist Analysis," *American Journal of Sociology* 85:12-13, 18, 1979.

2

The Jews of Yemen

Of all the Jewish commmunities dispersed throughout the world in 1948, those of Yemen and Habban were certainly among the most remote.[1] They were isolated from all other Jewish communities, those of the Mediterranean, Iraq, and Iran as well as Europe. The Jews of Yemen lived in a country which, like Tibet and Ethiopia, was physically inaccessible, largely closed to outsiders by religious and political barriers, and, for much of its history, off the main lines of international relations and commerce. In the twentieth century, as in earlier eras, its rulers expressly limited access to the country for fear of the political interests of outsiders and the influence of any religious doctrines other than their own Zaydi Shi'ite Muslim one. According to R. B. Serjeant, the ruler "wished to preserve the Yemen as a medieval Islamic state."[2] It was in this context that Yemen's Jews lived until after World War II.

There is evidence that Jews have resided in the southwestern corner of the Arabian Peninsula since at least the second century of the Christian era, five centuries before the birth of Muhammad and of Islam.[3] Their own legends suggest even earlier Jewish settlements there. Despite the isolation of the country, however, Jews from Yemen maintained contact with their coreligionists all over the world, sometimes for trade, but above all for religious reasons.[4] Throughout this millennium and a half the Jews remained loyal to their religion and its practices, kept up as much as possible with new developments in religious ideas and literature, corresponded with and helped support sages and academies in Spain, Iraq, Egypt, and Palestine, and maintained their identity as Jews. In fact, it is said that they always considered that they were only in temporary exile and that they lived always in the expectation that they would be returned to the Land of Israel by the messiah.[5] Nevertheless, their lives were lived in the context of Yemen's realities.

Yemen is a rugged, sometimes spectacular country of craggy mountains and rocky valleys. Many of its great slopes are completely covered with extensive rock-girt terraces, while its towns and villages are often set on the tops of the mountains, their multistoried houses perched at the edge of cliffs. The heart of the country consists of a plateau 7,000 to 9,000 feet high with mountains rising from it as high as 12,000 feet. The plateau and the mountains are surrounded by a coastal desert and the Red Sea on the west, and by the great Arabian desert, the Rub al-Khali, on the east. In the 1940s there were barely any roads suitable for wheeled vehicles, and almost all movement was by foot or on donkeys, horses, and mules. Even without the political restrictions which kept out foreigners, Yemen would have been relatively isolated.

Although rainfall in Yemen is unpredictable and failure of the rains often caused famine, its soils are capable of growing a wide range of crops on the intensively terraced slopes. Most of its people are, or were until recently, agriculturalists living in villages, but there are also a number of traditional cities, such as San'a, Ta'izz, Dhamar, Radah', Ibb, and Manakha, with markets and bazaars, impressive mosques, and palaces for the nobility and the imam. Yemen, known classically as "Arabia Felix," was not poor, but as Manfred Wenner puts it, "Yemen's inhabitants remained largely ignorant of the Industrial Revolution, modern technology, and the political, social, and economic theories and practices of the Western world. . . .Yemenis lived as they had for centuries, cognizant only of their own immediate surroundings, indifferent to all but their closest neighbors."[6]

The Status of the Jews in Yemen

Yemen is an Arab and a Muslim country, and throughout most of the last thousand years, until the revolution in 1962, it was ruled by Zaydi Shi'a imams according to their interpretation of Muslim law. In addition to the Zaydi Shi'a there were also many Sunni Muslims of the Shafi'i school, as well as a small Isma'ili Shi'a minority. But the Jews were the only non-Muslim population in Yemen.

The Jews lived among the Muslim Arabs as a *dhimmi*, a "protected people." As one of the "peoples of the book," but as non-Muslims, "Their personal safety and their personal property are guaranteed them at the price of permanent inequality."[7] This is according to Muslim law, under which these groups (Jews, Christians, and Zoroastrians) could practice their own religion and their own customs but had to submit to restrictions and humiliations. Anywhere in the Muslim world these special provisions might include the payment of a special head tax (*jizya*), a dress code, prohibitions on carrying weapons, building houses higher than those of Muslims or otherwise elevating themselves above Muslims, as, for example, by riding horses. But in the puritanical world of the Zaydi Shi'a this separation was often maintained particularly sharply, for the Shi'a look upon non-Muslims as unclean and polluting as well as being without rights.[8]

Although the Jews of Yemen could practice their own religion, leave their women unveiled, and make wine from grapes, they could not hold public office, bear arms, or testify against Muslims in legal actions. They had to depend for their protection upon local notables (*sayyids*, presumed descendants of the Prophet) and ultimately upon the imam.[9] Around San'a, the capital, and wherever his control was effective, the imam was the direct protector of the Jews.

The Jews were an endogamous group, different in religion and many customs, and were considered inferior to all Muslims both by law and tradition. They were also separated from most of their neighbors by their occupations, the majority of which were also looked down upon, or even considered defiling, by the mass of the population. For the Jews engaged primarily in the activities which the Yemenis call *suqi*. "The *suqi* niche comprises activities that are socially valuable while culturally defined as contemptible."[10] These include the activities of the marketplace, those of craftmanship, peddling, and selling. Like the highland Ethiopians, their neighbors across the Red Sea, the Yemenis look down on those who are neither nobles nor agriculturalists.[11] Many Jewish occupations, such as silversmithing, tailoring, and embroidering, were highly valued and seem, to western eyes, reasonably "clean." But the Jews were also forced into more obviously polluting work, which in India would be performed by members of pariah castes: the cleaning of latrines and sewers, the removal of carrion and manure from the streets, and the burial of non-Muslim travelers. (They were called upon to bury a member of Carsten Niebuhr's party who died there in the 1760s.) The Jews of San'a were ordered to do this work in 1806, and continued to do it until their departure from Yemen.[12]

Jewish Occupations

In Yemen the Jews were associated primarily with craftmanship and petty trade. They were the artisans who fashioned the decorative works of Yemen, as well as the producers of implements for fighting and working. S. D. Goitein claims that they engaged in as many as seventy different arts and crafts.[13] Raphael Patai gives a long list of these occupations, including goldsmiths and silversmiths, minters of coins, blacksmiths and workers in all other metals, armorers and gunsmiths, cabinetmakers, tanners, leatherworkers, cobblers and shoemakers, saddlemakers, embroiderers, weavers of cloth and carpets, dyers, tailors, potters, charcoal burners, soapmakers, millers, bakers, apothecaries, slaughterers and butchers, masons and stonecutters, carpenters, builders, painters, candymakers, winemakers, and distillers.[14] (The products of the last two industries were not supposed to be sold to Muslims.) Jews made the fancy tracery work in the windows of the great houses. Some were writers of amulets and charms, for Jews and non-Jews alike, to help in bringing rain, curing sick cows, and averting locust plagues. Still others were skilled scribes, *sofrei stam*, specializing in Jewish religious copying and calligraphy. They produced Torah scrolls and wrote the parchment inserts for the *mezuza*, which all Jewish homes have on their doorposts, and the *tfillin* (phylacteries), which men wear for morning prayers. Women had their craft skills as well, particularly in basket-making, sewing, and embroidery.

In addition to all these arts and crafts the Jews also worked as porters, donkey-drivers and guides, peddlers, shopkeepers, brokers, coffee dealers, and moneylenders. Most of their selling was done on a small scale, from shops or by peddling throughout the countryside. G. Wyman Bury noted that "The Jews run most of the better shops in Sanaa proper. . . ." Jews sometimes dealt in imported wares, and Bury claimed that in the bazaars of the Jewish Quarter one could find shops selling European calicoes and prints and various woolen fabrics.[15] An informant from San'a spoke of a Jew who opened a shop with wares from Russia and Japan in the 1920s or 1930s.[16]

Although the Jews lived modestly and many were actually very poor, a few did become wealthy and even powerful. Glaser records the story of a Jew from Manakha who made a considerable fortune in the coffee trade late in the nineteenth century.[17] Niebuhr tells of a Jew of San'a, whom he calls Oroeki, who "gained the favour of two successive [imams] and was for [twenty-eight years] comptroller of the customs and of the royal buildings and gardens; one of the most honourable offices at the court of Sana."[18] This man was Shalom Ha-Kohen Iraqi, whose family had come to Yemen from Egypt and subsequently played an important role in Jewish life and culture in San'a and Yemen. He also influenced the prayer of Yemen's Jews by introducing the Sephardi prayer tradition and distributing printed prayerbooks from abroad. This caused a split in the prayer traditions which continues to this day.[19]

In addition to craftmanship and trade, the Jews of Yemen were rather more closely connected with agriculture than was true of most Jewish communities in the diaspora. Many owned land and had rights to wells and irrigation channels. Some actually worked the land themselves, but it was more usual for them to lease land to Arab farmers or pay them to work the land. Goitein points out that even if few Jews actually engaged in agricultural work directly, they lived among farmers and were often paid, "not in cash, but with a specific part of the yearly harvest" and thus had considerable knowledge of and interest in the farmer's crops. In addition many Jews owned livestock in partnership with Arabs who tended them and shared the products and offspring.[20]

Almost all Jewish men knew at least one, and perhaps several, crafts. Trades were generally handed down through the generations, from father to son to grandson. As Yael Katzir notes, "every father was literally responsible for the tutoring of his son in the religion and the *melakha*, or craft."[21] Despite the demeaning work they might sometimes be called upon to do, Yemenite Jews were aware and proud of their roles as skilled artisans, craftsmen whose work in producing jewelry or daggers, or agricultural implements, was necessary and esteemed. Skilled artisans might be called *usta*, "craftsman" (Goitein says "master"), and get respect for this role. They might be trusted with gold and silver, given to them by clients to fashion into jewelry.[22] Even the most learned men, the rabbis, usually knew one or more of these arts, and at least some of the time made their living from it. This is in keeping with the tradition of rabbinical Judaism of Talmudic times and with the Yemenite Jewish injunction that a man should not live at the expense of the community.[23]

Jewish Communities and Religion

Until their mass departure for Israel in 1949 and 1950, the Jews of Yemen (about 50,000 at that time) were distributed throughout the country in more than 1,000 localities.[24] Possibly 25 percent of them lived in the larger cities of San'a (6,000), Radah' (2,500), Dhamar (2,000), Amran, Sa'da, Manakha, Ibb, and Yerim, usually in their own residential quarters, carefully separated from the sections of the Muslims.[25] The others lived in small towns and villages in the countryside, also usually in separate communities, apart from the Arabs. A good example of such a community was al-Gades, studied second-hand by both Goitein and Katzir. Al-Gades was a nucleated village of more than 1,000 Jews in a countryside of Arab communities. There were, however, some Jewish families "interspersed within the Arab population" beyond al-Gades.[26] These communities thus varied in size from quite large, to villages of fifteen to forty families, to those where only three or four Jewish families lived, isolated from others.[27]

The clear separation of the Jews from the Muslims, and the relative isolation of the former from the affairs of the latter, permitted the Jews to live their own lives as prescribed by Jewish law. According to S. D. Goitein, the Yemenite Jews "more than anyone else, have preserved rabbinical Judaism . . .," that is, the laws and practices of Judaism as established by the rabbis in the post-Biblical era, especially in the centuries immediately before and after the beginning of the Christian era. Life was lived according to the Jewish ritual cycle—six days of work and the seventh, the sabbath (*shabbat*), as the day of rest.[28] (This was an absolute value, firmly adhered to by all accounts.) The festivals of the Jewish year marked the annual cycle, and the observances of ritual circumcisions, weddings, and mourning marked the life cycle. The agrarian and artisan life they led permitted them to follow the precepts of the rabbis. As Goitein says, "This is a world centring around the synagogue, where simple people, craftsmen and labourers, are versed in religious lore and are able to follow arguments based on the Scriptures."[29]

In a world without modern education, where most of their Muslim neighbors were illiterate, most Jewish men were literate in Hebrew. In fact, if a man was not at least able to read the Torah and was not fully conversant with the book-bound Jewish prayer services, which must be recited word for word in Hebrew, it was a sign of extreme poverty and the inability of a father to educate his son, or of some other extraordinary problem. As Katzir says, "In effect, the men were walking books."[30] It was a principle of Yemenite Jewish life that a man was responsible for the education of his sons in the Torah, whether or not there were also teachers of children available in the community to instruct groups of boys. [31] In addition to the prayer services and the reading of the Torah in Hebrew, boys also learned to read the Aramaic translation of the Torah (by Onkelos), and, often, other important religious works, such as those of Rashi, Sa'adia Gaon, and Maimonides. The works of the Kabbalah and Talmudic study were available for the more advanced students, especially in the capital.

Professor Goitein also notes that "the Zaydi environment constituted a positive influence on the religious life of the Jews"[32] because that particular Muslim tradition also stresses the study of sacred texts. "The *imam* . . . is expected to be a scholar, and many .*imams* have indeed written learned treatises." There was thus precedent and example among the Muslim population as well as in Jewish tradition, and the possession of literacy enhanced self-esteem and did not detract from whatever prestige Jews had among their illiterate Arab neighbors. [33]

Women, however, did not learn to read or write, nor were they expected to be knowledgeable in Hebrew prayers. (Goitein says, however, that there were some "learned women of official standing.")[34] According to Jewish law they could not participate with men in public worship services, and so were not taught how to do so. It was not even expected that they would attend those services, although they might, especially on holidays or to celebrate weddings and other important occasions. (They would sit behind a cloth which kept them from the sight of the men.) They were, however, to be knowledgeable about the laws as they related to their realms. This meant knowing the Jewish dietary laws, and maintaining the proper conditions and atmosphere for the celebration of the sabbath and festivals at home. According to Goitein, "the women identified themselves entirely with the values of their men."[35] The importance of religious study and prayer for men was accepted, as was the woman's complementary role as supporter and maintainer of conditions for following the religious codes and practices. [36]

The Jews in their communities had a degree of local independence in the running of their own affairs. Although they were, of course, subject to more powerful outside authorities, such as local sheikhs and tribal leaders, the imam's agents, Turkish officials during periods of Ottoman rule, and the *sada* (*sayyids*), much of the time they could take care of their own internal affairs with their own leadership. These leaders included a local "headman," the *nasi* (Hebrew) or '*akil* (Arabic), who represented the community before the authorities and the non-Jewish neighbors, saw to order and peace, and to the collection and assessment of the head-tax.[37] Also of importance were the *mori*, men learned in religious tradition, who tended to the vital matters of the synagogues and kosher slaughtering, taught boys Hebrew, Torah, and prayer, and helped to interpret and apply Jewish law.

Goitein has written that the Jewish community was needed in order to permit the individual Jew to perform those obligations and good deeds (*mitsvot*) demanded of Jews by God. These *mitsvot* include public prayer (daily and sabbath), instruction in *aggadah* (the moral lessons of the rabbis) and *halakha* (the traditional laws and rules for maintaining Jewish life and society), arrangements for marriage and burial, the provision of *kosher* meat, the maintenance of a ritual bath (*mikveh*), and the teaching of sons.[38] This they attempted to do through the voluntary organization of synagogues and community associations. Men devoted their time, learning and expertise to these ends, for the most part without remuneration other than the esteem of their neighbors and kinsmen. Although teachers of children usually received some tuition fees from their students, often in the form of food or firewood, this was not enough to live on, and most also did other work. A weaver or other artisan might work while teaching.[39] Some of a specialist's services, such as slaughtering animals or copying marriage contracts, might be paid for, but most were given freely, without recompense, and brought only honor.[40] Even if the community could have paid for such services, it would not have been considered honorable for a person to live from them.

For men the center of the community was the synagogue, and here they spent much of their spare time, as well as their sabbaths, in prayer and study. It was in this setting that men could display their learning, skill, piety, leadership capacities, and wealth. So important was the synagogue and the role of leadership within it that most communities had competing synagogues. Any man who believed that he could regularly attract at least nine other men to form a *minyan* (quorum) for public prayer, and could afford to build one, could start his own synagogue. Even if such a man were not himself particularly learned he had the prerogative of giving out honors to others, dictating who could lead and read particular portions of services and the Torah. It was, therefore, a position of great prestige and importance. As Goitein notes, there was considerable rivalry and factionalism, and great passion, and sometimes actual fighting, over the matter of honors and control both within and between synagogues.[41] Sometimes Muslim authorities would step in to force agreement, so serious did disputes become.

Despite their importance and deep involvement in the material life and economy of Yemen, the Jews were able to live very much as a people unto themselves; nor did they desire to be close to the non-Jews. As Gamlieli puts it, "all they requested was to be left to live quietly and safely, within the framework of their religion and society, until the coming of Redemption."[42] It is clear that the Jews of Yemen, both in the larger cities and in their small highland communities, knew and lived by the rules of Jewish life, by *halakha*, and in the framework of the principles of worship and celebration.[43] Except for those who converted to Islam, either by choice or through force, Yemen's Jews knew no way to live other than in the context of Jewish practice and belief.

Sociopolitical Conditions

The extent to which the Jews were left in peace, however, is another question. It is not possible to generalize about the circumstances and conditions of the Jews over a period of almost two thousand years, and throughout the whole country of Yemen. Clearly there were times and places when relations with authorities and neighbors were good and when the economic situation of the community was stable. But there were many other times when this was not the case, when Jews were attacked, robbed, deprived of property and of rights they had enjoyed, and made to suffer in a variety of ways. Sometimes they were protected or avenged by powerful patrons,[44] but at other times there was nothing they could do against their opponents or oppressors. The imam was officially their protector, but no imam could control all his subjects, nor was there any guarantee that an imam himself would not cause troubles.[45]

In 1676 an imam ordered that the Jews be forbidden to engage in public prayer, and that all synagogues were to be destroyed. This was followed in 1678 by a decree expelling all Jews from San'a, the capital. These people were forced to live in the terribly hot and fever-ridden coastal lowland along the shores of the Red Sea. Evidently Jews from other parts of Yemen also had to move there, but after two years, following the death of the imam, they were allowed to return. The hardships were great, however, and have not been forgotten. When they returned to the highlands there were new restrictions placed upon them, and much of their property was lost.

The Imam Yaḥya ibn Muhammad al Mansur ibn Yaḥya Ḥamid ad Din, who ruled Yemen from 1904 until his assassination in 1948, apparently took his role as protector of the Jews very seriously, and older Yemenite Jews today often praise him and tell stories of his intercessions and his seriousness in applying Islamic law and seeing to it that the Jews followed *their* laws.[46] But in insisting upon the stricter enforcement of Muslim law, he increased certain of the hardships and humiliations. The laws regulating the status of *dhimmi* are old and basic in Islam, so he was not acting capriciously when he attempted to renew them with a decree in 1905, and this was understood by the Jews. This decree states, among other things, that:

> It is also . . . forbidden to them [the Jews] to help each other against a Muslim, and they shall not raise their houses above the Muslim houses, and they shall not disturb Muslims in their path and shall not encroach on their occupations . . . and shall not sit on saddles [any way] but sideways . . ., and shall not wink . . . and not raise their voices while praying. . . .[47]

Although these strictures might be interpreted harshly, for example by insisting that Jews take demeaning postures and walk in the gutter when meeting Muslims, they were more annoying than threatening to life and property. But another decree of Imam Yaḥya caused far more serious problems.

The "Decree of the Orphans," enacted as early as the seventeenth century and revived with special rigor in 1921, ordered that fatherless Jewish children below the age of puberty had to convert to Islam. At some times and places this actually involved a search for such children and their removal from the family, even if their mothers were alive. This caused great hardship and fear, the hiding of orphans and secret adoptions, and is remembered vividly and with great pain today. The prosecution of this decree, or the fear of it, was one stimulus to emigration from Yemen in the 1920s and 1930s—even though the imam had also decreed an end to travel to Palestine in the 1920s.[48]

Despite these prosecutions and hardships, there were times and places when life went on normally and was reasonably good, and many informants speak positively of their relations with their neighbors and their general standard and way of life in Yemen. Moshe Tsadok claims that Jews generally had a harder time with the Zaydi Shi'i city dwellers, who he says were "virulently hateful" to the Jews, whom their doctrine considered impure and polluting.[49] On the other hand "humble tribesmen" (*qabiliya*) in the countryside were more likely to get along well with the Jews.[50]

As noted before, there were even Jews who became wealthy, influential, and welcome at the palaces of the imams or other notables, who might even give them important posts. Nevertheless, their positions were basically unstable, and while this might be true of any men of position and ambition in the political world of Yemen, the downfall of a Jewish man of prominence often also meant problems for his people. The story of Oroeki (Iraqi), the prominent Jew mentioned by Niebuhr, did not have a happy ending. He fell into disfavor two years before Niebuhr's visit, and was imprisoned and fined 50,000 crowns. In addition,

> The disgrace of Oroeki had drawn a degree of persecution upon the rest of the Jews . . . The government ordered fourteen synagogues to be demolished. In their village are as handsome houses as the best in Sana. Of those houses likewise all above the height of fourteen fathoms were demolished, and the Jews were forbidden to raise any of their buildings above this height in the future. All the stone pitchers in which [they] used to keep their wines were broken. In short, the poor Jews suffered mortifications of all sorts.[51]

Prominent Jews of San'a found again in 1948 that they could easily be brought low when sixty were arrested on a mistaken charge, kept in prison for several months, and forced to pay large fines.[52] As one informant put it, no matter how good life was in San'a, no matter how successful you got, they never let you forget that you were a Jew and thus permanently subordinate.[53]

At best, when conditions were relatively stable, the Jews could live satisfying Jewish lives within their communities. In their separate quarters and villages they had their own way of life, and they could worship according to their own Jewish traditions, with their synagogues, holy books, educational system, and community leadership. The walls that kept the Jews from the Arabs also kept the Arabs from the Jews.[54] Informants told me that "it was forbidden to look on a *goy* (non-Jew) on *shabbat*," and this, they said, helped keep them a distinct people for all those centuries.[55]

Behind these walls they tried to live according to "the ancient Jewish code of law originally devised for just such an environment," that of

Middle Eastern agrarian communities and traditional towns and cities. Barer continues,

> They observed all its prescriptions dealing with the minutest matters of life, from the way in which meat should be cleaned before eating to questions of feminine hygiene and sexual intercourse. They might never have seen a bathroom shower, but they went to a primitive public bath because this is a prescribed religious ritual. The Ghetto in San'a might be a labyrinth of smelly, narrow lanes, the houses low, dreary, mud-baked structures, but they showed . . . "a high degree of cleanliness." The rooms might be bare of furniture, no chairs or beds, only carpets and mattresses on the floors, but the floors were scrubbed, the walls washed white.[56]

Apart from some European ethnocentrism in this passage, it points to a number of significant aspects of Yemenite life and culture which we shall encounter later: maintenance of the laws, cleanliness, and the general absence of furnishings in homes.[57]

It has often been claimed that the reason that Yemen's Jews always wore garments that looked modest and poor (aside from the sumptuary restrictions), that the streets of their quarter looked so dirty and unprepossessing, and that their houses were so bare of furnishings was because they would incur the envy of the Muslims if they were to look anything but wretched and poor.[58] According to Goitein, "Allah had ordained that Jews should be poor. Consequently, a Jew was not allowed to display even modest signs of wealth."[59] An informant gave another interpretation, however, when he told me a story of a rabbi who refused to bless a particularly fine new house in San'a. The rabbi said to the owner, "You are lengthening the exile by building such a fine house. It is written that the home in *galut* (exile) should be like a tent in the wilderness." Goitein believes that Yemen's Jews didn't feel degraded by the enforced modesty of their homes and dress because they considered themselves in temporary exile anyway.[60]

The apparent poverty of Yemenite Jewish everyday clothing, and aspects of their housing and furnishings, contrasted with the wealth of their religious, ritual, and ceremonial lives, their arts and, to some degree, their intellectual life. They had rich communal ceremonial life, based on *shabbat* and the traditional festivals and on the life cycle celebrations, especially ritual circumcisions (*brit mila*), engagements and weddings. These were accompanied by costuming, poetry, music, and dance of their own devising.[61]

The tradition of the Yemenite Jews included all the arts. As we have seen, many were professional jewelers, weavers, embroiderers, and experts at decoration. Vocal music played a central role in their religious and recreational life, and dance was extremely important in most Yemenite Jewish communities. Both the music and dance were distinctively Jewish, and not the same as those of the Arabs. They also had a rich corpus of poetic literature, much of it derived from the seventeenth and eighteenth centuries, and above all from the revered poet and philosopher, Shalom Shabazi. [62]

In addition they possessed a considerable religious literature. Most of this was shared with the rest of the world's Jewish communities, but there were also many treatises and theological studies which were produced in Yemen. [63] There were no printing presses in Yemen and printed books were rare, so people cherished hand copied books of all sorts.

Many communities had scholars, learned and pious leaders. San'a as the capital and the leading Jewish center was the site of the highest religious court (*bet din*), the home of some outstanding figures throughout the centuries, and, for a while, of the Turkish appointed religious leader of all the Jews in Yemen, the *ḥakham bashi*. (His authority was never accepted by all communities, however.) [64] And in the twentieth century San'a was the site of a schism between rationalists (the *Darda' im* [or *Dor-De' ah*]—Generation of Reason) who opposed belief in the mystical tradition of the Kabbalah, and those who continued to support Kabbalah. [65]

Despite the apparent simplicity of their surroundings and their poor and modest appearance, Yemen's Jews had created and maintained remarkably rich and diversified cultural traditions. With all of its problems, Jewish life in Yemen had a beauty and a richness which stands out even more sharply today, when remembered from a distance of more than thirty years, by people whose lives have not become perfect in the Holy Land to which they came in search of Redemption. There is a tendency to remember the beautiful things, and to regret, to some extent, that they and their children no longer live the pure and simple lives, according to *halakha*, that they did in Yemen; or that the ceremonial life, in which wedding celebrations would last for more than a week, has been very much attenuated by the requirements of earning a living in Israel. While so much has been gained through immigration to Israel, it is also important for many Yemenites to remember what was lost as well.

Notes

1. In general the term "Yemenite" or "Yemenite Jew" refers to people who originated in what is today called the Yemen Arab Republic, or North Yemen. Within the current boundaries of South Yemen, now the People's Democratic Republic of Yemen, there once lived two small but interesting groups of Jews. Each had its own identity and its own history and distinguishing characteristics, but each also shares a good deal with the Jews of Yemen proper and has been associated or identified with them as well. One of these communities lived in the city of Aden and was long involved in international trade. They were strategically located near the southern end of the Red Sea, on the international trade route from Europe and the Mediterranean to Persia and India. (For an interesting picture of the international connections of the Aden community, see S. D. Goitein, *A Mediterranean Society*, Vol. 1: *Economic Foundations*, University of California Press, 1967.) The other group of Jews lived in Habban, an area of South Yemen (Aden Protectorate) more isolated than most of those in Yemen proper. There they lived their own deeply Jewish lives amidst Arab tribesmen, very much cut off from other Jewish communities. For a recent study of a Habbani community in Israel, see Laurence D. Loeb, "Folk Models of Habbani Ethnic Identity," in Alex Weingrod, ed., *Studies in Israeli Ethnicity* (New York: Gordon and Breach, 1985).

2. R. B. Serjeant, "The Zaydis," in A. J. Arberry, ed., *Religion in the Middle East* (Cambridge: Cambridge University Press, 1969), p. 297.

3. See S. D. Goitein, *Jews and Arabs: Their Contacts Through the Ages* (New York: Schocken Books, 1964), p. 47. For a general study of the history and culture of the Jews in Yemen see Reuben Ahroni, *Yemenite Jewry: Origins, Culture and Literature* (Bloomington: Indiana University Press, 1986).

4. See, for example, Moshe Tsadok, *History and Customs of the Jews in the Yemen* (Tel Aviv: Am Oved, 1967), p. 27ff. [Hebrew]; S. D. Goitein, "The Jews of Yemen," in A. J. Arberry, ed., *Religion in the Middle East* (Cambridge: Cambridge University Press, 1969) p. 228; S. D. Goitein, *From the Land of Sheba: Tales of the Jews of Yemen* (New York: Schocken Books, 1973), pp. 6-20; Yosef Kafih, "The Ties of Yemenite Jews with the Jewish Centers," in Y. Yeshayahu and Y. Tobi, eds., *The Jews of Yemen* (Jerusalem: Ben-Zvi Institute, 1975) [Hebrew]; Mordechai Abir, "International Commerce and Yemenite Jewry; 15th to 19th Centuries," *Pe'amim* 5:4-28, 1980. [Hebrew]

5. See Jean-Jacques Berreby, "De l'Intégration des Juifs Yéménites en Israel," *L'Année Sociologique*, 3rd series:69-163; Yehuda Ratzaby, *Yemenite*

Jewry (Tel Aviv: Education Office, Israel Defense Forces, 1958), p. 49 [Hebrew]; Nissim B. Gamlieli, "The Arabs Amongst Whom the Yemenite Jews Lived: Islamic Sects, Their Inter-Relationships and Relations with the Jews," in Y. Yeshayahu and Y. Tobi, eds., *The Jews of Yemen* (Jerusalem: Ben-Zvi Institute, 1975), p. 179.

6. Manfred Wenner, *Modern Yemen: 1918-1966* (Baltimore: Johns Hopkins University Press, 1967), p. 17.

7. Gustave E. Grunebaum, *Medieval Islam* (Chicago: University of Chicago Press, 1946), p. 179.

8. See Hayyim Cohen, *The Jews of the Middle East, 1860-1972* (Jerusalem: Israel Universities Press, 1973), pp. 3-4; Moshe Tsadok, "Jewish-Arab Relations in Yemen," in Y. Yeshayahu and Y. Tobi, eds., *The Jews of Yemen* (Jerusalem: Ben-Zvi Institute, 1975), p. xvii. For similar attitudes in Iran, see Lawrence D. Loeb, *Outcaste: Jewish Life in Southern Iran* (New York: Gordon & Breach, 1977), pp. 16-20. Shalom Staub presents further perspectives on the complexities of Muslim-Jewish relations in Yemen in his dissertation: A Folkloristic Study of Ethnic Boundaries: The Case of Yemeni Muslims in New York City (University of Pennsylvania, 1985).

9. Wenner, *Modern Yemen*, p. 37; Gamlieli, "The Arabs Amongst Whom the Yemenite Jews Lived: Islamic Sects, Their Inter-Relationships and Relations with the Jews," in Y. Yeshayahu and Y. Tobi, eds., *The Jews of Yemen* (Jerusalem: Ben-Zvi Institute, 1975), p. 169ff.

10. Tomas Gerholm, *Market, Mosque and Mafraj: Social Inequality in a Yemeni Town* (Stockholm: University of Stockholm, 1977), p. 131. It is conventional in English to refer to the Muslim Arabs of Yemen as "Yemenis," while for some reason the Jews are called "Yemenites." I have followed this convention. In Hebrew they are referred to as *Teymanim* (pl.), i. e., those from *Teyman*, after the Biblical name for the country called in Arabic *Yaman*, or *al-Yaman*.

11. See Herbert S. Lewis, "Historical Problems in Ethiopia and the Horn of Africa," *Annals of the New York Academy of Sciences* 96:504-511, 1962.

12. See Tsadok, *History and Customs*, p. 82ff. The separation of the Jews from the Muslims of Yemen shows most of the characteristics of caste: (1) endogamy, (2) restriction of commensality (according to Shi'a law, "dishes touched by a non-Muslim become unclean and have to be smashed"), (3) status hierarchy, (4) concepts of pollution, (5) membership in each group ascribed by birth, (6) association with traditional occupations. These are six of seven characteristics cited by E. R. Leach. The seventh is the presence of the Hindu religion and is not applicable here. (See E. R. Leach, ed., *Aspects of Caste in South India, Ceylon and North-West Pakistan*, Cambridge, 1960, p. 2.) For discussions of "caste" in Yemen, see Goitein, "The Community Life of the Jews in the Land of Yemen," in *Jubilee Volume to Honor Mordechai Menahem Kaplan* (Philadelphia: Jewish Theological Seminary of America, 1953), p. 46

[Hebrew]; Yeshayahu and Tobi, *The Jews of Yemen*; Gerholm, *Market, Mosque and Mafraj*, p. 103ff.

13. Goitein, "The Transplantation of the Yemenites: The Old Life They Led," *Commentary* 12:25, 1951.

14. Raphael Patai, *Tents of Jacob: The Diaspora—Yesterday and Today* (Englewood Cliffs, N. J.: Prentice-Hall, 1971), pp. 226-227.

15. G. Wyman Bury, *Arabia Infelix, or the Turks in Yamen* (London: Macmillan, 1915), p. 79.

16. For a discussion of work and trade, see Erich Brauer, *Ethnologie der jemenitischen Juden* (Heidelberg: Carl Winters, 1934), pp. 233-263.

17. Gerholm, *Market, Mosque and Mafraj*, p. 84.

18. C. Niebuhr, *Travels Through Arabia and Other Countries in the East* (Edinburgh, 1792; repr. Librairie du Liban, Beirut), p. 378. See also *Encyclopaedia Judaica*, Vol. 8 (Jerusalem: Keter, 1972), p. 1462.

19. The Yemenites maintain two distinct prayer traditions: the original one, called *baladi* (local, of the country), and *shami*, based on the Sephardi tradition. The *shami* tradition spread widely, but it remains a minority tradition. (See Chapter 6.)

20. Goitein, "The Transplantation of the Yemenites," p. 25; Goitein, "Portrait of a Yemenite Weavers' Village," *Jewish Social Studies* 17:13-14, 1955.

21. Yael Katzir, "Preservation of Jewish Ethnic Identity in Yemen: Segregation and Integration as Boundary Maintenance Mechanisms," *Comparative Studies in Society and History* 24:275-276, 1982.

22. Yosef Kafih, *Jewish Life in Sana* (Jerusalem: Ben-Zvi Institute, 1969), p. 229 [Hebrew]; S. D. Goitein, *From the Land of Sheba*, p. 24.

23. Goitein, "The Community Life of the Jews," pp. 54, 56; Goitein, *From the Land of Sheba*, p. 25.

24. Goitein, "Jewish Education in Yemen as an Archetype of Traditional Jewish Education," in C. Frankenstein, ed., *Between Past and Future* (Jerusalem: Henrietta Szold Foundation, 1953), p. 112.

25. Yosef Tobi, *The Legacy of the Jews of Yemen: Studies and Researches* (Jerusalem: Bo'i Teman, 1976), p. 67. [Hebrew]

26. Yael Katzir, "The Effects of Resettlement on the Status and Role of Yemeni Jewish Women: The Case of Ramat Oranim, Israel," (doctoral dissertation, University of California, Berkeley, 1976), p. 33.

27. Goitein, "The Community Life of the Jews," p. 44.

28. The observance of the sabbath, the seventh day, as a day of absolute abstention from work and creative activity, including the lighting of fires, cutting, and writing, is a central institution and value in Judaism. The observant Jew is enjoined to engage in religious worship and study, to gather with family and friends to eat, sing, discuss religious matters, and generally devote oneself to familial, social, and spiritual renewal. *Shabbat* was of the greatest importance

to the Yemenites. It is significant that Rabbi Yosef Kafih's book on the life of the Jews of San'a devotes the very first chapter to the observance of *shabbat*.

29. Goitein, "The Jews of Yemen," in Arberry, p. 228.

30. Katzir, "Preservation of Jewish Ethnic Identity in Yemen," p. 272.

31. Goitein, "Jewish Education in Yemen," p. 118.

32. Goitein, "The Jews of Yemen," p. 230.

33. Niebuhr noted that in San'a in 1762, "Writers go about with their desks, and make out brieves, copy-books, and instruct scholars in the art of writing, all at the same time." (See Niebuhr, *Travels Through Arabia*, Vol. I, p. 375.)

34. Goitein, *Jews and Arabs*, p. 187.

35. Goitein, "The Jews of Yemen," p. 231.

36. See Goitein, "Jewish Education in Yemen"; Katzir, "The Effects of Resettlement," p. 54ff.

37. Yehiel Nahshon, "Jewish Leadership in Yemen," in Y. Yeshayahu and Y. Tobi, *The Jews of Yemen* (Jerusalem: Ben-Zvi Institute, 1975), pp. 75-76. The volume *The Jizya Poll Tax in Yemen*, by Rabbi Shalom ben Sa'adya Gamliel, ed. M. M. Caspi, contains documents and census notebooks pertaining to the collection of these taxes. These throw light on disputes and factions within the San'a community. Rabbi Gamliel was one of the two community leaders appointed by the imam to collect the *jizya* from one faction during the 1930s. (Jerusalem: The Shalom Research Center, 1982.)

38. Goitien, "The Community Life," p. 48.

39. Goitein, "Portrait of a Yemenite Weavers' Village," p. 18; Katzir, "Preservation of Jewish Ethnic Identity," p. 276.

40. Goitein, "Portrait of a Yemenite Weavers' Village," p. 19.

41. Goitein, "The Community Life," p. 50ff.

42. Gamlieli, "The Arabs Amongst Whom the Yemenite Jews Lived," p. 179.

43. *Halakha* is the body of literature which comprises the legal system of Judaism. Based on the Five Books of Moses (Torah) and on the commments and interpretations of the rabbis, especially from the Second Temple and Talmudic periods, it consists of directions for religious and ethical matters as well as for personal status, social behavior, and civil and criminal law.

44. See Shlomo Barer, *The Magic Carpet* (London: Secker & Warburg, 1952), pp. 126-129.

45. Bat Ye'or's book contains two documents, one from a Jewish source and one from the Arabic chronicles, that give a vivid picture of the punishment meted out to the Jews in 1666 when they became agitated by the news that the messiah had risen in Jerusalem. This was the result of the activities of Shabtai Tsvi, the "false messiah." Bat Ye'or, *The Dhimmi: Jews and Christians Under Islam* (Rutherford, N. J.: Fairleigh Dickinson University Press, 1985), pp. 361-364.

46. Cf. H. Cohen, *Jews of the Middle East*, p. 64; Tsadok, "Jewish-Arab Relations in Yemen," pp. 158-163. For a fuller list see Bat Ye'or, *The Dhimmi*, p. 341, also pp. 341-343.

47. H. Cohen, *Jews of the Middle East*, pp. 62-63. R. Ahroni, *Yemenite Jewry*, pp. 117-120.

48. Goitein, "The Jews of Yemen," p. 230; cf. Y. L. Nahum and Y. Tobi, "R. Yosef Shemen's Pamphlet *Hayei haTemanim* (On the Distress of Yemenite Jews in the Twentieth Century)," in Y. Yeshayahu and Y. Tobi, *The Jews of Yemen* (Jerusalem: Ben-Zvi Institute, 1975).

49. Tsadok, "Jewish-Arab Relations in Yemen," p. 147ff.

50. Cf. Goitein, "Portrait of a Yemenite Weavers' Village," pp. 16-17; Yehuda Nini, "Immigration and Assimilation: The Yemenite Jews," *Jerusalem Quarterly* 21:86, 1981.

51. Niebuhr, *Travels Through Arabia*, p. 379.

52. See Barer, *Magic Carpet*, p. 120; H. Cohen, *Jews of the Middle East*, p. 64.

53. Cf. Grunebaum, *Medieval Islam*, p. 182.

54. "The Jews . . . have to clear out [of San'a proper] before night and go back to their quarter, as no Jew is allowed to live in sacred Sanaa," wrote Bury, *Arabia Infelix*, p. 79.

55. Cf. Goitein, *From the Land of Sheba*, p. 56; Katzir, "Preservation of Jewish Ethnic Identity in Yemen."

56. Barer, *Magic Carpet*, p. 137.

57. Cf. Joseph B. Schechtman, *On Wings of Eagles: The Plight, Exodus, and Homecoming of Oriental Jewry* (New York: Thomas Yoseloff, 1961), p. 44; Carl Rathjens, *Jewish Domestic Architecture in San'a, Yemen*, Oriental Notes and Studies 7 (Jerusalem: Israel Oriental Society, 1957), p. 46.

58. See Barer, *Magic Carpet*, p. 126; Rathjens, *Jewish Domestic Architecture*, p. 17; Katzir, "The Effects of Resettlement," p. 30.

59. Goitein, "Portrait of a Yemenite Weavers' Village," pp. 14-15. This problem is nicely illustrated by a Yemeni Muslim theologian's discussion of the expulsion of the Jews from San'a in 1678. Ibn ar-Rijal wrote, "But if the Jews ignore these conditions and conduct their funeral processions in broad daylight and embellish and beautify their synagogues to make them look like wedding canopies, outshining our mosques . . . then they must be humiliated by the destruction of their synagogues." Quoted in Bat Ye'or, *The Dhimmi*, p. 340.

60. Goitein, *Jews and Arabs*, p. 75.

61. The richest description of custom and ceremonial is found in Kafih, *Jewish Life in Sanà*. A fine introduction to Yemenite Jewish musical heritage is given in Yehiel Adaqi and Uri Sharvit, *A Treasury of Jewish Yemenite Chants* (Jerusalem: The Israel Institute for Sacred Music, 1981). [Hebrew]

62. See Ratzaby, *Yemenite Jewry*.

63. See Goitein, "The Jews of Yemen," p. 233; *Encyclopaedia Judaica*, Vol. 16, pp. 745-746.

64. See Nahshon, "Jewish Leadership in Yemen." *Ḥakham bashi* was "a title conferred by the Ottomans on the chief rabbi appointed in a conquered country." Yosef Tobi, "The Authority of the Community of San'aa in Yemenite Jewry," in S. Deshen and W. Zenner, eds., *Jewish Societies in the Middle East: Community, Culture and Authority* (Washington, D. C.: University Press of America, 1982).

65. Tsadok, *History and Customs of the Jews of Yemen*, pp. 123ff; Nini, "From Joseph Halevy till the *'IQSHIM* and *DARDA'IM* Dispute in 1914" in Y. Yeshayahu and Y. Tobi, eds., *The Jews of Yemen* (Jerusalem: Ben-Zvi Institute, 1975). This important religious and intellectual movement continues to influence the ideology, attitudes and practices of its adherents and opponents today. For the background, see Ahroni, *Yemenite Jewry*, pp. 154-156.

3

The Exodus from Yemen

The Nineteenth Century

We have seen that Yemen's Jews lived for almost two millennia with the idea that they were only in exile in Yemen and that their true home was the Land of Israel. Sooner or later they would be redeemed and would return there. Much of the poetry of the beloved Shalom Shabazi, so widely known and so often sung and cited, dealt with the love of Zion and redemption (*geula*). They bore humiliation and disenfranchisement with this in mind. Yehuda Nini writes, "When pressures increased the Yemenite Jew would murmur *ba-ḥata'enu* ('for our sins'); yet, despite his humiliation, he would always remember that he was the son of the matriarch (Sarah) and as such, superior to the son of the maidservant (Hagar)."[1]

During these millennia there were sporadic contacts between Yemen's Jews and the outside world, and occasionally an individual or a family would actually leave Yemen and go to live in Palestine.[2] (Amram Korah lists seventy-two rabbis who went to Erets Yisrael between 1690 and 1946.)[3] In fact some people even went to live in other countries, such as Egypt, but these were rare occurrences, and Yemen's Jews continued to live in Yemen, with all of the problems this presented. In the second half of the nineteenth century, however, some new influences and prospects began to awaken ideas of more immediate redemption among the Jews of Yemen.

Although Yemen remained very isolated, a difficult place to visit largely closed to outsiders, there were growing influences from the rest of the world in the nineteenth century.

1. In 1839 the British conquered and began to rule Aden and its hinterlands. This put the British on the doorstep of Yemen and gave the Jews an outlet to the rest of the world. The Jewish community of Aden, closely related to that of Yemen, increased in well-being and

importance under British rule, and they and the Yemeni community
gained more access to the wider Jewish world. By the 1850s and
1860s they were in contact with such important Jewish institutions as the
Board of Deputies of British Jews and the Alliance Israelite Universelle
(founded in 1860).[4]

2. In 1849 the Ottoman Turks started to occupy Yemen, and by
1872 they had captured San'a and controlled much of Yemen. (The
Turks had ruled part of Yemen in the sixteenth century, but lost it in
the seventeenth. They never controlled all of it fully in the nineteenth
century either. The imams were always able to hold on in at least certain
portions of the northern highlands.) Because Palestine was also part of
the Ottoman empire at this time, there was a closer connection between
Yemen and Palestine. It apparently facilitated visits by emissaries from
the Jewish community of Erets Yisrael, and resulted in several trips by
Jews from Yemen to Istanbul and elsewhere in the empire, on behalf of
their communities.[5]

3. There was an increasing number of travelers and traders coming
to Yemen. Some were non-Jews, some were ex-Jews seeking Jewish
communities to convert to Christianity, and some were emissaries
(*shlihim*) sent by the Jewish community of Palestine to seek financial
and moral support and to strengthen the links between their communities.
(A large part of the Jewish community of the Holy Land at that time was
dependent upon donations from abroad.) Prominent among the *shlihim*
were Jacob Sapir, who wrote an important book about Yemen's Jews,
and Haim Jacob Feinstein of Safed.[6] These travelers were able to tell
Yemen's Jews about new developments and prospects for the settlement
of Palestine, and tell the rest of the world about Yemen's Jews.

4. The years from 1840 to 1880 were ones in which an increasing
number of European Jews began to think in terms of the settlement
of the Holy Land as a possible solution to "the Jewish problem." Sir
Moses Montefiore of England threw his energy, wealth, and influence
into the idea. He worked to influence the prevailing governments,
especially the Ottomans, and he bought land in Jerusalem which he
gave to Jews for settlement. In 1860 this land was the site of the first
Jewish settlement outside the walls of the Old City. The Rothschilds also
made contributions from an early period. In 1870 the Alliance Israelite
Universelle established an agricultural school, Mikveh Yisrael, to train
and encourage Jews in agricultural pursuits. And still other Jews, and

some non-Jewish British Zionists, talked of purchasing larger amounts of land in Erets Yisrael, to be given for Jewish settlement.[7]

According to Nini, in 1873 the emissary Haim Jacob Feinstein brought news of the idea of establishing Jewish settlements in the Land of Israel.[8] And in 1875 a Yemenite Jewish emissary, Yosef Ben-Shlomo Mas'ud, who was sent from San'a to Istanbul, went to Jerusalem where he learned of other plans for buying land and settling Jews there. Through these channels and others the Jews of Yemen were stimulated to believe that immigration to Erets Yisrael (*aliya*) might actually be possible, not in the far distant future but immediately.

5. The middle of the nineteenth century was a period of heightened messianic expectation among Yemen's Jews. They had a long tradition of messianism, expecting a messiah whose appearance would usher in "the end of days." They had had a messianic movement in 1172 which was the subject of Maimonides' famous communication, *Iggeret Teyman* (Letter to Yemen). He cautioned them that this messianic era might be close, and that the tribulations then being suffered by the community might be a sign of the nearness of redemption.[9]

Later they were also avid followers of the movement of Shabtai Tsvi, the powerful and widespread Jewish messianic movement of 1665-66. (Bat-Zion Klorman-Eraqi argues that the Jews of Yemen were influenced, in part, by the eschatological expectations of their Muslim neighbors, who also awaited the coming of the *mahdi*, "the divinely guided one.")[10] And in the 1860s and 1870s Yemen's Jews were very impressed by two more false messiahs. Klorman-Eraqi claims that consistent with the pattern of active messianism of the Yemenite Jews was the idea that the very act of immigration to the Land of Israel, and settling there, was "essential to accomplish the full realization of redemption."[11] Most writers agree that this messianic tradition played an important role in the subsequent immigrations of the Yemenite Jews to Israel.[12]

6. Granted the very significant role of messianism in the decision to leave Yemen for Erets Yisrael, the prevailing political and economic conditions were also important. The middle of the nineteenth century had been a particularly difficult time, marked by great political instability, struggles for the imamate, and revolts by various tribes. The false messiahs thrived in this context. Conditions varied from place to place, but often they were worst for the Jews in the cities.

The coming of the Turks to San'a in 1872 gave new hope to the Jews of that city. It seemed possible that the new regime might make basic changes in their situation and treatment, and at first the Jews willingly aided the Turks.[13] In the beginning of the occupation their economic situation did improve markedly, and the community grew both from natural increase and as others were attracted to it from the surrounding countryside.[14] The Turks also made the task of cleaning the latrines and streets less onerous by paying reasonable wages to those willing to do the work.[15] But the optimism was short-lived, for the basic disenfranchisement of the Jews did not change, and their Arab neighbors came to dislike them even more in the new sociopolitical context.[16]

On top of this, the Turkish regime heaped still more burdens on the Jews. A heavy head tax was levied on the community; it remained a source of trouble for years. The Jews were also ordered to bear wounded Turkish soldiers on the long and arduous walk from the highlands down to the port of Hodeida on the Red Sea.[17] And a particularly difficult situation resulted from the decree that the Jews had to grind grain for the food of the Turkish soldiers. At first there weren't many soldiers and it wasn't such a problem, but as they grew in numbers it became increasingly difficult for the Jewish women to grind the grain on their hand millers at home.[18] No grain mill was established in Yemen until 1910.[19]

The Turkish occupation also resulted in worrisome changes in social and moral life, above all by stimulating prostitution. Some Jews provided entertainment and drink for Turkish soldiers. Erich Brauer writes that "in the towns Jewesses were often sold to the Turks" and some "even went over to Islam."[20]

The coming of the Turks brought many new things to the Jews, such as the use of kerosene and, according to Tobi, showed the Jews some of the ways of modern life. Part of this role was played by the Jewish merchants and medical officers who accompanied the occupying forces.[21] But above all it was the disappointment which the Jews of San'a experienced as a result of the Turkish occupation, and the decline in their economic and social situation, that stimulated them to heed the signs and take the new opportunities which were opening up for them.[22]

The First Aliya—*E'eleh b'Tamar*

In 1881 a rumor spread among Yemen's Jews that Rothschild, whom they thought of as the king or the great rabbi of the Jews, had bought a lot of land in Erets Yisrael and was going to give it, free of charge, to Jews from all over the world who would come to settle on it and engage in agriculture. It seems most likely that the basis for this rumor is the fact that the British non-Jewish Zionist, Laurence Oliphant, was then negotiating with the Turkish government, seeking rights of settlement for Jews in Palestine. Oliphant hoped that rich European Jews would finance his scheme to settle poor Eastern European Jews in Palestine.[23]

In fact Oliphant's scheme did not succeed, but on the basis of the rumor and the hopes it aroused, more than 100 families from San'a and its hinterland left Yemen and, with great difficulty, made their way to Jerusalem. Two families left first, starting out in May 1881; others arrived in August 1881 and the rest in August 1882.[24] The first settlers from Yemen arrived in Palestine in exactly the same year as the first organized group of Zionist settlers from Europe, the so-called Bilu.

The emigrants tried to sell their houses and most of their tools and other possessions, but they had few takers. The Muslims had little use for houses in the Jewish quarter or for tools specific to Jewish trades. And many Jews had hopes to make *aliya* themselves. In fact, many Yemenite Jews saw the year 1881-82 as the beginning of the messianic era.[25]

The year 1881-82, 5642 in the Jewish calendar, is called *Tarmab*, after the Hebrew letters which stand for the numbers of the year. The Song of Songs, which is known to all Yemenites and is full of symbolic meaning, contains within it the phrase "Amarti e'eleh b'tamar," which means "I thought [or said] I would climb a palm tree" (7:8). But the word *e'eleh* also means "I will go up to Erets Yisrael." (The root *oleh*, the source of *aliya*, means "to ascend," including "to go up to Israel" or to Jerusalem.) This sentence from the Song of Songs could thus be taken to mean "I thought I would ascend (to the Holy Land) *b'tamar*," and by a simple reversal of the letters *b'tamar* (a date palm) becomes *tarmab*—1881-82! Thus for those reading the signs, as the Jews of Yemen were, the year *Tarmab* could indeed be taken to be a significant one, perhaps the beginning of the redemption.

The Yemenites in Jerusalem

After the difficult trip, which took some immigrants many months to complete and usually exhausted all of their funds (for passage, bribes, protection, and living expenses), their reception in the Holy City must have been yet another disappointment. There was no free land from Rothschild, no place to live, and very little work.

In 1881 the Jewish community of Palestine numbered about 25,000 (out of perhaps 300,000 total inhabitants), and the country as a whole was very poor, undeveloped, and a backwater in all respects. Although Jerusalem had a small population of Jewish merchants, primarily Sephardim, an elite who had long lived in the Near East, many of the city's European (Ashkenazi) and Middle Eastern Jews were members of religious communities living from charity collected from Jewish people in the diaspora, including Yemen. Although there were the beginnings of a few Jewish settlements outside the walls of the Old City in the 1870s, Zionist nationalist settlement, oriented toward the rebuilding of the land and the establishment of a national home for the Jews, was only just about to begin.

The Jews who arrived from San'a in 1881-82 endured many hardships in the early years. At first they were hardly even recognized as Jews. With their distinctively different costumes, their dark complexions, and their Yemeni Arabic speech, they were at first taken for Arabs by many Jews. [26] They couldn't communicate with the Ashkenazi Jews who spoke Yiddish, a Jewish dialect based on German, but not Hebrew. But worst of all they were forced to live at first in the open air, under temporary shelters in summer, and in caves and rock shelters during Jerusalem's often unpleasant winters. There was no other housing available. [27] Within its walls the Old City was very crowded, conditions were poor, and the rents were high.

In the early years the newcomers were aided by the efforts of a Russian-born newspaper editor, Yisrael Dov Frumkin, who had already had contact with Yemenite emissaries in the 1870s. [28] He publicized their plight and organized a fund for their relief. One of its aims was to arrange for the newcomers to learn new trades for their livelihoods. He also managed to acquire a parcel of land outside the walls of the Old City, not far from the Western Wall (the so-called "Wailing Wall") where they were able to build their first houses. They did their own building, using materials obtained with the aid of the fund. The village of Shiloah, right next to the site of the ancient city built by David, remained the home of many Yemenites from 1885 until the 1930s, when they were forced to abandon it as a result of Arab anti-Jewish riots. In the succeeding years a number of other primarily Yemenite residential sections were built in Jerusalem. [29]

It was not easy for them to find work in their old occupations. Some were able to work as jewelers and other artisans, or as scribes, but many more had to find new forms of work. Many women went to work as housekeepers. Druyan points out that some Yemenites did low-status work, "the most despised work," which was not a problem for them since they were already used to it from Yemen and were not opposed to it by their values. Soon they got a reputation for not rejecting any kind of work. [30] Of great importance, however, were the building trades. These were just about to become very important as a result of the new immigration, and the Yemenites played an important role in them. Fifty men were taught to be stonecutters (almost all building in Jerusalem is in stone), while others went into other aspects of building. Before long they were a major element in the building trades, and some Yemenites even became successful contractors. [31]

By 1908, according to Druyan, of 572 Yemenite men, 36.5 percent were engaged in the building trades. [32] Almost 16 percent were engaged in various skilled and semiskilled trades as tailors, weavers, printers, blacksmiths, shoemakers, tilers, bakers, and plasterers. Jewelers accounted for another 7 percent, while peddlers and shopkeepers represented just 5.4 percent. Those engaged in service occupations (at schools and hospitals) dropped from 12.7 percent in 1887 to just 4.2 percent in 1908, and those listed as "receiving charity" (*tsadaka*) dropped from 20.3 percent to 2.4 percent! Seventeen percent are listed as students of higher religious studies in *yeshiva*, while about 11 percent were engaged in other religious professions, as religious teachers, "wisemen" (*hakhamim*, curers), religious scribes, and kosher slaughterers.

The picture which emerges from this list, as well as from other sources, is one of an industrious community, working with their hands as they had in Yemen, but also devoting a good deal of time, effort, and money to religious pursuits. Despite their original difficulties, they did not remain economically dependent upon others for long.

A very high percentage of Jerusalem's Jews in the 1880s and 1890s were dependent upon donations from Jewish communities abroad, who maintained these representatives of the faith living in the Holy City. When the Yemenites arrived in Jerusalem, all the different Jewish "ethnic" communities were organized into institutions for the distribution of donations (*halukkah*), and to care for the general welfare of the groups and look after their interests. There were such organizations (called *kolel*) to represent the Jews who had come from Poland, from Holland and Germany, from Hungary, from Georgia, from North Africa, and elsewhere. There was also one for the "Sephardim," those Jews, mostly from various countries in the Middle East, who trace their origins back to Spain (*Sefarad* in Hebrew), whence they were evicted during the Inquisition in the 1490s.[33] It was this last *kolel* to which the Yemenites were attached when they first arrived, and to which they had to turn for aid and support.

The relationship between the Yemenites and the Sephardi *kolel* was never easy. The common pot was small, and there were inevitable conflicts over the distribution of funds. The Yemenites could not even claim to be Sephardim, but on the other hand the Jews of Yemen had been sending donations to this *kolel*.[34] It very soon became apparent that the situation was not satisfactory, but it was not until 1907 that they finally managed to organize and establish their own independent *kolel*.

By 1912 the Yemenites of Jerusalem had grown in number to 2,874, through continued immigration and natural increase. This community maintained twenty synagogues, two schools for the education of children, two institutions for higher religious studies (*yeshivot*), a cemetery, and a slaughterhouse.[35] They had developed prominent religious leadership, and under the direction of Rabbi Avraham Ḥaim el-Nadaf. Yemenite editions of the prayer book, the Torah, and numerous other religious books were published.

The Second Aliya

The *aliya* from San'a to Jerusalem was not the only early Yemenite settlement in Erets Yisrael. By the turn of the century there was a small colony of Yemenites living in Jaffa (Yafo) that was soon to play a role in the building of Tel Aviv when that city was founded in 1909 as a suburb of Yafo. An important development began in 1907 when new groups of Yemenites came to Palestine from the northern provinces of Yemen, from Sa'da and Haydan. These people did not come from the cities of the central districts of Yemen, but from small villages where they had been familiar with agriculture and had lived relatively secure and satisfactory lives amidst the northern tribes, who protected them reasonably well. In fact, they were even used to bearing arms themselves.[36]

According to Zekharya Gluska,[37] a man named Yosef Qarḥash went to Jerusalem to spend his last days and be buried there. "When he reached the Holy Land, he was deeply impressed by the new Jewish agricultural settlements, and in 1906 he came back to his homeland to tell the news of the settling of the land and, in Gelusqa's words, 'he made up his mind to return to Yemen and to announce redemption.'"[38] His advice was heeded by many, and between 1907 and 1909 several hundred Jews from the north and, almost at the same time, a number from the south of Yemen had come to settle in Palestine. They specifically sought to settle in the new Jewish agricultural communities and seek work in agriculture, as Qarḥash had suggested. They made their way to the newly established Jewish settlements of Reḥovot, Petaḥ Tikva, Rishon LeTsion, and Hadera, and to the farming communities near them, where they looked for work and a place to settle their families.

The beginnings were hard for these settlers, too, as they had been for those in Jerusalem. They had to live in storerooms, cellars, barns, and the open air until they were able to build their own homes. They were met with prejudice and contempt by some of the other settlers and the farmers for whom they would work. The work was hard and the pay was very poor, but they soon established themselves in an important way. They had come at a critical juncture in the development of the Jewish community and its institutions.

By 1906 the attempts of the first wave of European Jewish settlers to create agricultural colonies had shown mixed results. Progress was being made in production, but at the cost of hiring cheap Arab labor. The idealism of the first farmers had encountered the realities of agricultural production and had given way to economic considerations. The local Arabs were familiar with the work and either had their own farms and thus could work for low wages as a supplement, or, if they had no other options, could still be hired cheaply. On the other hand, the newly arrived Eastern European immigrants of the Second Aliya—young, idealistic, socialistic, and anxious to work the land—were unattractive workers for the Jewish farmers who were expected to hire them. They had no farms or other families to support them, were used to a higher standard of living, and demanded higher wages. They were also imbued with ideas of equality, socialism, and pioneering Zionism, and were quick to demand their rights. They wanted to be represented in local

administrative bodies and "constantly served to remind the farmers of
their sins; for the latter, too, had been fired with the same idealism and
integrity of purpose before their bitter experiences robbed them of their
enthusiasm and turned them into sceptical bourgeois."[39]

This was the setting into which the new settlers from Yemen intruded
themselves, looking for work in agriculture! It was soon clear that
they could work for as little as the Arabs; even if they were not used
to the particular farming techniques and crops in the settlements, they
were excellent workers and could tolerate the heat and other difficult
conditions that bothered the Europeans. Wives and children often
worked along with the men. Some farmers were soon happy to hire
them, and to the leaders of the Second Aliya it seemed like a partial
solution to a major problem. Here were Jewish workers who could take
part in what was called *kibush ha' avodah*, the "conquest of labor."[40]

The idealist pioneers who had come to Palestine at this time were
under the influence of Tolstoy and "popular socialism," and they believed
in the "ennoblement of labor." They argued that the Jews would forfeit
their moral right to the land if they allowed it to be worked, on behalf of
Jews, with the cheap labor of non-Jews. Before many years had passed,
some of these young people would be successfully working the land
themselves, in the newly developed communal settlements (*kibbutsim*),
but at this point the coming of the Yemenites seemed to be just what the
Zionist movement needed. (The first *kibbuts* was established in 1909.)

The Yemenite settlers were so successful as agricultural workers, and
adapted to their new environment so well and so rapidly, that leaders
of the Zionist workers' movement decided to recruit more immigrants
from Yemen, especially young workers. An emissary, Shmuel Yavnieli,
was sent for this purpose in 1911.[41] Speaking in secular terms about
the national redemption of the Jews through work on the land and the
upbuilding of Erets Yisrael, Yavnieli tried to give his listeners a realistic
sense of the shortages, difficulties, and hard work which awaited them
in Palestine. He eased the way for them by arranging special rates on
the ship up the Red Sea, and by covering some expenses for those who
couldn't afford the trip otherwise. In this way he stimulated hundreds
to leave for Palestine, and he seems to have set off another round of
messianic expectations. Even though he purposely couched his appeal
in modern Zionist words, he was aware quite early that his coming was
seen by many as a harbinger of the messianic age.[42]

Yavnieli's mission caused great excitement and a flood of potential immigrants was apparently about to develop when he was suddenly told, in 1912, to halt his activities and stop the flow of immigrants. It seems that the leaders of the Poalei Tsion (Zionist Workers) movement, including David Ben-Gurion, Rachel Yannait, and others, were deeply concerned about the implications of bringing in the Yemenite workers. Some were concerned that these apparently tractable and uncomplaining workers were being exploited and given second-class status. Others worried that their lack of secular socialist ideology would water down and weaken the Zionist workers' movement. Still others feared the potential conflicts between the groups of settlers.[43] In any case, Yavnieli, to his great distress and embarrassment, had to tell those Yemenites who wanted to leave that the time was not right and that they should wait. The emigration slowed down and, with the coming of World War I, was practically cut off for a while.

In the meantime, despite the early problems, the new Yemenite immigrants settled down and had soon created their own little communities adjacent to the newly developing agricultural settlements and towns. Here, as in Jerusalem thirty years earlier, the Yemenites showed the same preference for settling in ethnically homogeneous communities. They chose to do so at least in part in order to enable them to maintain as much as possible of their own way of life. Many of the settlements which they established in those few years are still major Yemenite communities. These include Sha'arayim in Rehovot and Shivat Tsion in Rishon LeTsion, both established in 1910; Mahane Yehuda in Petah Tikva (1912); and Nahaliel in Hadera (1914).

The new settlers craved their own little piece of land and their own houses. "They hoped that the houses would turn them into permanent citizens, and the portion of land promised to establish and complete their needs for times of unemployment and their old age."[44] The Palestine Office of the World Zionist Organization and the Jewish National Fund, whose task was to aid land purchase and immigrants, aided some settlers with grants of land, making possible their first settlements in Rehovot and Rishon LeTsion.[45]

The years 1904 to 1914 were the time of the Second Aliya, the epic period of pioneering for Jewish immigrants in Palestine. The Jewish community (*yishuv*) was growing, and the Yemenites had to deal with at least three kinds of European Jews. Yisrael Yeshayahu, a prominent

Yemenite leader and Labor Party politician, described the situation as follows:

> . . . in the cities (Jaffa and Jerusalem) the religious people lived from alms received from foreign Jewish communities. In the [new agricultural] settlements the small farmers sought to find manual laborers for the lowest price. [These were the "bourgeoisie" of the First Aliya.] Between these two extremes fought the young socialist Zionists burning with the ideal of building the country.[46]

The Yemenites and the young European Jewish socialist pioneers comprised "two separate worlds," but the Yemenites received a certain amount of aid and support from the socialist pioneers, especially those of the HaPoel HaTsair (Young Worker) movement. At that time some Yemenites became associated with that party and the wider labor movement of which it was a part. As Ratzaby notes, "despite everything they (the socialists and the Yemenites) had a common language: love of the land (Israel), love of labor, and the revival of the (Hebrew) language."[47] In fact, at this time there developed the beginning of a split between those Yemenites who chose to ally themselves with the socialist labor movement, while eschewing its secular outlook, and those who affiliated with, or at least sympathized with, the religious Zionist Mizraḥi party.[48]

Despite the aid and the positive relationships which some Yemenites had with HaPoel HaTsair, in general it was a difficult time from every point of view: physically and economically, politically and socially. Their health suffered and children were sick and died. Conditions were difficult in most cases for the new settlers from Europe, too, but they at least had the wholehearted support of the political machinery of the Zionist movement, and had their parties and their ideology to sustain them. There was much greater suffering for the Yemenites who were often exploited, looked down upon, and badly mistreated by the farmers, workers, and townspeople.[49] In addition the Zionist settlement agencies were not generous in granting land to the Yemenites. They gave smaller plots to Yemenites than to others[50] and refused to establish a Yemenite farming community until 1933, despite repeated requests for years. In part this was due to the conflict of interest with the other settlers, who were closer to the agencies, but in part it was a question of ideology and policy. The establishment was committed to the ideal of communal and cooperative agriculture, so they were not anxious to grant land to those Yemenites who wanted to form their own farming communities based on individual family enterprise.[51] As Yehuda Nini points out in a related context,

> The Yemenite Jews were not simply the victims of discrimination. They rather suffered from two general tendencies resulting from the building of Zionism along party lines. One was the preference understandably accorded by the parties to their own members and supporters abroad over individuals without party affiliation. The other was the desire to create a new kind of Jewish society, which implied a preference for Jews sharing in this ideological vision over those who would merely add to the "old" *yishuv*. These two preferences served to work not only against the Yemenite *olim* (immigrants) as a group, but also against nonpartisan individuals from Eastern Europe, or people with a traditional outlook.[52]

Whatever the reason, it was a difficult time. Nini quotes one Yemenite worker as having said, "There [in Yemen] we were exiles in body; here, in *Eretz Israel*, we are exiles in both body and soul."[53] The difficulties and struggles of those times are remembered today with some bitterness, which is certainly not eased by the fact that standard Israeli history celebrates the struggles of the other pioneers while ignoring the even more disappointing and avoidable travails of the Yemenites, so many of which were caused by the cruelty and insensitivity of their Jewish brethren.

The First World War and the Mandate Period (1914-48)

World War I made immigration from Yemen to Palestine almost impossible, and conditions in the ensuing years were not much better. In 1920, under the influence of Palestinian Arabs, especially the Grand Mufti of Jerusalem, the imam decreed an end to emigration to Palestine. It is also said that he was concerned about the loss of the skilled Jewish artisans who were so important to his country's material culture. On the other hand, the "Decree of the Orphans" was being prosecuted vigorously, and fatherless Jewish children were being taken from their families and communities and brought up as Muslims. This and other economic and social difficulties merely increased the fear of the Jews and added to their desire to leave Yemen and join their kinsmen in Erets Yisrael. (From the first days of the first *aliya* there had been frequent exchanges of correspondence, and the Jews still in Yemen were aware of the lives of their kinsmen abroad. Sometimes the emigrants tended to make their situations sound far more satisfactory than they actually were.)

During their rule the British mandatory government severely restricted Jewish immigration to Palestine, and after 1939 they forbade it altogether. The Jewish Agency (by then the executive arm of the World Zionist Organization) put the Jews of Yemen very low on their priority list of those who should receive the few entry permits.[54] Nevertheless, despite the difficulties about 16,000 Yemenite Jews managed somehow to get to Erets Yisrael during the years from 1920 to 1948. By 1948, on the eve of the declaration of the independence of Israel, there were an estimated 28,000 Jews of Yemenite descent living in the country, out of a total Jewish population of 650,000.

The Veteran Yemenite Community

The Yemenites of the prestate community remained rather heavily concentrated in unskilled and semiskilled occupations.[55] Many worked in agriculture, some as farmers but more as farm laborers. The building trades continued to be important, and many Yemenites worked in related fields as tile setters, painters, plasterers, carpenters, plumbers, electricians, and mechanics. They were overrepresented in the menial work of the *yishuv*, as porters, garbage collectors, and street cleaners. Women frequently worked as laundresses and, above all, as housemaids in the homes of the more affluent Jewish urban and farm families. Joseph Schechtman observed that Yemenites were often thought of primarily as "destined to do the coarsest, most difficult, poorly paid manual work."[56]

There were, however, Yemenite teachers, clerks, civil servants, and religious officials, as well as party and labor officials. There were rabbis and editors and authors among them, as well as jewelers, artisans and artists, musicians, scribes, and rabbis. Some women went into teaching and nursing as professions. Shopkeeping and business were not popular enterprises among Yemenites, but there were successful building contractors and other wealthy businessmen, especially in the greater Tel Aviv area. (Percy Cohen's list of Yemenite occupations in Sha'arayim in 1955-57, when 75 percent of the population were still veterans of the prestate period, is reasonably representative of the situation at the time of the founding of the state.)[57]

In 1948 Yemenite Jews were to be found residing primarily in Jerusalem, Tel Aviv-Jaffa-Holon, and in neighborhoods of their own in or near most of the major Jewish towns and cities, such as Reḥovot, Rishon LeTsion, Ḥadera, Petaḥ Tikva, Netanya, Herzliya, Zikhron Ya'akov, and Nes Tsiona, as well as in some smaller villages. Until 1948 they had been granted only two substantial farming villages, or *moshavim*, of their own. These were Elyashiv in 1933 and Geulim in 1938. (Raphael Patai discusses three older small settlements which had some acreage for agricultural production, although they were intended primarily as residential areas for workers.)[58]

Wherever possible the Yemenites continued to live in their own communities. It seems clear that this was largely self-segregation by choice. Nitsa Druyan writes that the majority of Yemenite immigrants preferred to live with their own brethren. They were not inclined to adapt to the ways of other communities but preferred to continue the way of life they were used to in Yemen. Thus they clustered in their own neighborhoods and "maintained a way of life similar to that which they had led in their country of origin."[59] There they established their own synagogues, ritual baths, slaughterhouses, schools, and leadership to represent them in the wider Jewish community.

There is, however, another motivation for the community self-segregation, a reactive one. If it was partly chosen out of positive attraction for kinsmen and fellow countrymen, and to perpetuate a valued way of life, it was intensified as a result of the insults, the affronts, and the bad treatment they suffered at the hands of others, including private citizens, local governments and the Zionist establishment. Berreby quotes the important Yemenite leader, Yisrael Yeshayahu, arguing that "Little by little there crystallized, in the midst of the *yishuv*, this sort of minority group, demanding its part on every occasion, and even its part in political life, as a minority."[60]

Berreby continues:

> In the *moshavot* [the Jewish towns] the Yemenites, settled in separate quarters, cloistered themselves voluntarily; they refused to pay municipal taxes; they engaged in lawsuits with the local councils and for a long time deprived themselves of all community services. In the cities they were also concentrated in distinct quarters. This social retrenchment reinforced in them the desire to differentiate themselves totally from all those who surrounded them. 'They opposed with all their might all foreign influences which penetrated their quarters.'[61]

Whatever the motivations, the Yemenites underlined and maintained their separate identity. Neither Ashkenazi nor Sephardi, with different traditions and history, as a community they acted to keep significant ethnic markers and boundaries. Many men and women emphasized the differences by continuing to wear their traditional costumes, while many men and boys retained the traditional side-locks (*pe'ot*) as they had in Yemen. Endogamy was the rule, and they held firmly to their distinctive pronunciation of Hebrew, as well as to their religious, folklore, and artistic traditions.

On the political side, in addition to gaining recognition as a separate community (*kolel*) in Jerusalem in 1907, some younger Yemenites began participating in Zionist politics as a distinct unit as early as 1911, by joining the Young Worker movement. They established a number of Yemenite political organizations, some affiliated with other Zionist movements and some completely independent of, and often at odds with, the others.[62] The Organization of Yemenite Jews in Israel was founded in 1923.

Reading about this era one feels an interesting contradiction. On the one hand writers, Yemenites among them, invariably stress the Yemenites' almost mystical love of Zion, their willingness to trust in God and to work hard and suffer privations cheerfully and philosophically. On the other hand, the literature is full of bitter complaints by Yemenites, of attacks on the Zionist establishment and local authorities and councils, and very real evidence of political organization and pressure. Patai quotes at length from a resolution by the Council of Yemenite Laborers, in 1920, expressing their great bitterness at their situation in Palestine at that time.[63] Schechtman cites other examples of the expression of resentment,[64] while Poulos gives a particularly bleak—and overstated—picture of their anger and potential dissidence.[65] (The case of Sha'arayim, discussed in Chapter 8, offers a prime example of hostile intercommunal relations.)[66]

The truth seems to lie in a combination of these two competing images. To judge from the literature, the Yemenite settlers were deeply devoted to the Land of Israel, and they were capable of undergoing suffering while maintaining their faith in God. But they were not so simple and foolish that they did not understand that their lives could be made better both by hard work and saving and by organized attempts to influence the political and economic environment in which they lived. As a community they had considerable political awareness. As Patai noted in 1953, "They are the best organized of the Oriental Jewish communities in Israel."[67] Indeed, until the 1980s they were virtually the only Jewish ethnic group to contest elections with an openly ethnic appeal, and they were, until recently, the only country-of-origin group to have successfully elected Knesset members on an ethnic slate (in 1949 and 1950).[68]

There is a similar ambivalence in the literature about the image and reputation of the Yemenite Jews within the *yishuv*. To some extent they were admired for their thrift and industriousness and for their willingness to work hard and responsibly at difficult and low-paid menial labor. They were also given credit for their faith, their respect for learning and the maintenance of their religious tradition, and for their beautiful artisanry, music, and dance. Their arts played a very important role in the development of the culture of Jewish Palestine.[69]

On the negative side, the socialists did not appreciate their religiosity, the maintenance of the religious traditions which these secular-minded modernists were themselves leaving behind in the diaspora. Nor did they care for Yemenite "individualism."[70] The Ashkenazi religious establishment, on the other hand, was not appreciative of the subtle differences in Yemenite interpretations of law and of worship and presumably did not care for the competition and loss of control.

In the years just before the establishment of the state the Yemenite image was affected by the frequent battles between Yemenite communities and their neighbors (as, for example, the case of Sha'arayim versus Reḥovot). In addition there were some cases of aggressive and "antisocial" behavior by young Yemenites, of a type uncommon within the Jewish community.[71] A disproportionate number of Yemenite and other "oriental" youths participated in the Revisionist political movement, with its Betar youth group. They joined the Irgun Tsvai Leumi nationalist underground military organization, led by Menahem Begin. Those Jews who were not supporters of this group looked upon it as a dissident terrorist organization, and the reputation of Yemenite youths in the 1940s was influenced accordingly.

Finally, a good many people simply considered the Yemenites "primitive." As Berreby noted, a majority "recognizes all their qualities; they are intelligent, hard-working, economical, good patriots, but *they are not adaptable*. They call them 'the Blacks.' They like them *on condition that they stay 'in their place*,' at the bottom of the economic-social scale."[72] Although Berreby reckons that this view changed considerably after the war of independence, it does undoubtedly summarize the feeling of many people in the 1930s.

It is clear that the Yemenites had an impact upon the image of the Jewish community of Palestine. No other non-European Jewish community had anything like their visibility and prominence. This was not merely a matter of numbers (they were only about 4.3 percent of the Jewish population), but was based on the combination of elements enumerated above, both positive and negative. They captured the imagination. In the late 1930s the image many people had of the Jews of Palestine was a tripartite one: (1) the pioneers on the kibbutzim; (2) the old religious Jews at the Western Wall, living from charity; and (3) the Yemenites—colorful, hard-working, praying, and making silver jewelry.[73]

As for their actual economic situation at this time, it is difficult to evaluate. The majority worked at low paying labor, but the tendency for most able-bodied members of the family to work, their propensity for saving, for home ownership and the acquisition of real estate (houses and apartments—evident even from an early period), and their unwillingness to display their wealth, suggest that their condition was not as poor as it often appeared.

In summary, by 1948 there was a Yemenite community of about 28,000, dispersed throughout the country in a number of distinct settlements. They had established their identity in Palestine especially through their contribution to agriculture, building, and the arts. They made some mark on the political scene and, in addition to a traditional elite of learned rabbis, had produced a small but significant group of writers, intellectuals, political leaders, and artistic figures, especially prominent in music and dance. There were not many wealthy Yemenites, but there were a few. And the Yemenites played a significant role in the movement for liberation from British control of Palestine. Many Yemenite youths had joined the dissident Revisionist political movement and the Irgun Tsvai Leumi, while others joined the Palmakh units of the Haganah, associated with the labor movement. It is Berreby's estimation, from what he learned in 1954, that "their patriotism and heroism in combat, their stoicism, and their capacity for work, their small but authentic elite" had won the sympathy and admiration of even those who had previously scorned them.[74]

Independence and Operation on Wings of Eagles

In May 1948 the Jews of Palestine declared their independence from Great Britain and officially established the State of Israel. The political organizations and agencies of the Jewish community were transformed into the machinery of a government, and an administration was established in the midst of an armed struggle against invading Arab armies.

The immigration of Jews to Israel ("The Ingathering of the Exiles") was a major priority of the new state. Of primary importance, of course, was the need for manpower for industry and agriculture, for the war effort against a far more numerous enemy, and to populate the new country. Of almost equal importance was the fact that there were Jewish communities in distress in various parts of the world, apparently in need of rescue. Displaced persons who had survived the war in Europe were still living in refugee camps in Europe and in internment camps in Cyprus, under British control. The Jews of Iraq, Egypt, and Libya were in danger from mobs as well as from governmental action, especially once Israel was declared a state. In China almost a thousand Jews were caught up in the turmoil of the revolution, mostly around Shanghai. And in the Arabian Peninsula, Yemen's Jews were in difficult economic straits, hoping to emigrate. Thousands of Yemen's Jews were being kept in a desert camp near Aden, having being stopped en route to Palestine by the British authorities in that Crown Colony.

In 1939 the British government in Palestine had issued the White Paper which forbade Jewish immigration to Palestine. When this happened, even those Yemenite Jews who had managed to reach Aden previously on their way to Palestine, in defiance of other bars to emigration and immigration, were stopped and held there in camps. Some were forced to spend years in Aden with no real homes or work. In 1946 the British authorities permitted the American Joint Distribution Committee to open camps for these homeless Jews several miles from the city, at Hashed. The two camps housed about 2,700 people at first, but as more of Yemen's Jews tried to leave, their numbers had grown to 7,000 by a few months after the State was established.[75] The British in Aden considered these camps a problem and were threatening to have their inhabitants repatriated to Yemen. It was clear that something had to be done quickly.

The Israeli government issued visas for 3,500 of these refugees and contracted with some American pilots to fly that number of Yemenites from Hashed to Israel. At first they took just the elderly, the sick, and the children, for the British would not permit men of military age to go. But by March 1949 young men, too, were allowed to leave. The flights did not succeed in emptying the camps, however, because thousands more of Yemen's Jews began streaming to Aden to leave for Israel!

In May 1949, for reasons which are still not understood,[76] the imam of Yemen (the son of the murdered Yahya) decreed that the Jews of Yemen should be permitted to leave for Israel in peace. The British had agreed by this time not to interfere with the evacuations, and the mass exodus of Yemen's Jews began. Jewish families and communities from all over the country and from Habban left their homes and began trekking toward Aden and the transport planes. The camps at Hashed swelled to over 7,000 by September 1, 11,000 by September 14, and 13,000 by September 20, 1949. The nurses, doctors, and other officials and workers at the camps did their best to supply medical treatment and nutritious food and to issue clothes to the refugees before loading them onto the converted World War II military transport planes for the trip to Lydda airport in Israel. At the height of the airlift "68 flights evacuated 8,864 Yemenites (in September 1949) and 11,445 were flown in 89 flights in October."[77]

The story of this exodus was often told through Israel's press and radio and was commemorated by stamps and anniversaries, but it is worth sketching briefly once again.[78] In a little over one year, on over 400 flights, 48,000 Jews left the country where they and their ancestors had lived for so long. They came from every corner of the country, and even from distant, isolated Habban, responding to rumors and partial information hardly understood because they knew so little about the events which were taking place. The imam first permitted radios in the late 1940s, and they had not reached far into the countryside. Newspapers arrived only on rare occasions, and did not often get out of San'a. But they heard "There is a government in Israel," "There is a king in Israel," "There is an army in Israel," and "Let's go up to Erets Yisrael."[79]

Wherever possible they sold their houses and their goods to their Arab neighbors for whatever they could get. Some just abandoned everything and left.

All over the Yemen, that summer, Jews abandoned villages and fields and cemeteries, locked up their synagogues and schools, buried holy books and old manuscripts and scrolls and jewellery and valuables in the ground, and packed other scrolls and other books and the rest of their belongings, rugs, mattresses, kettles, tin pans and water pipes, into boxes and bundles, provisioned themselves with dry cakes and boiled butter and dried meat and spices and coffee and flour, and wandered away. [80]

For most the journey was undertaken largely on foot, although some could ride part of the time on animals, and many made the last lap of the trip, from Ta'izz to Aden, by truck. For some it was a journey of a few days or a week, but it took others as long as three months over mountain trails. The country is rugged and difficult, and most had to sleep outside at night during their long trek. Many arrived in poor condition, and a number died en route.

On the way they were forced to pay ransoms and transit or protection fees to local sultans, sheikhs, customs officials, or anyone with the power to extract something from them. Those with resources paid for those without. Many were robbed and cheated, and a few arrived with little more than their clothes. If they were lucky some women arrived at the camp in Hashed with their jewelry and special costumes, and men brought prayer books, Torah scrolls, manuscripts, and other religious articles, including a *shofar*, the ram's horn used to announce the new year, and perhaps a *narghila* (water pipe).

Once in the camps at Hashed, even if the camps were crude, understaffed, and overtaxed by the unexpected thousands who poured in, their basic needs were cared for, medical treatment was provided, and they were safe. Most left on the planes within a few weeks or even sooner. By September 1950 the stream of emigrants had more or less ended, Yemen had been emptied of all but 1-2,000 Jews, and the operation called "On Wings of Eagles" was officially ended. [81]

Many commentators have noted that these 48,000 people, few of whom had ever seen an automobile, had calmly and quietly entered the air transports and flown to the Holy Land, eight hours away. The easy acceptance of the flights was apparently due to their remembrance of God's words in Exodus 19:4: "You have seen what I did to the Egyptians, and how I bore you on wings of eagles and brought you to myself." It seemed, quite reasonably, a fulfillment of prophecy.

Developments in Israel (1948-55)

Once Israel was declared a state and was opened to Jewish immigration, the Knesset passed "The Law of Return," granting every Jew the right to come to live in Israel. Its population grew as perhaps no other country's in history. From May 1948 to September 1951 the Jewish population of Israel had doubled with the addition of 665,000 immigrants. Within thirteen years it had tripled, to more than 1,980,000 at the end of 1961. In addition to the 48,000 Yemenite Jews, who came "On Wings of Eagles," more than 120,000 Jews were brought from Iraq, in a larger airlift called "Operation Ezra and Nehemiah" from May 1950 through 1951. By the end of 1952 almost 35,000 Jews came to Israel from Libya, another 35,000 from Egypt, 33,000 from Turkey, and, by 1958, almost 40,000 from Iran, in "Operation Magic Carpet."[82] Although the major part of the Moroccan *aliya* came somewhat later, by 1958 there were more than 150,000 immigrants from Morocco and 40,000 from Tunisia. From Poland came 103,000 Jews, from Romania 119,000, and from Bulgaria 37,000.[83]

From May 1948 through the end of 1952 more than 346,000 Jews came to Israel from Asia and Africa, while 342,000 came from Europe and the Americas. Israel had come through a difficult war that had lasted more than a year and had to build its economy, develop the country's infrastructure, and find housing, training, work, food, and all other necessities for its veteran population as well as for the immigrants who poured in daily. Few of these immigrants brought any wealth with them; many were sick or were too young or too old to work even if there had been work for them. The Yemenites in particular were suffering from malnutrition and numerous medical problems.[84] Many of those coming from Europe were in very bad psychological condition from their experiences in the Holocaust and during their long internment afterwards in Europe and Cyprus. A large percentage of those coming from African and Asian countries were without modern education or training in occupations that were necessary for Israel's developing economy. (This was less true of most of those from urban Iraq and Egypt.)

In 1948 and 1949 new *olim* who could not be settled in existing Jewish communities moved into abandoned Arab dwellings wherever possible, in order to find shelter. Soon these were no longer available and the government set up camps at the reception centers, using old British army barracks and tents. Yemenites were brought primarily to reception centers at Rosh Ha'Ayin, Ein Shemer, and Pardessiya. Although they received food, clothing, shelter, medical aid, and education for children, there was usually no work around the camps, and the idleness and dependence that developed was clearly not good. New camps were therefore built in areas in which work might be found, usually on the outskirts of established cities and towns. These were called *ma'abarot*, "transit camps."[85]

Those immigrants who had no other choices, or who could not cope on their own, were sent to *ma'abarot*. According to Deborah Bernstein, 57 percent of the immigrants from African and Asian countries between 1948 and 1951 spent some time in *ma'abarot*.[86] At the end of 1951 a quarter of a million people were living in 127 *ma'abarot*, in tents and in corrugated iron and wooden prefabricated shacks. And many Yemenites were among them.

This was a time of austerity for the whole country, and in the camps it was worst of all. The tents and prefabs were not adequate to the climate in winter or summer, and there were floods during the winter rains. There was little work during the first few years, and what there was had to be divided among the heads of families, so that many might work only three days per week. Much of the work consisted of afforestation, road building, and other public works projects, although some found work in industries, factories, agriculture, and construction. Many women went to work in domestic service in the towns, which was relatively well paid.[87] The new immigrants had to depend upon the camp authorities, governmental officials, and staffs of voluntary organizations for almost everything. Food was tightly rationed and not at all satisfactory for the varied cuisines from all the countries represented there.

Aside from the physical difficulties it was a time of disappointments, surprises, and cross-cultural misunderstandings. It was also a time of learning, especially for the Yemenites, who had come from so far away, geographically and socioculturally. The most obvious problems, which the press was quick to publicize, had to do with the material culture and domestic practices of the new world to which the Yemenites had come. According to Jean-Jacques Berreby,

> The principal task was much more basic, less specialized and more difficult than medicine. It was to teach the Yemenites the use of the fork, that many threw away after wounding themselves; to demonstrate that a bed is a comfortable accessory—if you sleep on it and not under it; that sheets aren't intended for the manufacture of shawls or dresses.

To teach them the use of a chair, of a table, of a washbasin; of a
garbage can; to prove that the use of a latrine is, from all points of
view, preferable to the "open air"; and that stones have a disastrous
effect on the drainage of latrines. . . . Running water amused them;
the shower amazed them.[88]

Medicine was not a minor problem at first. Many of the newcomers
from Yemen were in poor physical shape. According to Constantine
Poulos, one out of three had acute malaria, while many suffered from
tropical ulcers, skin diseases, and trachoma.[89] Tuberculosis, venereal
diseases, and bilharzia were also common.[90] Many children were
suffering from chronic malnutrition, but "it took some time for the camp
authorities to overcome the stubborn refusal of the mothers and fathers
to entrust their children to the nurseries and clinics."[91] Women often
refused to be examined unclothed by male doctors, and as of the time
Poulos was writing, "not one expectant mother [had] been willing to
have her baby delivered in a hospital."[92] Raphael Patai noted that even
dangerously ill patients would sneak out of the hospital as soon as they
were able, or their kin would sneak them out.[93]

There were other problems as well, however, as the newcomers faced
a whole new world of laws and customs, social expectations and statutes.
Polygyny and child marriage, common in Yemen, were not sanctioned in
Israel. Correctly or not, the Israeli authorities and social workers, largely
European in origin, thought that the Yemenites had a very powerful
patriarchal family structure. Giora Yosephthal, a leader of the Labor
Party and the head of the Absorption Department (charged with caring
and planning for the new immigrants) was very concerned about these
problems. He wrote,

> . . . we have given a high priority to expanding our social services,
> primarily for the benefit of those who were most neglected in the
> social structure of their lands of origin: the children and the women.
> We fought—and not unsuccessfully—against the patriarchal structure
> of the backward countries, in which the father was the unchallenged
> potentate in the family in whom all rights and privileges repose, and we
> tried to create a Western type of social climate, one which is centered
> around the education of the child. . . . I have in mind mainly (the)
> Yemenites (whom, rightly, we all so love) . . .
>
> The transformation from an authoritarian to a modern society, to a
> critical, democratic society, in which a person's status is determined by
> his ability, character, and achievements, and not by family connections,
> cannot be achieved in a few years. The struggle between the patriarchal

society and the child-centered society was waged in order to allow the child to pass childhood in conditions conducive to normal maturation. We tried as best as we could to change the living patterns the immigrants brought with them. [94]

This statement very nicely states the position of Israel's establishment vis-à-vis "traditional society," a view much influenced by the social science of that era. But if Yosephthal saw the Yemenite social patterns as a problem and a challenge, we must assume that to some extent the Yemenite fathers saw the attempts to weaken their families as a problem. Aside from the planners and the social workers, the political parties, too, fought over the Yemenites—and *all* the immigrants—in order to influence them and gain their votes and support. While the religious parties played on their strong religiosity, the socialist parties, especially Mapai, strove to get their children into the secular schools, or into youth groups, and indoctrinate them with the ideals of secular socialism. [95]

Considering all that they had to learn, it is noteworthy that the Yemenites were among the earliest to leave the *ma'abarot* and move into new settlements. First, the government set up twenty-seven "work villages" in areas where agricultural and other labor was needed, as in the Emek Hefer region near Ḥadera. Families who went to these new communities were each given tiny houses on small plots of land. They had enough land to plant trees and gardens but not enough for extensive agriculture. They also received chickens and perhaps some other livestock. Twenty-one of these villages were settled exclusively by Yemenites. [96] Yosephthal attributes the "distinct communal [i.e. ethnic] character" of these work villages to "chance," but it seems likely that it can be better explained by the willingness of the Yemenites to do agricultural labor on the lands of others, as well as their very strong desire to settle in their own, Yemenite, communities. [97]

By the end of 1953 the government established more than 250 smallholders' cooperative agricultural villages for immigrants. Yemenites moved into more than fifty of these new communities, called *moshavim*, which permitted each family to farm its own land intensively. [98] The Yemenites, who represented 6.5 percent of the immigrant population, at that time provided 24 percent of the settlers (14,000 people) for these new pioneering villages which were situated primarily on the borders and in underdeveloped districts. [99]

Wherever possible new immigrants went to live with veteran relatives who had come before 1948 and were already established in the country.

Thus the old Yemenite settlements in Jerusalem, Tel Aviv, Rehovot, Netanya, Petah Tikva, and elsewhere grew with the addition of new immigrants. New Yemenite neighborhoods developed in towns like Kiryat Eliahu, the site of this study. Very few Yemenites went to the all-new, planned "development towns"—places like Ashdod, Dimona, Kiryat Gat, or Kiryat Shmona—because by 1955, when most of these new cities were established, they had already settled into the *moshavim* and the older cities and towns. One completely new all-Yemenite city was established on the site of the Yemenite *ma'abara* at Rosh Ha'Ayin, four kilometers from Petah Tikva. [100]

By 1955 the vast majority of Yemenite immigrants had found jobs, most had their own homes (as small and inadequate as these might be in comparative perspective), most children were in school, and most men (but few women) were serving in the Israel Defense Forces. [101] There was still austerity, but despite the overwhelming difficulties, both the nation and the immigrants had managed to cope remarkably well.

The sources on this period reveal a two-sided view of the Yemenite reaction and reception similar to that reported earlier for the prestate settlers. On the one hand we learn that they were happy to have come home to the Holy Land, to have prophecy fulfilled. They were cheerful, optimistic, and invariably answered the question "how are you?" with *barukh ha-shem*, "praise God." As Raphael wrote, "the Yemenites of Rosh Ha'Ayin have, on the whole, shown themselves to be industrious, adaptable, and co-operative." [102] They generally took any work that was offered, no matter how menial or back-breaking, and they accepted low wages without apparent complaint. Indeed, sometimes they sought work outside the framework of the labor bureaus, accepting lower wages. This, of course, incurred the wrath of the General Federation of Labor (the Histadrut), and of some organized workers. [103]

On the other hand we read of riots and outbreaks of violence in the camps; bitter laments from Yemenites about their situation; and allegations of discrimination, especially in the assignment of work, jobs, and land. There was also resentment against the authorities. As with the earlier settlers, it seems that their faith in God, their appreciation for their redemption, their cheerfulness and ability to endure travail did not keep them, or at least some among them, from recognizing injustice, acting in their own interests, and asserting themselves when they felt justified.

Once again it is clear that the Yemenites established themselves, by their own behavior both before and after arrival in Israel, as deeply religious people, hard workers, and good people to hire and trust. In the words of Joseph Schechtman,

> . . . the Yemenites can be considered the most thoroughly integrated Jewish community in Israel, firmly rooted in the land. They are the commonly acknowledged outstanding success of Israel's absorption effort.
>
> This success is due in the main to the Yemenites' own qualities . . . their boundless love for and attachment to the Holy Land. . . . They never spurn any kind of work and possess the rare quality of being satisfied with their lot. Among them complaints about the economic hardships are heard much less frequently than among any other section of the population. [104]

On the other hand, despite this positive Yemenite image, there were still many Europeans who carried over negative attitudes formed earlier regarding the veteran Yemenite community:

> European Jews, even when sincerely praising the Yemenite immigrants as industrious, honest, and patriotic, were doing so with an undertone of patronizing benevolence. Remarks to the effect that the Yemenites were childish, shiftless, averse to cleanliness, and unwilling to do steady work, were circulated with an outstanding lack of tact and insight. [105]

Today it is clear that the positive evaluation is the overwhelming one. Yemenites have proven themselves so thoroughly in the eyes of others that one rarely hears critical remarks about them. Nevertheless, in the 1970s the Yemenites still remembered with pain the earlier attitudes, and they still had their sensitivities and their doubts about how others viewed them.

Despite the prejudice they encountered, and despite the difficult conditions, the new immigrants knew that they were now full citizens, among other Jews, in their own homeland—a homeland that had been promised to them by God. Despite the complaints, the fact was that complaint was now legitimate, as was voting, and participation in political parties, and running for election on party lists. They bore arms and served in the military—in a Jewish army. This *was* something new. [106]

Today there are more than 165,000 Israeli citizens who were either
born in Yemen (52,000) or were born to fathers who were born there
(112,000). (The Central Statistical Bureau reports ethnicity in this
manner.) The Yemenites constitute about 5.1 percent of the Jewish
population of Israel. In the next chapters we shall narrow our focus to
deal with the Yemenites of just one small city, Kiryat Eliahu.

Notes

1. Yehuda Nini, "Immigration and Assimilation: The Yemenite Jews,"
Jerusalem Quarterly 21:86, 1981.

2. *Ibid*, p. 85.

3. Amram Korah, *Whirlwind of the South: History of the Jews of Yemen*
(Jerusalem: Rav Kook Institute, 1954), pp. 173-174. [Hebrew]

4. Yosef Tobi, *The Jews of Yemen in the Nineteenth Century* (Tel Aviv:
Afikim, 1976) [Hebrew]; Nini, "Immigration and Assimilation," p. 87.

5. *Ibid*, p. 88.

6. See Yehuda Ratzaby, *Yemenite Jewry* (Tel Aviv: Education Office, Israel
Defense Forces, 1958), p. 74 [Hebrew]; Moshe Tsadok, *History and Customs
of the Jews in the Yemen* (Tel Aviv: Am Oved, 1967), p. 95ff. [Hebrew]

7. See Ben Halpern, *The Idea of the Jewish State* (Cambridge, Mass.:
Harvard University Press, 1969).

8. Nini, "Immigration and Assimilation," p. 88.

9. See Bat-Zion Klorman-Eraqi, "Messianism in the Jewish Community
of Yemen in the Nineteenth Century" (doctoral dissertation, University of
California, Los Angeles, 1981), p. 16ff.

10. *Ibid*, p. 49ff.

11. *Ibid*, pp. 9-10.

12. See Ratzaby, *Yemenite Jewry*, p. 74; Nini, "Immigration and
Assimilation," p. 87. Klorman-Eraqi's dissertation consists of an extensive
discussion of messianism in Yemen and its role in the nineteenth-century
immigrations. Shalom Medina has published a novel, *The Messiah from Yemen*,
about messianism in this era. (Tel Aviv: Aviner, 1977.) [Hebrew]

13. Tobi, *The Jews of Yemen*, p. 76.

14. Ratzaby, *Yemenite Jewry*, p. 68.

15. See Nitza Druyan, *Without a Magic Carpet: Yemenite Settlement in Eretz
Israel* (1881-1914) (Jerusalem: Ben-Zvi Institute, 1981), p. 12. [Hebrew];
Korah, *Whirlwind*, pp. 43-44.

16. For a touching account of the troubles of the late nineteenth century see
the letter from San'a (in English) published in the Jewish Chronicle in 1873,

reprinted in Yehuda Nini, *Yemen and Zion: The Jews of Yemen, 1800-1914* (Jerusalem: Hassifriya Haziyonit, 1982), pp. 296-307. [Hebrew]

17. Korah, *Whirlwind*, p. 31.

18. *Ibid*, p. 38.

19. Ratzaby, *Yemenite Jewry*, p. 69.

20. Erich Brauer, "The Yemenite Jewish Woman," *The Jewish Review* 4:42, 1933.

21. Tobi, *The Jews of Yemen*, pp. 118-119.

22. *Ibid*, p. 120. This period is discussed in Ratzaby, *Yemenite Jewry*; Tobi, *The Jews of Yemen in the Nineteenth Century*; and Druyan, *Without a Magic Carpet*. Also Nini, *Immigration and Assimilation*, pp. 72-99.

23. See Ratzaby, *Yemenite Jewry*, pp. 74-75; Eric Macro, *Yemen and the Western World* (London: C. Hurst, 1968), p. 85. Yehuda Nini suggests a slightly different origin for the rumor, but the principles and the implications are basically the same. He argues that the Yemenite emissary Yosef Ben-Shlomo Mas'ud had learned of the similar schemes of John Cox Gawler and Haim Gedaliah.

24. Klorman-Eraqi, *Messianism*, p. 193.

25. See Ratzaby, *Yemenite Jewry*, p. 75; Klorman-Eraqi, *Messianism*, p. 199ff.

26. See Tsadok, *History and Customs*, p. 226ff; Druyan, *Without a Magic Carpet*, p. 19ff.

27. Ratzaby, *Yemenite Jewry*, p. 76.

28. Druyan, *Without a Magic Carpet*, p. 23. American Christians living in the American Colony of Jerusalem also gave them aid in the form of medicines, money, and food, cooked by a Jewish woman who followed the laws of *kashrut*. As they got work they would come, one by one, to thank the Americans and to say that they no longer needed aid, until only a few old people still came for help. After some time the missionaries were presented with a "beautifully scribed" testament of thanks, written by a Yemenite who couldn't use his hands but wrote with his feet. Bertha Spafford Vester, *Our Jerusalem: An American Family in the Holy City, 1881-1949* (Garden City, N. Y.: Doubleday, 1950).

29. *Ibid*, p. 24ff; Yosef Tobi, *I Will Ascend in Tamar: One Hundred Years of Aliyah and Settlement* (Jerusalem: Ben-Zvi Institute and E'eleh B'tamar Association, 1982), p. 31ff. [Hebrew]

30. Druyan, *Without a Magic Carpet*, p. 17.

31. See Raphael Patai, *Israel Between East and West: A Study in Human Relations* (Philadelphia: The Jewish Publication Society of America, 1953), p. 189; Tsadok, *History and Customs*, pp. 229-230; Druyan, *Without a Magic Carpet*, p. 64ff.

32. *Ibid*, pp. 66-69.

33. *Encyclopaedia Judaica*, Vol. 7 (Jerusalem: Keter, 1972), pp. 1207-1215.

34. Tobi, *I Will Ascend in Tamar*, p. 9. Nini discusses attempts of the Yemenites in Jerusalem to work with the North African Jewish community there. *Yemen and Zion*, pp. 239ff.

35. Tsadok, *History and Customs*, p. 231.

36. See Patai, *Israel Between*, p. 187; Ratzaby, *Yemenite Jewry*, p. 80.

37. Zekharya Gluska, *On Behalf of Yemenite Jews* (Jerusalem: Y. Ben-David Gluska, 1974), pp. 91-92. [Hebrew]

38. Klorman-Eraqi, *Messianism*, p. 206.

39. Alex Bein, *The Return to the Soil: A History of Jewish Settlement in Israel* (Jerusalem: Youth and Hechalutz Department of the Zionist Organization, 1952), pp. 42-43.

40. In a recent article N. Druyan offers a more complex and mixed view of Yemenite characteristics as agricultural workers ("natural workers") and of their relations with the Eastern European immigrant workers. "'Workers Born and Bred'—Yemenite Immigrants in Agricultural Settlement," in Shalom Seri, ed., *Se'i Yona: Yemenite Jews in Israel* (Tel Aviv: Am Oved, 1983), pp. 195-210. [Hebrew]

41. Patai, *Israel Between*, p. 187ff.

42. Klorman-Eraqi, *Messianism*, p. 209ff.

43. Nini, "Immigration and Assimilation," pp. 90-93.

44. Ratzaby, *Yemenite Jewry*, p. 82.

45. See Norman Berdichevsky, "The Impact of Urbanization on the Social Geography of Reḥovot" (doctoral dissertation, University of Wisconsin, Madison, 1974), p. 71. This period of settlement on the land, and the establishment of the first Yemenite settlements outside of Jerusalem and Jaffa, is discussed in Tsadok, *History and Customs*; Pinḥas Kapara, *From Yemen to Shaarayim, Reḥovot* (Reḥovot, 1978) [Hebrew]; Druyan, *Without a Magic Carpet*; and Tobi, *I Will Ascend in Tamar*, among others.

46. Jean-Jacques Berreby, "De l'Intégration des Juifs Yéménites en Israel," *L'Année Sociologique*, 3rd series: 93, 1956.

47. Ratzaby, *Yemenite Jewry*, p. 82.

48. See Berdichevsky, *Impact*, p. 67; Dina Greitzer, "The Settlement of Yemenite Immigrants at Kefar Marmorak—Between Separatism and Integration," *Cathedra* 14:144ff., 1980. [Hebrew]

49. See Patai, *Israel Between*, pp. 197-198; Mishael Caspi, "Nahliel—Relations of Neighbors in Its Early Years," *Pe'amim* 10:71, 1981. [Hebrew]

50. See, for example, Caspi, "Nahliel," p. 70; Nini, "Immigration and Assimilation," p. 91.

51. See Berreby, "De l'Intégration," p. 94; Tsadok, *History and Customs*, pp. 243-244; Greitzer, "The Settlement," p. 121.

52. Nini, "Immigration and Assimilation," p. 93.

53. *Ibid*, p. 93.

54. *Ibid*, pp. 93-96.

55. Israelis use the term *vatik* (veteran) to refer to people and communities who were in Israel before 1948. It can also be used in a relative sense to separate old-timers (*vatikim*) from new immigrants (*olim* or *olim ḥadashim*).

56. Joseph B. Schechtman, *On Wings of Eagles: The Plight, Exodus, and Homecoming of Oriental Jewry* (New York: Thomas Yoseloff, 1961), pp. 355-356.

57. Percy Cohen, "Alignments and Allegiances in the Community of Shaarayim in Israel," *Jewish Journal of Sociology* 4:14-38, 1962.

58. Patai, *Israel Between*, p. 202.

59. Druyan, *Without a Magic Carpet*, p. 79.

60. Berreby, "De l'Intégration," p. 95.

61. Yisrael Yeshayahu, quoted in Berreby, "De l'Intégration," p. 95.

62. Patai, *Israel Between*, pp. 209-210. Shimon Rubenstein presents a picture of the political awakening and alliances of the Yemenites of Petaḥ Tikva from about 1913 to 1919. See "'Gibeonites'?" in Shalom Seri, ed., *Se'i Yona: Yemenite Jews in Israel* (Tel Aviv: Am Oved, 1983), pp. 211-230. [Hebrew] Hanna Herzog has written about the origins of Yemenite political ethnicity and organizations. See, e. g., "Ethnicity as a Negotiated Issue in the Israeli Political Order: the 'Ethnic Lists' to the Delegates' Assembly and the Knesset (1920-1977)" in A. Weingrod, ed., *Studies in Israeli Ethnicity: After the Ingathering* (New York: Gordon and Breach, 1985); also: *Political Ethnicity: The Image and the Reality* (Tel Aviv: Yad Tabenkin, 1986). [Hebrew]

63. Patai, *Israel Between*, p. 198.

64. Schechtman, *On Wings*, p. 358.

65. See Constantine Poulos, "The Transplantation of the Yemenites: In the New Land," *Commentary* 12:33, 1951.

66. Mordechai Tabib's novel, *As the Grass in the Field*, contains an example of Yemenite expressions of their grievances in Reḥovot in 1917. See the English excerpt, "1917" in M. Z. Frank, ed., *Sound the Great Trumpet* (New York: Whittier Books, 1955), pp. 237ff.

67. Patai, *Israel Between*, p. 209.

68. See Herbert S. Lewis, "Yemenite Ethnicity in Israel," *Jewish Journal of Sociology* 26:5-24, 1984.

69. See Lewis, "Yemenite Ethnicity in Israel," pp. 13-15; also below, Chapter 8.

70. Berreby, "De l'Intégration," pp. 94-95.

71. *Ibid*, p. 96. Yemenite elders had long complained that they did not have the time or ability to properly train and control their sons as they had in Yemen. See Ratzaby, *Yemenite Jewry*, p. 82.

72. Berreby, "De l'Intégration," p. 95.

73. This is nicely exemplified by a 1947 volume, *A Palestine Picture Book* (New York: Schocken), with photographs by Jakob Rosner. Along with sections on the look of the land, the pioneering in the agricultural settlements,

and the modern sectors of Tel Aviv and Haifa, there are sections devoted to the Old City of Jerusalem and to the Yemenites. Of the sixteen pictures of Yemenites, seven stress religion and religious learning among old men and young children, and two show arts and crafts. Other pictures stress the old ways: grinding grain, wearing traditional costumes, and smoking water pipes.

74. Berreby, "De l'Intégration," p. 98.

75. Nissim B. Gamlieli, "The Arabs Amongst Whom the Yemenite Jews Lived: Islamic Sects, Their Inter-Relationships and Relations with the Jews," in Y. Yeshayahu and Y. Tobi, eds., *The Jews of Yemen* (Jerusalem: Ben-Zvi Institute, 1975). [Hebrew]

76. See Shlomo Barer, *The Magic Carpet* (London: Secker & Warburg, 1952), p. 177ff.

77. Schechtman, *On Wings*, p. 70.

78. See Barer and Schechtman for accounts of the exodus.

79. Ratzaby, *Yemenite Jewry*, p. 88.

80. Barer, *Magic Carpet*, p. 205.

81. Schechtman, *On Wings*, p. 71. It is estimated that there are from 2-4,000 Jews still in Yemen.

82. The airlift which brought the Yemenites is commonly referred to as "The Magic Carpet." Even Shlomo Barer uses this for the title of his book. But it has been pointed out by Yehuda Nini, among others, that the Yemenite operation should correctly be called "On Wings of Eagles," and this distinction is meaningful to the Yemenites.

83. See Zvi (Yaron) Zinger, "State of Israel (1948-72)," in *Immigration and Settlement* (Jerusalem: Keter, 1973), pp. 52-55.

84. See Poulos, "Transplantation," p. 30.

85. See Ben Halpern and Shalom Wurm, eds., *The Life and Opinions of Giora Yosephthal* (New York: Schocken Books, 1966), pp. 98-99; Zinger, p. 57ff.

86. Deborah Bernstein, "Immigrant Transit Camps—The Formation of Dependent Relations in Israeli Society," *Ethnic and Racial Studies* 4:29, 1981.

87. See Fanny Raphael, "Rosh Ha'Ayin: The Development of an Immigrant Settlement," in C. Frankenstein, ed., *Between Past and Future* (Jerusalem: Henrietta Szold Foundation, 1953), p. 197.

88. Berreby, "De l'Intégration," p. 105.

89. Poulos, "Transplantation," pp. 30-31.

90. See Raphael, "Rosh Ha'Ayin," p. 197.

91. Poulos, "Transplantation," p. 31. Apparently they feared that their children would be taken away and given to others. See footnote 2, Chapter 7.

92. *Ibid*, p. 31.

93. Patai, *Israel Between*, p. 193. Cf. Phyllis Palgi, *Socio-Cultural Trends and Mental Health Problems in Israel* (Jerusalem: Ministry of Health, 1969), p. 39.

94. Halpern and Wurm, *Life and Opinions*, p. 268.

95. See Barer, *Magic Carpet*, p. 262; Raphael, "Rosh Ha'Ayin," pp. 206-207.

96. See Berreby, "De l'Intégration," p. 125.

97. Halpern and Wurm, *Life and Opinions*, p. 120.

98. For a list and discussion of these settlements, see Tobi, *I Will Ascend in Tamar*, pp. 109-110.

99. Berreby, "De l'Intégration," p. 125.

100. Fanny Raphael gives a picture of problems and progress at Rosh Ha'Ayin, as of June 1953, in "Rosh Ha'Ayin."

101. *Ibid*, p. 212.

102. *Ibid*, p. 211.

103. See Berreby, "De l'Intégration," p. 106; Schechtman, *On Wings*, p. 360.

104. *Ibid*, p. 360.

105. *Ibid*, p. 357.

106. Cf. Barer, *Magic Carpet*, pp. 266-267.

4

The City of Kiryat Eliahu

Kiryat Eliahu[1] is an unprepossessing place in the opinion of many of those Israelis who have heard of it, or ever visited it. It was established just at the end of World War II and has no significant historical associations, no outstanding physical charm, no social or cultural features not shared by any city of similar size in Israel. More negatively, it can only be reached by routes through some unattractive industrial areas. It has a reputation as a working class community with more than its share of criminal activity. (This last belief is not borne out by the statistics on crime and delinquency.)[2] It isn't even one of the most famous "development towns" whose inhabitants Israelis know should be respected and sympathized with because of the hardships and threats they endure on the borders or in the Negev desert. The people of Kiryat Eliahu do not suffer from the problems of those in Kiryat Shmona, Shlomi, Yeruham, or Mitspe Ramon.

But Kiryat Eliahu, for all its ordinariness, is a remarkable example of the "miracle" that Israel represents for the Jewish people. After more than 2,000 years of praying daily to God to "gather together our dispersed exiles and assemble us from the four corners of the earth,"[3] the Jews have, in fact, returned to the Land of Israel, and today this city contains more than 35,000 people who have come to it from all over the world. They have come from India and Poland, Uruguay and Yemen, Singapore and Egypt, Romania and Morocco, Lithuania and Libya, Algeria and Argentina, England, Hungary, Czechoslovakia, Tunisia, Iraq, Iran, Syria, Burma, Turkey, the United States, the Soviet Union and many other countries.

What is more, in Kiryat Eliahu these people from five continents and thirty-five countries live in remarkable harmony, with no organized ethnic clashes and very few unorganized ones, within only a few years of having been brought together. A shopkeeper from Casablanca sells next door to a bakery run by new immigrants from Russia, around the corner from the hardware store of a couple from Iran, across from the bank in which former Egyptian, Moroccan, Yemenite, Rumanian, Russian, and Polish Jews work amicably. Although they are all Jews, they differed considerably from each other, only ten to fifteen years ago, in their respective countries of origin. The extent of the original differences should not be underestimated, and neither should the degree of mutual accommodation and coexistence which exists among these people. They work and shop and go to school together despite the fact that they pray in different synagogues (if they go at all), speak different languages at home, and may even feel that they have different values from the others.

In this sense Kiryat Eliahu is a remarkable place, although it is not unique. The pattern is common in Israel among the Jewish population. But Kiryat Eliahu is above all a place of new immigrants, with virtually no "veteran" (prestate) elite or core to anchor it. In 1972 approximately 97 percent of its people were born abroad or were the young children of those who were.[4] And its Jewish population profile resembles that of the state as a whole.

History of the City

Although a private company built a few houses there in 1939, and the British established a military camp on the site during the war, the real beginnings of Kiryat Eliahu dated from the first days of independence in 1948 when the immigrants began arriving in the new state. There was work to be had quite near the new town, for it is located within a few kilometers of a major industrial zone and only a little further away from one of Israel's major cities. New immigrants were therefore sent to live on the sand dunes of the still unnamed place, just as soon as shelter could be provided.

The first arrivals were Holocaust survivors from Europe, whose housing consisted of small, one-story houses shared by four families, one family to a room, with shared kitchen and toilet facilities. At the end of 1948 there were just 900 people living in these homes and in the older housing in the town. They shared one grocery store, but for bus service they had to walk to the next town.

By 1949 thousands of immigrants were arriving in Israel each day, and the government began a crash program of building in Kiryat Eliahu, as it did all over the country. Massive machines were brought in to produce huge concrete slabs to make the walls and roofs of simple houses that could be erected as quickly and cheaply as possible. A total of 1,800 such units were built. The immigrants who came now received apartments of 28 to 35 square meters (a room and a half or two) with their own bathrooms and kitchens. By now the newcomers were coming from Yemen, Turkey, Egypt, Morocco, Tunisia, and Iraq as well as from Poland, Romania, Czechoslovakia, Germany, and elsewhere. By the end of 1950 the new town's population had grown to 7,800! And in 1951 Kiryat Eliahu received its first recognition as a political entity, taking on the status of a local council, *moatsa mkomi*, with an elected council whose chairman functioned as mayor.

The population continued to grow each year with the addition of ever more immigrants, some coming directly from abroad and others moving to Kiryat Eliahu after brief residence in other parts of the country. About 1958 a nearby *ma'abara* was closed down and its inhabitants, who had been languishing in the camp for some years, moved into another hastily constructed section of the growing town. (Many of these people came from Iraq and Morocco.) More Egyptian and Hungarian Jews came in 1956, after the Suez Crisis and the Hungarian uprising. Moroccan Jews came in increasing numbers in the late fifties; Romanians and Moroccans came steadily throughout the sixties and seventies, although in relatively smaller numbers. By 1965 the population had reached 14,300.

Jews from the Soviet Union, some from Russia and Lithuania, others from Georgia and Azerbaijan, have been arriving since the early 1970s. In the 1980s they were joined by the new immigrants from Ethiopia. Smaller numbers are still coming from North and South America, India, and elsewhere. Today the population is over 35,000 and still growing. There are plans for Kiryat Eliahu to absorb a population of up to 50,000. When its population passed the 25,000 mark, in 1976, Kiryat Eliahu was granted the status of a municipality (*iriya*).

Ethnicity and Integration

Kiryat Eliahu's population is representative of the Jewish population of Israel as a whole in terms of country of origin. As of 1972 approximately 55 percent of its people were born in Africa (35 percent) or Asia (20 percent), or their parents were, while 45 percent originated in Europe or America. This compares with the national figures of 52 percent African-Asian (26 percent and 26 percent) and 48 percent European and American.

As for the representation of individual countries of origin, the Moroccans are the largest single group, as they are within Israel as a whole. They are somewhat overrepresented in Kiryat Eliahu (24 percent vs. 14 percent) as they are in most new development towns. The next three largest ethnic communities, those from Romania, Poland, and the Soviet Union, are found in the national population in about the same proportion. Only the Iraqi Jewish community, of the largest ones in Israel, is underrepresented in Kiryat Eliahu (2 percent vs. 8.8 percent). There are substantial percentages derived from Turkey (6.3 percent), Egypt (5.8 percent), Yemen (5.3 percent), and Algeria/Tunisia (3.5 percent), with many smaller groups each contributing from 1 to 2 percent of the city's population, as is also the case nationally.

From its inception Kiryat Eliahu has served as home for all comers from abroad, as a place for *kibbuts galuyot*, "the in-gathering of the exiles," and for *mizug galuyot*, the "fusion of the exiles," into one new Israeli population. (These are both key concepts in Israeli ideology.) This is a point of pride, a challenge, and something which is spoken of on all ceremonial occasions by the mayor and other elected officials, and by those representatives of the national government who now and then attend dedications and celebrations in the city. There is, of course, awareness of the potential for interethnic tension and considerable satisfaction at the apparent absence of such conflict. Objectively, the population of Kiryat Eliahu has attained a fairly high degree of integration, at least in terms of the potential for individuals to interact with those of other backgrounds and to take advantage of the facilities and opportunities the town offers.

The city today stretches for about 2 1/2 kilometers by 1 kilometer. It is compact, on absolutely flat land, and it is easy to get around on foot, bicycle, or bus. Its facilities are well distributed; some are centrally located and others are duplicated in different sections. Although there are certainly differences in income and well-being within the population, there are no major, glaring gaps, and, above all, these are not readily visible in ethnic terms. Although various neighborhoods have particular reputations and characteristics, for the most part these are not connected with ethnic differentiation.

Residence and Neighborhoods

As the country grew in economic capacity, the size and quality of the available housing improved.[5] Although part of one section of town

has been built by private firms, most of the housing in the the other
seven-eighths of the town (about 75 percent of the city's apartments)
has been built at the initiative of the government through the Ministry
of Housing. Government-built apartments grew to 54 square meters,
then 76 square meters, and by 1976 to 85 square meters and four
rooms. These are either sold outright or are rented with an option to
buy. The government rental and management agency, Ami-Gur, is in
charge of sales, rental, and maintenance, especially to new immigrants.
(In a number of communities Ami-Gur has replaced the earlier agency,
Amidar. Ami-Gur is run by the Jewish Agency, the *Sokhnut*, which
deals with immigrants and their needs.)

Styles of building have changed through the years, and one who
knows Israel can immediately tell the age of a street or quarter by its
buildings. The newer sections feature high-rise apartments, either three
or four stories tall without elevators, or six to eight stories with elevators.
These may alternate with one- and two-story "cottages" (*kottajim*),
much larger and better than those of twenty-five years ago, and more
expensive.

The coincidence of waves of immigration with government building
projects means that most new immigrants first settled in the housing
which was then becoming available. To some extent this produced a
clustering of people of the same origin in the same sections. That this
has not, for the most part, resulted in ethnic segregation is due to several
factors. Each wave of immigration was sufficiently heterogeneous that
a number of groups would be housed in each neighborhood. If one
building, or one section of a building, contained people predominantly
from one country, the next section or building had people from another.
This is true also in the newest section of town, which contains Georgians,
Russians, Latin Americans, Indians, and Moroccans. In many cases
original residents move out, either by means of their own resources or by
successful appeal to the housing authorities for larger or better housing.
Those who move in to replace them may be of different backgrounds.
This urban succession is taking a new form today, as young couples from
outside Kiryat Eliahu have been attracted to the city by its successful
development and relatively low costs. These young people, often Israeli-
born, have been buying both the newer housing, and, in some cases,
older housing which they intend to renovate. While many people who
were first sent to Kiryat Eliahu moved on, it has been more stable than

many new towns and has increasingly attracted new immigrants and more veteran Israelis.

There are, however, a couple of minor and partial exceptions to the patterns of heterogeneity in residence. In one case, which will be discussed at length below, the Yemenites have generally continued to live in the section of town to which they first came, and to acquire more apartments in that neighborhood for their children. There is thus a sort of "Yemenite quarter" (*shkhuna*), even though they probably do not comprise a majority of the population in the area. Their neighbors come from many other countries.

The other exception is Yosephthal Street, a long street on one side of which there are eight huge, rather forbidding four-story apartment blocks built in the late 1960s. These contain almost 300 apartments, about 60 percent of which are occupied by families from Morocco. Together with a smaller but still substantial percentage of Moroccans on the other side of the street, this section comes closest to being an ethnic aggregation. Even in this case, however, "segregation" is limited, because (1) there is a substantial and varied non-Moroccan element on this street; (2) perhaps 75 percent of the city's Moroccan families are dispersed throughout the rest of the town; and (3) a walk of only one block leads the resident of this street into the wider ethnic world of the city. There is a good deal of movement in and out, with Moroccans, as well as others, moving to more attractive parts of town.

All other sections of town are ethnically heterogeneous, with no one group comprising a majority of any of them. Any given building may be heavily Moroccan, or Ashkenazi, or Georgian, but the one across the street will usually be quite different, and most larger buildings are also quite mixed. The apartment house my family lived in may serve as an example of the mix in one of the newer, high-rise buildings attracting young couples. It contained families whose members came from Algeria, Austria, Bulgaria, Czechoslovakia, Egypt, France, Germany, Hungary, Libya, Morocco, Poland, Romania, Russia, Tunisia, and Turkey, in 41 apartments. The composition of the next building was quite similar, although there were several others nearby with heavy concentrations of new immigrants from Georgia.

Integration in Education

In 1975-77 Kiryat Eliahu's students attended seven primary schools (grades 1-6) and two "comprehensive" secondary schools (grades 7-12). This arrangement is the result of a national educational reform which took place in 1969-70, in an attempt, in part, to integrate students from different neighborhoods into heterogeneous schools earlier than ninth grade, as had been the case previously.[6]

Israel's Jewish educational system has two main public school options. Two-thirds to three-quarters of Jewish students attend primary schools run by the government as secular institutions, while the other one-third to one-quarter attend state-supported schools which are specifically designated as religious schools (*batei sefer memshalti dati*). The latter, in addition to the regular secular school curriculum, lay heavy emphasis on religious education and on the observance of religious practice and prayer. (There is also a small independent school system run by the ultra-orthodox Agudat Yisrael party, that caters to about 6 percent of the Jewish students in primary schools and a much smaller number in secondary and middle schools.) This division into different school systems affects the distribution of Kiryat Eliahu's children.

In 1975-77, four of Kiryat Eliahu's five secular primary schools were integrated ethnically in much the same way as the neighborhoods they drew upon. They had balanced representation of students whose parents came from Europe and America, and from Asia and Africa. The fifth was located very near Yosephthal Street, however, and about 60 percent of its students were of Moroccan origin. (By 1981 this school had been closed and its students were integrated into two other schools, one of them newly built.) These schools accounted for 80 percent of the primary school population.

The two religious schools drew their students from the more religiously observant part of the population, and this gave them a less heterogeneous student population. Very few Yemenites sent their children to the secular schools. Most preferred to send them to one of the two religious schools. That school was thus about 35 percent Yemenite and 43 percent Moroccan, with the remainder drawn from the more orthodox Ashkenazim, Libyans, Georgians, and Tunisians. The second religious school, close to Yosephthal Street, was not favored by the Yemenites and was about 75 percent Moroccan, with the remainder primarily Georgians.

There was (and still is) a similar picture with regard to the secondary schools. The secular high school, with about 1,300 students, contained a representative distribution of members of all the ethnic groups, except for the Yemenites. The religious high school had relatively few students of European or American origin. The vast majority came from Asia and Africa, with Moroccan students comprising from 40 to 50 percent of the student population.

The general picture of school integration may be summarized as follows: five of the six secular schools were well and truly integrated, while the sixth was subject to neighborhood-based ethnic overrepresentation in 1975-77. Two of the three religious schools were reasonably integrated within the limits imposed by the choice made by parents to seek religious education for their children. The third was also subject to neighborhood- based ethnic imbalance.

In these two cases the ethnically unbalanced schools were predominantly Moroccan, but children of Moroccan origin were also represented in every other school as well. Moroccans are not only the single largest population group, they are also a very young population. On the average, Moroccan families have the largest numbers of children.

In the critical areas of residence and education, Kiryat Eliahu presents a clear picture of ethnic integration. With the exception of the "Yosephthal cluster," which partially affects perhaps a quarter of the Moroccan population, neighborhoods and schools are ethnically mixed in ways very similar to the distribution of the population of the city as a whole. Where this is not the case it is usually due to conscious decisions on the part of parents to send their children for religious education.

Work and occupation

According to a 1975 report on the development of the city, support for 5,700 families was estimated to come from the following sources:

Local commerce, business:	600
Local industry:	100
Local educational and cultural institutions:	500
Work outside the city:	4,500

It is immediately apparent that more than three-quarters of the town's economic support comes from work outside the city. While this includes many who are employed in shops, offices, schools and businesses in the nearby city, a good proportion are engaged in industry in the enterprises of the industrial zone. There are factories producing chemicals, shoes, glass, cement, electronics, electric wire, and military equipment as well as building firms and a host of smaller enterprises. Those who are employed in these industries are not necessarily assembly-line workers, for there is work for specialists, technicians, bookkeepers and accountants, clerks, and skilled workers (including metal workers, electricians, carpenters, mechanics, and crane operators), as well as unskilled laborers. Whereas once the city's population may have consisted largely of skilled and semiskilled workers, the growth of the younger generation, mobility on the part of some of the older people, and the in-migration of higher-status veterans and young couples have diversified and raised the status of the labor force. There are more engineers (or higher-level technicians) and clerical workers, as well as teachers, commissioned officers in the military, nurses, and others of a middle educational, income, and status level who derive their livelihoods from outside the city.

The numbers engaged in local commerce have risen recently because of the further development of the town's shopping facilities. In 1977 there were three shopping centers (two with supermarkets) containing arcades of shops selling clothing, electrical appliances, hardware, household goods, sporting goods, books, stationery, and furniture, in addition to butcher shops, fruit and vegetable stores, groceries, and bakeries. There were also several pharmacies, photo stores, opticians, and record shops. In 1975 there were five banks, branches of the major Israeli banking firms, but new branches were opening as the town's commerce expanded. In addition to the three major shopping centers there were also quite a few other smaller clusters of shops throughout the town. Development is continuous, and by 1982 there was considerable expansion of the newer centers. The town is not yet a shopping center like the three great cities, or even like Netanya or Rehovot and the other cities with populations of 75,000 to 150,000, but its shops can handle a good many of its citizens' regular needs.

There are, of course, barbers, hairdressers, watchmakers, shoe repairers, and other service workers, as well as a number of peddlers who sell fruits and vegetables from carts and wagons. Local industry, as the figures above indicate, is another minor source of income. Most of Kiryat Eliahu is residential, and the only industrial area consists primarily of small workshops of independent metal workers, carpenters, glaziers, and electricians.

In Kiryat Eliahu, as elsewhere in Israel, it is true that people of European origin are better represented, on the average, in the higher income and status occupations than are those of African and Asian origin. There is, however, considerable variation within each country-of-origin group, and a great deal of overlap between these groups. And although no ethnic group has anything like a particular occupational specialty, an ethnic ecological niche, there are certain evident occupational preferences and avoidances among members of ethnic groups. For example, people from Egypt are frequently to be found working as clerks, bankers, bookkeepers, and accountants. Although Moroccans engage in virtually every occupation represented in the town, and are found in every status, they show a striking preference for the ownership of stores and for selling. At one end of the scale there are many who engage in petty selling and peddling from carts or from stands. At the other, a large proportion of the city's stores and services are owned and operated by Moroccans as well. Yemenites in Kiryat Eliahu, as we shall see, avoid and disdain this way of earning a living.

Government and Administration

Since the inception of the council and local self-government, Kiryat Eliahu has been administered by this council and local officials who deal with such things as tax collection, expenditure, education, building engineering and planning, sanitation and water supply, licensing businesses, and the supply of services, usually in conjunction with outside agencies and ministries. Until 1982 the Israel Labor Party had always won a majority of the votes and supplied a majority of the council members, as well as the mayor and vice-mayor (drawn from the council members). In 1973 there were seven Labor members, two from Menahem Begin's Gah'al (Likud's name at the time), and one each from the National Religious Party (NRP) and the Independent Liberals. By 1976 the council had grown to thirteen members, eight from Labor, two each from the NRP and the Likud, and one from the Independent Liberals. In 1982 there were six from Labor, three from Likud, three from the NRP and one from "Dash," the new party led by Yigal Yadin. The mayor was still from Labor.

The government of the town has been stable, in contrast to the problems and upheavals of some towns of this size which have suffered from persistent factionalism, ineffectual administration, or corruption. Although individuals may grumble about unequal services or pass on rumors of corruption, there has never been a scandal or a serious attempt to prove one, and the town must be credited with a reasonably clean administration. Kiryat Eliahu had the same mayor from 1955 to 1982, and although he made enemies and sometimes acted in partisan and high-handed ways, it seems clear that his constant attention to the job and his political skill were important contributing factors in the town's progress.

The mayors have all been European born, and, in 1975-77, so was the first vice-mayor, who is also the head of the local Worker's Council of the General Federation of Labor, the Histadrut. The second vice-mayor at that time was Moroccan-born. The council included: six Ashkenazis, three Moroccans, two Iraqis, one Egyptian, and one Yemenite. In 1982 there were four or five Ashkenazis, three Moroccans, two Yemenites, and one member each of Egyptian, Turkish, and Iraqi origin. In 1987 there were three Yemenites on the council, one of whom was the deputy mayor.

Services and Facilities

Just as the housing in Kiryat Eliahu has improved over the years, so have its appearance and its facilities. Within and between its residential sections are gardens, parks, and landscaped isles down the centers of the larger thoroughfares. There are plazas with public buildings such as the community center, the municipality and library buildings, and the main motion picture theater and shopping center.[7] The upkeep is far from perfect, and it is difficult and expensive to maintain the foliage on the sandy ground and in the face of neglect and vandalism on the part of some, but the concern and the progress are evident. The community depends for its physical facilities, its appearance, and its services on the municipality and various governmental and voluntary agencies. There is little private initiative. But the range of these services is impressive.

Education and "Culture"

In addition to the seven primary schools and two secondary schools noted above, in 1975 the city maintained thirty-four nursery schools and kindergartens for children below the age of six. In 1975 there were also four day care centers with places for 255 children from six months old to nursery school age, but many more have been built since then as the need became clear. (The day care centers and some of the nursery schools were supported in whole or in part by various organizations such as WIZO [Womens' International Zionist Organization], Na'amat [a woman's organization of the Histadrut], the National Religious Party through its women's auxiliary, and individual charitable donations.)

To further aid in education there are social workers, psychologists, and a variety of programs meant to deal with the learning disabled, troubled youth, truancy, and special programs of education, work, and training for those teenagers who can no longer stand school and for whom classroom work is no longer appropriate. In the summer the city maintains *kaitanot*, day camp programs, with sports, recreation, games, and trips. These are quite inexpensive to the users, and there are discounts and grants available to poor families and those with many children.

Beyond school hours and ages, various organizations compete to provide after-school activities and continuing education. The most significant institution for this is the community center, the Matnas, a new development in the 1970's in Kiryat Eliahu as it is all over the country.[8] Working out of a brand new building (donated by a family in the United States), the staff organizes an amazing range of activities for all who are interested. It acts as a "music conservatory," offering instrumental music lessons, jazz ensembles, folk and other dance groups, and choruses (one of them specifically for "oriental" music, led by Yemenite, Moroccan, and Egyptian Jewish musicians). Through the community center one can take lessons in judo, gymnastics, ceramics, painting, macrame, sewing, metal enameling, and beauty care. There is a bridge club, a chess club, and ping pong, tennis, and basketball groups. Boys can prepare for their *bar mitsvahs*, and adult groups meet with leaders to discuss the Torah and Talmud. The staff of the center tries to arrange for any activities for which there is both a demand and available guidance.

The community center of Kiryat Eliahu, with help from the Ministry of Education, organized classes to teach mothers how to play and interact with their babies and children. This is meant especially for mothers from cultures in which toys of any kind, let alone educational toys, are hardly known. They lend the toys to families as one would lend books from a library. The center has youth workers and maintains after-school clubs for schoolchildren, nighttime activities for teenagers, and a senior citizens' group. They have attempted to organize young couples' groups as well. The Matnas staff brings visiting speakers and performers and organizes holiday parties, ethnic festivals, open houses, and all kinds of activities. There is a director with experience in community work and a staff of social and community workers, and other leaders and instructors are hired as needed.

The community center is in competition with other institutions, such as the Histadrut House, which also offers extension courses, clubs, lectures on economics, Hebrew lessons for new immigrants, and a program of entertainment (Arts for the People), which brings shows and concerts to town. Their women's organization, Na'amat, has a new building at which it offers courses in child care, nutrition, cooking, sewing, and other domestic subjects. HaPoel, the Histadrut sports federation, organizes the local soccer and basketball teams, and other athletics.

There is a Technical Club, which permits school children to work in technical fields, crafts, photography, and all sorts of hobbies after school hours. It had twenty-two activity groups in 1975. (The schools also have some clubs of this sort.) And there are youth groups connected to the Labor Party (Mahnat Olim), the National Religious Party (Bnei Akiva), Likud (Betar), and the Zionist left (HaShomer HaTsair). There is also a separate club and program for old people, as well as chapters of the Rotary Club and Bnei Brith. The public library occupies a fine new building and in 1975 contained more than 30,000 volumes in Hebrew, English, French, German, Romanian, Russian, and a few other languages. It has a children's section and a good reference room used by more serious high school students. In 1975 it had 5,000 subscribers.

There is one major theater in town which shows American, Israeli, and European films, and live shows in Hebrew and occasionally in Yiddish. It also shows Indian movies once a month or so, drawing customers from the Indian communities of Kiryat Eliahu and neighboring towns. The theater is located on a plaza which also features shops, an ice cream parlor, and a pizza stand. The plaza is the scene of a great informal Saturday night, post-sabbath assembly each week when the weather is good, as families, couples, and teenagers—indeed people of all categories—walk, talk, snack, and go to the movies.

There is also a small, old movie house which plays Turkish and Indian films and an occasional martial arts epic from Hong Kong. It caters primarily to teenagers, almost all of Middle Eastern origin or descent.

There are other clubs, organizations and activities besides these, but it should be clear that the city does not lack for educational, social and cultural opportunities and activities. What cannot be supplied right in town, however, can be found in the surrounding area or in the big city, half an hour away by bus.

Public Health and Welfare

There are a few private doctors in town, but most people depend upon the three clinics maintained by the Kupat Holim (the "Sick Fund"), which is also a part of the Histadrut. Each maintains a staff of medical personnel and a pharmacy, and treats the sick on an outpatient basis. More serious cases are referred to Histadrut run facilities and affiliated specialists outside the city, or to the hospitals in the big city.

Kiryat Eliahu also maintains three "stations for the care of mothers and children," staffed by nurses. These offer classes for expectant parents, instruction for new mothers, well-baby care, and screening and inoculation. Doctors see babies there several days a week, and the nurses keep records on the progress and problems of the babies and families. The nurses and social workers try to keep track of problems, offer advice, and serve an important function, especially in cases of troubled families and those without education or ability to cope with a wide range of problems.

The welfare office is located in the municipality building, and it is there, and to a branch office in another part of town, that those in need of financial support go to present their cases to the case workers. The social workers also concern themselves with the problems of troubled and broken families, troubled marriages, the aged, the mentally ill, and the retarded. They try to coordinate their efforts with those of the school social workers, and with the social workers affiliated with such other institutions as Ami-Gur, the government housing agency.

Religious Life

As is true in Israel generally, Kiryat Eliahu's population contains within it a range of observance. There are many Jews who are not religiously observant in any way, and others who would call themselves "traditional," meaning that they keep the dietary laws, that men may attend synagogue on the important holidays and sometimes on the sabbath, but that they do little else. Then there are those who are rightly considered fully observant, or orthodox (*dati*). The men of such families attend synagogue regularly on sabbath and all holidays, observe the sabbath proscriptions, and wear the skullcap (*kipa*). Such families observe the dietary laws and other central practices of Judaism. They usually send their children to the local religious schools or even to religious boarding schools outside the city.

For the most part the members of the city council have been secular socialists, members of the Labor Party, but the municipality also has a Council of Religious Affairs which is supposed to concern itself with the needs of the religiously observant. There are two chief rabbis for the city, one Ashkenazi and one "Sephardi."

The municipality has contributed to the building of several synagogues. The "Central Bet Knesset," which is the largest by far, is an Ashkenazi synagogue. While one may question the tactfulness of making the central synagogue the Ashkenazi one, it is true that all the Ashkenazi, in theory 44 percent of the population, can use the same synagogue, while the various "Sephardim" (African and Asian groups) may be as different from each other as they are from the Europeans. Thus there are synagogues built by the council for Moroccans, Yemenites, Georgians, and "Sephardim"—Jews from Turkey, Greece, and Bulgaria. (These are the "true" Sephardim who speak Ladino, a Judeo-Spanish.) In addition, there is one synagogue which aims to be a synagogue of *all* the ethnic communities, in which Ashkenazim, Moroccans, Yemenites, and Sephardim can pray together. The compromise has worked, but not too easily. The members of different ethnic groups pray in separate synagogues, not merely because they are "clannish," but because there are significant differences in the melodies, pronunciation, and styles of prayer. These seem like minor differences compared to all that is shared—they might not show up through a comparison of the prayer-books at all—but they are important. Religious Jews take the recitation of prayers very seriously indeed. The melodies and pronunciation are known by heart and are deeply imbedded in the mind. It can be extremely upsetting to such a worshipper to find himself unable to follow the prayers and to hear only alien sounds.

Aside from these six synagogues there are many more which are privately maintained by individuals and groups with little or no official support. There are two other large Yemenite synagogues and three smaller private ones. Moroccans maintain about six others, and there are Tunisian, Iraqi, Egyptian, and Indian congregations, as well as a second Georgian one and two small Ashkenazi synagogues.

Ethnicity and Public Life in Kiryat Eliahu

Ethnicity is not normally flaunted in public and in ethnically mixed settings like stores, workplaces, schools, and offices. An observer who is aware of accents, names, physical features, and style (bearing) will be aware of the remarkable diversity, but these differences are usually submerged in the common enterprise in which participants are engaged. Moreover, these institutions, and the city itself, have their own special activities and celebrations in which all are expected to partake. These include performances and parties in schools, the celebration of national and Jewish holidays, and other "rites of intensification."

The Day of Remembrance (*yom zikaron*—memorial day) and Independence Day (*yom ha-atsma'ut*) are good examples of such national and city-wide events. The Day of Remembrance takes place 24 hours before Independence Day and is observed at night with a mass gathering in the plaza by the municipality building. All ethnic groups and all ages are represented, both in the crowd and among the various performers, speakers, and wreath-layers, as well as on the honor roll with the names of those who were killed in the defense of Israel from 1948 to the present. It is a somber and impressive event, as thousands stand patiently and listen to speeches and appropriate music in darkness which is relieved by electric lights and torches.

The Independence Day celebration which follows the next night is even better attended. The municipality sets up a great stage in the plaza of the main shopping center and both local and outside paid performers put on shows. Thousands watch, mill around, buy *felafel*, steak, *shashlik* and drinks from hastily erected food stands, and perhaps continue wandering around town and partying until late at night.

In daily life and on these special occasions, people of all origins participate as citizens of Kiryat Eliahu and Israel. But there are other less general activities and events—ethnically based ones—which are known and recognized primarily (or only) by the participants themselves.

As we shall see in detail, the Yemenites have their own synagogues, celebrations, social life, their own neighborhood in fact, about which most outsiders are largely ignorant. Moroccans have two special types of celebration which are gaining in importance these days: *mimouna* and *hilula*.

Mimouna is celebrated right after the ending of the Passover holiday as people from Morocco spread their tables with marvelous decorations—flowers, cloths, candlesticks, and candles—and with great displays of food and drink. They then hold open house for all comers and go visiting in their turn. (Israelis have become aware of *mimouna* celebrations the following day, as Moroccans and others go out to parks and picnic in the tens of thousands, but the home-based celebration the night before is less commonly known.) *Hilula* involves pilgrimages to sacred sites, such as the tombs of great and wonder-working rabbis. These are frequently organized tours, as buses are chartered to take scores of families and individuals to these sites, especially in the Galilee region.

The Georgians make their presence felt in another way. They have developed their own street and backyard community life. Where large numbers of Georgian families live together, they make use of the public areas between and under apartment blocks like no other ethnic group. Teenagers and young men play soccer, old men talk and play chess, girls and boys comprise separate little social groups, playing games and talking among themselves. On Fridays, before the sabbath, Georgian (Gruzini) women congregate around improvised outdoor pita ovens, baking and talking. Weddings are frequently celebrated in the sheltered area underneath buildings and in the surrounding parking areas. In contrast to Moroccan areas where it is mostly the young and teenagers who congregate outside around the building, with the Gruzinim it is all ages and both sexes.[9]

These few examples may give some sense of the centrifugal-centripetal nature of ethnicity and integration in Kiryat Eliahu. The forces for acculturation and assimilation are real and strong, but there is scope as well for the maintenance of ethnically specific activities and social relations.

Summary

Kiryat Eliahu must be considered a successful new town, despite its lack of prominence and its reputation among the more snobbish—who may never have seen it, or remember it as it was 20 years ago. The Ministries of Immigrant Absorption, Interior, Housing, and Education, as well as the Histadrut, have put resources into its development. Its stable local government and its good location have produced a growing community with a reasonable standard of living to offer its residents. It is not home to the social, economic, and intellectual elite, but there is work, reasonably good housing, schools of quite a good caliber, and access to food, consumer goods, health care, and cultural activities and entertainment. As such it occupies the middle range on the scale of Israeli life and communities, between the better sections of Israel's large and middle size cities, and the poorer sections of those cities and the less successful development towns.

In one area Kiryat Eliahu is exceptional, though not unique. This is the area of ethnic heterogeneity and integration. Perhaps because almost everyone was originally working class, or possibly because, in contrast to Ayara,[10] the Ashkenazim were not veteran Israelis or *kibbutsnikim* but were new immigrants themselves, there was less conflict from the beginning. Perhaps it is the balance between East and West and the very heterogeneity that accounts for the integration. In any case, it is a fact of life in Kiryat Eliahu. For most people, their lives in the neighborhood, in school, in the shops, at work and in the army is, or can be, spent in the company of others who come from the most amazing variety of backgrounds. My favorite example is of the staff that worked for Ami-Gur in 1977. The team in charge of liaison with tenants consisted of one person from each of the following places: Morocco, Soviet Georgia, Romania, Egypt, India, Poland, and Kurdistan. They worked under the direction of a man from Yemen.

This is the context in which the Yemenites of Kiryat Eliahu live. And this heterogeneity and ethnic integration make even more striking the strength of Yemenite ethnicity in this city.[11]

Notes

1. Kiryat Eliahu is a pseudonym for the city. The name is created after the pattern of such community names as Kiryat Ḥaim ("Ḥaim's Town") and Kiryat Shmona ("The Town of the Eight") and simply means "Eliahu's Town." It is a firm tradition in Israeli social science, as in American community studies, to disguise the actual name of the community. There are scholarly drawbacks to this, and it will disappoint many who had hoped to see their community discussed in a book, but there are good reasons to respect the tradition. The description of the city is less exact and vivid than it could be, and some not insignificant details have been left out in order not to make the identity of the place too obvious.

2. See *Social Profile of Cities and Towns in Israel*, Part 2 (Jerusalem: Ministry of Social Welfare, 1977). [Hebrew]

3. This phrase appears in each of the three daily prayers in the Jewish liturgy.

4. Central Bureau of Statistics (CBS), 1972 Census.

5. Cf. Shlomo A. Deshen, *Immigrant Voters in Israel: Parties and Congregations in a Local Election Campaign* (Manchester: Manchester University Press, 1970), p. 21.

6. See Aharon F. Kleinberger, *Society, Schools and Progress in Israel* (Oxford: Pergamon Press, 1969), pp. 146-150, 189. By 1987 there were several new primary schools in developing sections of the city. Because I do not know how this changes the distribution of the children I shall discuss only the seven I studied in 1975-77.

7. By 1987 there had been almost a quadrupling of the extent of the shopping center, and a substantial secondary one had been built elsewhere in the city.

8. "Matnas" is an acronym for *Merkaz l'tarbut, noar, u'sport*, "Center for Culture, Youth, and Sport." The community center movement, stimulated and supported by Jewish community centers in the United States, has been developing during the past decade and is still growing. There are new buildings going up to house these institutions in communities all over the country.

9. Indian films provide the primary secular basis for aggregation among Jews from India. Once a month the local theater shows Indian movies, and many Indian Jews from nearby communities come to the town to see them and to meet relatives and friends. These films are attended by whole families and all ages.

10. See Deshen, *Immigrant Voters*, p. 18.

11. By "integration" I do not mean that everyone is identical in behavior, attitudes, choices, etc., I mean that all may have equal access to the public facilities, the educational and economic resources and opportunities, the shops— and to members of other ethnic groups in such public settings as the school, workplace, shops, army, etc.

5

The Yemenite Community of Kiryat Eliahu

The History of Settlement

Almost all of the Yemenite families of Kiryat Eliahu came to Israel in the 1949-50 exodus from Yemen. The majority had come from the cities of San'a, Dhamar, and Amran and their hinterlands. Most came directly to Kiryat Eliahu after a residence of some months to a year or more in the reception camps such as those at Ein Shemer. Although some years later a group of families came from a more homogeneous and less developed Yemenite community, the vast majority of Kiryat Eliahu's Yemenite families came there as soon as housing became available, in 1950 or 1951. They came as families, about 400 people of all ages, and moved into the tiny apartments which had been so hastily erected in the newest section of the town.

They were not alone in this neighborhood, however, for there were also new immigrants from Turkey, Egypt, Morocco, Poland, Romania, and several other countries of Central Europe and North Africa. The early 1950s were a time of great difficulty and scarcity in Israel. A long war had ended, immigrants were flooding in, and the country was unable to produce the food or other products its people needed. In Kiryat Eliahu all of the newcomers faced more or less the same hardships together. All had to learn the new language, adjust to the new environment and culture, and live with every sort of shortage, including the most basic foods. But informants of all ethnic backgrounds speak of these as the good old days, when all the *eydot* (ethnic groups) were together, with a considerable degree of integration, mutual interaction, and accommodation. Yemenite, Ashkenazi, and Turkish informants all agree on this point. It is a common perception that things began to deteriorate to some extent when the large group of Moroccans and others was brought en masse from the nearby *ma'abara* in 1958. This group is believed to have been less adaptable, more sunk in poverty and a pattern of dependency, and to have had a negative effect on the growing community.

Most of the older Yemenites could no longer follow their previous occupations and had to find new ways to make a living. The crafts that they had practiced in Yemen were not in demand in the new country. Even a man who had been a candy manufacturer in San'a, who had received a license to produce it in Kiryat Eliahu, couldn't get enough sugar because of rationing to make a living that way. And so most started as unskilled laborers, some in road work or afforestation, others in building and factory work. Some worked in sanitation—and a few still do. Many women went to work outside the home, which they never would have done in Yemen. Many worked as cleaning women in the nearby city and its suburbs.[1]

In time, however, some Yemenite men became skilled or semiskilled workers: painters, plumbers, electricians, plasterers, metal workers, and tile setters. They settled into stable and responsible positions in the industries outside of the town. Several men got jobs as custodians at schools, one became a milkman, while several took up the scribal art, writing Torah scrolls, *mezuzas*, and other sacred manuscripts. Not many attempted to open shops, but three did establish very small grocery stores. One started a *felafel* stand, and another gave up a craft to become a real estate agent. Still another man, who came at the age of thirty and began working in afforestation, took a course and succeeded as a clerk in a Histadrut enterprise.

The youth attended the same school as all the other immigrant children. There was just one school, but it was divided into secular and religious "streams." At that time Yemenites were in the great majority in the religious part of the school, as they were also in the Bnei Akiva youth movement. (This is the movement of the religious party, HaPoel HaMizrachi.) While a few young Yemenite men became prominent in the socialist youth movement, most of the Yemenite teenagers belonged to Bnei Akiva, and some were leaders in it. They learned about the new country through trips and hikes (*tiyulim*) and other activites, and formed an informal social group (*hevra*), with some Ashkenazi, Moroccan and other youth, in which they played leading roles—as young Israelis.[2] Then most of the young men went into the army at the age of eighteen. The young women did not because they were religious, and observant women are excused from military service.

From an early period several political parties and movements bid for the loyalties of the Yemenite community. The Histadrut and the Labor Party, with its youth movements and its Council of Workers, and its control of the local council, was in a position to offer some inducements. The religious parties, the Agudat Yisrael and the HaPoel HaMizrachi (one of the parties which now makes up the National Religious Party) tried to work with the strong religious sentiments and needs of the community. Labor and the NRP still play some roles, but members of the community are, on the whole, wary of politics and politicians. While they are willing to make use of politicians and parties wherever possible, most people in the mid-1970's were not happy to take sides or to get involved, perhaps as a legacy of the competition and the political deals of the early days.

Despite the hardships of those years—and to some extent because of them—it is the consensus that the Yemenite community of Kiryat Eliahu had a good start in the new country. As they remember it, their relations with other *eydot* were good, they had access to the local elites and to members of other ethnic groups from whom they could learn a great deal. They often contrast their own community in this respect with other, more isolated and homogeneous Yemenite communities, such as Rosh Ha'Ayin and the *moshavim*, which they believe could have benefited from the example of, and competition with, other ethnic groups. In Kiryat Eliahu the Yemenites were among the pioneers, sharing the difficulties equally with others, and they now recollect this as a time of camaraderie. Although there were certainly individual traumas and failures, for the community as a whole this time is seen in a positive light, and it is a source of pride.[3]

The Community Today

There are over 1,200 people of Yemenite origin in Kiryat Eliahu today. In 1972 they numbered 1,058, 5.3 percent of the city's population. They are not dispersed throughout the city, however; about 90 percent live in the same compact neighborhood to which they originally came thirty-six years ago. Although members of other ethnic groups move out when they rise in the world economically, most of the Yemenites do not. Their Ashkenazi, Egyptian, and Moroccan contemporaries leave, but most newly married Yemenites establish themselves in the *shkhuna*, the neighborhood.

Shikun Amidar, as this housing development was once called, was established in an area of about 600 by 400 meters. Approximately 235 two-story buildings were arranged along fifteen lanes, divided into two sections by a main street. Each building contained either four or eight tiny apartments, and normally each family received one apartment, regardless of the size of the family. The government management agency, Amidar, rented the houses until such time as the owners wanted to purchase them. Although there are still quite a few units owned and rented by Ami-Gur (Amidar's successor), the overwhelming majority of the Yemenites own their own apartments. In fact, only a few aged people (whose rent in most cases is paid by welfare) and a handful of families with other problems do not own their own homes.

The neighborhood is not fashionable socially, nor is it impressive to look at, but it is preferred as a place of residence for a number of reasons. Because most members of the Yemenite community are religious, they cannot ride on the sabbath or most other religious festivals and holy days. This means that they must be within walking distance of their synagogues and the homes of their parents, close kin, and friends. The use of the telephone and transportation is forbidden to them on these days, although they may travel before the start and after the end of the holidays, if they can arrange to stay with others for the duration. Loyalty to family and to religious precepts is thus a central part, but only a part, of loyalty to the neighborhood.

Yemenites generally express a preference *not* to live in multistory housing. They prefer to live at ground level or one flight up and, if possible, to have a small garden. This is not to say that they are necessarily avid gardeners (in Kiryat Eliahu most are not), but many at least keep a small herb or flower garden and express the desire for private land around the house. This is possible for many in the Yemenite *shkhuna* because the rows of buildings were built quite far apart and there is much open space between them. This preference for one- or two-story housing has been noted elsewhere in the literature,[4] and such housing typifies every Yemenite community in Israel that I have seen. There are attractive new high-rise buildings within a few minutes walk of the synagogues, but only a handful of families has moved into them. A somewhat larger number has, however, begun buying one- or two-story houses and apartments a short walk from the *shkhuna*.

The original one and one-half room, 35 square meter apartments have been greatly modified and enlarged over the years. Although there are still some that are unchanged, most families have expanded their apartments in a number of ways. In the course of time many homeowners have been able to buy the apartments next door to their own, or perhaps downstairs, and to link these units. It is very common for families to build additional rooms, adding them to the front, the rear, or the side, if one has an apartment at the end of a building. This may result in apartments whose floor plans are outlandish, as first one additional apartment is added, then a room built, and so on, but it may produce apartments of five and six rooms, as large as 125 square meters. In 1976, a young married man was given a one and one-half room apartment by his father and then acquired the apartment next but one to his own. He planned to build on the outside of the building in such a way as to connect his two apartments, while biding his time until his neighbor chose to sell the intervening apartment. As one friend said, "We Yemenites add on a balcony and then enclose it, then add on another balcony and enclose that one, and so on. And all around the house there are piles of sand and gravel for the next construction."

From an economic point of view it is true that these apartments, which have been acquired over thirty years, are relatively cheap and are thus a good value. But non-Yemenites are more likely to sell and move out, or in some cases never bought these apartments but rented and then moved on to new rental housing. The Yemenites bought, and they stay. (The Yemenite push for home ownership and real estate has been noted elsewhere.[5] Eisenstadt quotes a new immigrant on his ambitions in Yemen, "I always wanted to be rich, and to have houses and to study Torah. . . .")[6] In addition there are a number of families with several apartments, acquired as rental properties and to hold for their children. There are quite a few families wealthy enough to move easily to other neighborhoods or to some of the "better" nearby towns, just as many of the early Ashkenazi settlers have done. The Yemenites, however, are loyal to the neighborhood, their families, and the Yemenite community as a whole.

This is not to say that no Yemenite ever forsakes Kiryat Eliahu. Over the years a number of young people have left, as marriage, work, or study has drawn them to other parts of the country. There are even Yemenites from Kiryat Eliahu in Brooklyn. But when they leave they tend to seek out and settle in Yemenite communities in the new areas. This is not always possible, of course, and there may even be some who try to get away altogether.[7]

There is a new small "colony" of Yemenites in a section at the opposite end of Kiryat Eliahu. This part of town, which had once housed the British army camp, has been developed lately by private builders who put up well-constructed two-story houses; there are also small older houses available for improvement. In the mid-1970s a number of young couples with more than average education and relatively high status positions have moved here. They could still return to their parents and old friends fairly easily, but they usually attended the synagogue in that area—the one that attempts to create an ethnicity-free congregation. These young Yemenites were very welcome there, especially because most of them could act as cantors (*hazanim*) and Torah readers since their religious education and skills were greater than those of most others. Nevertheless there was talk, at the time I left, of starting a young Yemenite synagogue in this neighborhood. (The idea of the mixed synagogue was appealing, but the reality was not very satisfactory.)

The Neighborhood

Aside from the synagogues and the people themselves, the *shkhuna* is not rich in ethnically based services and attractions. The only meeting places are homes and synagogues. Shopping is done mostly at the small but convenient local commercial center which is multiethnic. (The sellers there are predominantly Moroccan, Turkish, and Eastern European.) Except for three tiny grocery stores and two *felafel* stands there are no Yemenite shops, and a Yemenite cafe or restaurant would be a contradiction in terms for this community. They do not feel that cafes are proper places for nice people, and some express very strong feelings against eating at restaurants. This may seem ironic to those who are familiar with Yemenite restaurants in the Tel Aviv area, but it is the case here.

The wide areas of open ground between rows of houses present a mixed, but superficially unappealing, prospect to the outsider. There seems to be no zoning, and anything goes. In addition to pleasant little playgrounds behind nursery schools and some nicely tended gardens, there are old shacks used for workshops and storage by local artisans, and messy empty lots. But it is a quiet and peaceful area, and young children are often seen playing in small groups in the lanes. Although the Yemenites are not in the majority in this area, many of the others are older people or childless young couples starting out in small apartments, so most of the children are Yemenite, and their play tends to be rather quiet and controlled. Their parents and kin are generally nearby and ready to call them to account if things get out of hand. There is not the vandalism or rowdiness that is found in some other nearby areas of town, especially in the heavily Moroccan area along Yosephthal Street. What the neighborhood lacks in modern housing, lawns and trees is compensated for by the quiet, the security, and the sense of community— at least for the Yemenites.

Housing and Furnishing

As indicated above, the majority of Yemenite apartments in this area have been constructed and rebuilt bit by bit and thus may take very odd forms. In some cases great skill and imagination have gone into the finishing of interiors with wood trim, fancy louvres, and other decorative touches, but more often the rooms are left quite simple, functional, and clean but relatively unadorned. Indeed, a Yemenite home in Kiryat Eliahu is almost instantly recognizable by the lack of wallpaper, the barrenness of the floors, and the sparseness of the furnishings. This contrasts very strongly with the typical Moroccan apartment, which often is brightly and heavily wallpapered, full of rugs, furniture, curtains, appliances, and knicknacks.[8]

Apparently homes in Yemen were relatively large but sparsely furnished.[9] The mats used for sitting and sleeping were rolled up and put out of the way when not needed. One gets the same sense from many Yemenite homes today, because the furniture is often arranged around the walls, frequently leaving a large expanse of floor. There is not likely to be a great dinner table with six or eight big chairs set in the middle of the room as is typical of Moroccan households. A small table suffices. Meals are often eaten alone or in small groups, except on the sabbath, and the table can always be moved to the center of the room and more tables and chairs brought to it. It is especially easy to move furniture because the floors are bare or have only thin rugs which are easily moved aside.

The most common form of wall decoration consists either of simple geometric designs, incised and painted on the walls, or of pale painted or stenciled designs. Although wallpaper (*tapetim*) was very much the fashion in Israel in the mid-1970s, it was rarely found in Yemenite homes in Kiryat Eliahu. In fact the word *tapetim* is not infrequently used metonymously to signify something like "chasing after the externals of modernity." Similarly, the full Israeli living room/dining room complex, including drapes, rugs, heavy upholstered sofas and chairs, buffet, dining room set, and fancy coffee table, is rarely encountered in Yemenite homes. Even people with good incomes and status are likely to furnish their homes sparsely, with light, moveable furniture, and perhaps to make do with old and worn things. Although there are likely to be few knicknacks around the rooms, there is almost always a prominent bookshelf with religious works and probably a set of encyclopedias and history books.

This pattern of furnishing is not the product of poverty or of a lack of awareness, nor is it fortuitous. It is a distinct pattern which marks most Yemenite homes.[10] Just as E. O. Laumann and his colleagues found ethnic and class patterns of furnishing in Detroit homes, so the observer can see them in Kiryat Eliahu.[11] The Yemenite pattern of furnishing and decoration may derive from the empty rooms of Yemen or even from the need to hide one's wealth there. Perhaps it comes partly from the functions of the Yemenite home and living room and the need to keep them adaptable to accommodate visitors. But it is also consistent with the thrift of the Yemenites, their desire to save for other things, and with the attitude called in Hebrew *histapkut b'mu'at*, contentment with little, an important theme to which we shall return later.

A number of Yemenite attitudes and characteristics come together and seem to be expressed through the medium of furnishing and decorating apartments. There is a preference for open and uncluttered space rather than for the things that others might put into that space. Bright colors and heavy furnishings are avoided in favor of a spare, simple, sometimes even undecorated motif. (Yemenites often refer to their style, their way, as *adin*, "refined" or "delicate," rather than crude or gaudy. They mean it to refer to a wide range of arts and manners.) In addition there is a definite sense of the avoidance of show in material goods and an expressed preference to make do with the simple and old. Sometimes this may be taken as the ability to do without when there is no choice. At other times it seems clear that a choice is being made and that expenditure on furnishings has a low priority compared to other uses for income.[12] We shall discuss this subject more extensively in Chapter 7.

Work and Occupations

The men who were heads of families, or were in their late teens or early twenties at the time of their immigration, had little choice but to go to work as laborers or as workers in building and industry, either unskilled or semiskilled. They had little or no education or training which was of use to Israel's economy. Those men born after 1930, however, were able to fill a wider range of jobs. The youngest ones received some years of schooling, and all had more opportunity to learn skilled trades. Whereas as many as 65 percent of those born before 1930 were unskilled laborers, for those born between 1930 and 1939 the figure drops to below 20 percent. In 1976, 40 percent worked in various skilled and semiskilled crafts (metal work was particularly popular), while more than 30 percent were engaged in teaching and held clerical and administrative positions. Several workers had risen to the position of foreman.

These trends continue for those born after 1940 and before 1954. The proportion of unspecified factory laborers drops under 5 percent; skilled workers account for 51 percent and technicians account for 10 percent. In this age group we find that teachers (11.7 percent), clerks (5.8 percent), and managers (4.4 percent) account for 21.9 percent of the male labor force, but we also find professionals (engineers, a lawyer, an accountant, a rabbi) comprising 8.8 percent.

A clear pattern of occupational choice emerges both from the work that is adopted and that which is not. Of those men born between 1930 and 1954, more than 11 percent have chosen teaching as a profession, whereas only 4 percent (five individuals) are engaged in any sort of selling. Not a single man can be considered to be working in a service industry, while 46.4 percent are skilled workers, primarily in industry. Thirteen percent are bureaucrats (*p'kidim*, clerks) and managers. The preferences are for skilled crafts in industry and technical work, for teaching and education, and for clerical and management work.

The Yemenite avoidance of shopkeeping and other selling is quite marked, especially in view of the frequent adoption of these trades by people from Morocco, Turkey, and Europe. Moroccans, for instance, sometimes express a desire for the independence that selling brings and impatience with the discipline of the factory and industry. There is a suspicion of shopkeepers among Kiryat Eliahu's Yemenites, however, and those few who do sell are not envied or emulated and even show unease about the profession themselves. Two who had opened stores in

1977 had closed them by 1979. One of them had been very successful, made a lot of money fast, sold the business, and went back to the university to study.

If we look at women in the labor force in 1977, the preference for education and clerical work is even more striking. Although some older women worked as cleaning women, and a few younger women may still do such work from time to time, when we look at those women born after 1930 who work outside the home we find the following: of seventy women, forty-eight are in education (forty-two teachers, from nursery school and kindergarten to teachers' seminary, two youth leaders and four teachers' aides); twelve are clerks (office workers); and three are seamstresses. The others include an architectural engineer, a bookkeeper, one each in the army and the police force, one nurse, and one worker in a beauty salon. By 1982 at least five more women had become teachers, but the range of choice was widening as more young women continued their studies in universities. (See Postscript.)

For both men and women, therefore, we find avoidance of selling and of service work, a preference for education and clerical/office work, as well as for skilled craft and technical work among the men. Very few are self-employed, but most work in firms, schools, offices, or the military. In part this is related to the structure of occupations in the area, but not completely. They live within a diversified modern economy, and opportunities for independent enterprise exist for those who are anxious for them. Many Moroccans make such choices. Independence does not seem to be a high priority for Kiryat Eliahu's Yemenites, even though in Yemen they were almost all independent craftsmen and sellers. Security seems more important.

From the economic point of view, skilled labor in industry provides a reasonably good and steady wage, with neither the returns nor the risks of business enterprise, while offering a better income than is normally available through the service sector or saleswork.[13] Teaching and clerical work offer similar rewards. In any case, work in these areas and careful saving have provided almost all Yemenite families with their own homes, while quite a few families have been able to purchase second or third apartments, some of which bring in rental income. In 1975-77 very few owned automobiles compared to the general population and perhaps also to Yemenites in other communities. This seems to have been the result of rational economic decision rather than of inability to acquire cars. Most workers could use either public or company-supplied transportation to and from work, and very few travel on the sabbath. Since Israel generally has a six-day work week, this leaves relatively little need for a motor vehicle. Apparently by 1982, however, there was a considerable rise in automobile ownership among the young. Young couples are now buying small, used automobiles. As one explained it, (1) salaries are now higher; (2) once they have homes they can consider buying a small car; (3) those who work for the government or certain private firms can get allowances for the purchase or upkeep of a car; and (4) because they don't drive on the sabbath, they get lower insurance rates.

Occupational Status and Social Mobility

Social and occupational mobility has been a major topic for Israeli social scientists, especially in light of the apparent inequalities of status and income between those of African and Asian background and those from Europe and America.[14] The findings show that whereas there has indeed been educational and consequent social mobility among those whose fathers were born in Asia and Africa, the relative gap between the African/Asian and the European/American portions of the population remains, with the latter moving still more rapidly into higher prestige fields.[15] Regardless of the *relative* ranking of Kiryat Eliahu's Yemenite labor force in 1976, the *absolute* rise in occupational status within one generation is undeniably very striking.

Starting with a male labor force which was almost entirely composed of unskilled laborers who were forced to abandon most of the craft skills they had previously utilized for their subsistence, we find, less than 30 years later, that the sons of these men are almost all skilled workers, technicians, clerks, bureaucrats, or teachers. The daughters of the cleaning women are increasingly involved with education as teachers and clerks.

Using the Occupational Prestige Scale (Social Grading of Occupations) devised by Vered Kraus for Israel,[16] we may estimate the aggregate occupational prestige score of those men born between 1920 and 1929 at 15.8 on a 100 point scale. The score of those born between 1930 and 1939 doubles to 33.65, while those born between 1940 and 1954 have a score of 40.2. These scores can be compared for those which Kraus has reckoned for all of Kiryat Eliahu—31.225, and all of Israel—37.554.[17]

These figures thus show striking progress in occupational status within the Yemenite community itself over three decades. We may expect this rise in status to continue, probably even more sharply, because more students are staying in school longer. In 1977 there were more than twenty Yemenite students from Kiryat Eliahu in universities, and this number had increased greatly by 1982. Furthermore, the many teachers among them will have a profound effect upon their own children and on those of their families and the community more generally. In twelve of fifty-five younger families in the sample at least one parent is a teacher.

The aggregate figures showing percentages of people employed in different types of activity, and the prestige scores, convey a sense of the general direction and pace of social mobility and occupational change. It will give a more vivid picture if we cite some of the striking cases of occupational and social mobility during the first generation in Kiryat Eliahu.

1. When Moshe Levi arrived in Israel, the oldest of his four sons and four daughters were in their late teens. The youngest was born in 1953, four years after arrival in Israel. Until his retirement, Moshe Levi held a laborer's job in industry. Three of his four sons went into education. To date, one of them is an inspector in the Ministry of Education, a second has been a vice-principal and currently instructs teachers, while the third has begun a university teaching career. Two sons are pursuing doctorates. One daughter is a clerk, and two of the others are in education, one as a nursery school teacher. The other had become a regional inspector of nursery schools in the Ministry of Education.

2. Shlomo Cohen had been a jeweler in Yemen but had to give that up when he arrived in Israel. Starting as a laborer, he tried other unskilled jobs until fairly recently, when he turned his religious knowledge and manual skills to the difficult but rewarding art of religious scribe. Today his nine children range in age from about forty to twenty years old. Five of them chose education as a profession, as, it would seem, will the sixth, who is still working towards a master's degree. Two daughters are clerks, and the last one has yet to choose a profession.

3. Yisrael Medina made in living in Israel, at least in the last few years, from a small grocery store. In 1976 his sons worked respectively as an engineer, a major in the air force, and a clerk. One daughter was a teacher, another a bank clerk, and a third was still a university student.

4. David San'ani had to give up his old-country work as a candy maker and work at various unskilled jobs until he, too, opened a small

grocery. He has five daughters and two sons. One daughter is a construction engineer, two are teachers, one is a bookkeeper, and one a clerk. One son works in a defense industry and the other is a *pakid*.

5. Reuven Damari's children include two teachers, one of whom has become a school principal; a university student; and a son who gave up a successful small business to attend law school. His brothers' children include one nursery school teacher, two clerks, and a retired air force lieutenant colonel, now the manager of a small bank.

Most of these achieving sons and daughters are married to spouses of equivalent status, especially to other teachers or *p'kidim*. Most are married to other Yemenites; a few to Ashkenazim.

These cases are not "typical," but neither are they exceptional. I could easily have added a number of other such families as well as many individuals who stand out within their families. As the aggregate data show, the trend is toward rapid mobility within the first thirty-five years, and I have every reason to think it is a continuing process. The horizons of younger people are much broader and resources are more extensive. They can stay in school longer, they know of more career options, and their home environments offer much greater knowledge of the Israeli social, cultural, and economic world than was true for their parents and older siblings. (See Postscript.)

In the cases I have cited, the children of immigrant laborers used the educational system and the opportunities offered by the economy and institutions of Israel to move into positions of relative economic security and reasonably high social status. I am not suggesting that these gains were made easily or without costs. These young people, especially those who are today in their mid-thirties and early forties, were pioneers, the first in their families to continue in education and to leave the known world of manual labor. Many of them had to work during the day and go to school at night. They could not count on much help from home in the early days, either financially or with the content of their studies. They moved into very different intellectual and social worlds from those of their parents. They also had to confront a largely Ashkenazi world which, aside from its prejudices, presented a forbidding environment to many of these young Yemenites. But it did not stop them, and it is now far easier for those of the younger generation who are in seminary and university. They have their older siblings and cousins as role models and supporters.

Before leaving the subject of the achievements of the younger generation, it may be worthwhile to say something about the origins of the families mentioned above. Although in most cases the parents were not distinguishable in terms of economic, educational, or occupational origin (most had been artisans in the old country and workers in the new, while the mothers were either house-bound or cleaning women), the most successful families seem to have come originally from San'a and Dhamar.

As we noted previously, the people from San'a have considerable pride in their origins, a sense that they are more serious, more refined, the elite, from the capital of Yemen. Those from Dhamar feel the competition, the problem of being deemed second best. Whether or not these distinctions will be continued into the next generation we cannot say, but they are by no means unimportant for the generation now in its late thirties and older. The achievements of these sons and daughters of San'ani parents, those immigrating to Israel in their youth or born within the first years after *aliya*, are so striking as to warrant the suspicion that the sense of pride and tradition, if not other values as well, have played some role in their success. It is clear that they were brought up to feel that they should achieve more. As one San'ani man, now in his forties, expressed it, "San'anim think a lot of themselves and you grow up thinking that you are special: more cultured, more able, more enlightened (*maskil*). You feel that you must achieve."

Education

Learning was held in high esteem among the Jews of Yemen. The only learning they knew was religious, but respect for books and for the learned man was marked. They possessed a considerable corpus of religious scholarship, including the writings of major non-Yemenite Jewish scholars such as Maimonides and Sa'adia Gaon, various works of Kabbalah and religious poetry, and treatises on religious topics produced by Yemenite scholars.[18] Goitein notes that love of books was an outstanding characteristic of Yemenites, even those from remote villages,[19] and we have seen that books were among the only possessions brought with many families on the exodus.

Goitein writes, "The Yemenite community [in Yemen] laid great stress on the education of boys. Public opinion brought very strong pressure to bear upon every father to give his son a certain amount of instruction in Jewish subjects."[20] Such religious instruction remains today an outstanding characteristic of the Yemenite community of Kiryat Eliahu. Each *shabbat* one can observe virtually all of the fathers with their sons between the ages of six and thirteen seated together in the synagogue. The father will have prepared the sons at home each week so that they can follow the services and the reading of the weekly Torah portion. They teach their sons to read from the Torah publicly, which the boys begin to do as soon as they are able, perhaps at the age of seven. This learning is religious rather than secular and is directed only to the sons. What of the daughters and of secular learning?

Schooling is compulsory for both boys and girls until the age of sixteen, or through the tenth grade, and in Kiryat Eliahu it is free through the twelfth grade. Although they have a choice between the secular and the religious schools, virtually every Yemenite child in Kiryat Eliahu goes to just one religious school, the one which grew out of the "religious stream" in the town's first school.

As for secondary school, from grades 7 to 12, even though it is widely believed that the nonreligious school is academically superior, most parents still prefer to send their children to the city's religious school or to send them away to religious day schools or boarding schools with better reputations in other towns. This is something for which parents will sacrifice and save, or even turn to the welfare office for scholarship aid.[21] Parents are concerned about the quality of their children's schools, but in the absence of better alternatives they still choose the religious high school over the secular one.

Unfortunately I do not have figures to indicate how many students go away to school, or how many finish twelve grades, and what sort of certification they receive when they leave school.[22] (There are several levels of school-leaving certificates: full academic certification [*bagrut*]; completion certificate for those who finish various nonacademic vocational training courses [*gemer*], and a third carrying a lower level of certification.) One indication of the numbers of students that are sent to other schools may be found in the fact that whereas the number of Yemenite students in the six primary classes in 1977 averaged just over twenty, those in the three intermediate grades averaged under thirteen, and those in the highest three grades just over nine. Since the larger drop occurs between primary and middle grades, at an age when school is still compulsory, we must assume that they are being sent away to other schools at about this time. Because there is virtually no problem of early dropout and truancy in the Yemenite community, this plays no role in these figures. In the upper three grades half of the Yemenite students in 1976-77 were enrolled in the academic (*iyunit*) course, while the other half chose vocational "streams," including secretarial, electrical, and mechanical specializations.

It is also clear that an increasing number of young people are continuing on to university. Whereas the older brothers and sisters, those now in their late thirties who were born abroad or in the first difficult years after immigration, made their way through teachers' seminaries and perhaps to further course work later, relatively few were able to afford the luxury of bachelor's degrees. Now, however, while there are still a good number of young women in teacher training, in 1977 there were more than twenty students enrolled in baccalaureate courses at Israel's universities, and even some who were continuing for advanced degrees. By 1981 this number had risen very rapidly, and in my sample of twenty-one recent graduates fourteen had gone on to further study, ten at universities and four at teachers' seminaries. While a few chose technical and scientific fields, it was more common for them to be drawn to the study of Hebrew and Semitic languages, Jewish history and the Bible, and the social sciences. They have a great advantage over other students in some of these fields because of their intensive training at home as well as their attendance at religious schools. Students and teachers agree that they are very good at the study of Hebrew and history, but rather weak in English and mathematics. Technical and scientific fields seem to be growing in popularity, however, and the 1981 group includes students of medicine and biology as well as law, engineering and business administration.

Attitude to Education

It would be misleading to portray Kiryat Eliahu's Yemenites as a community of scholars or as determinedly middle-class people seeking their fortunes through higher education, although the trends of the last five years may be leading rather more in this direction. (See the Postscript for the trends of the late 1980s.) In the mid-1970s the community was more mixed than this, and, when asked, many people responded that they were more concerned with religion and with their children's future happiness and right conduct (*derekh erets*) than they were with their occupational and educational attainments.[23] Nor is learning for its own sake necessarily regarded highly by all. On the other hand, the tendency toward education as a vocation is certainly very marked. Aside from the teachers, the educational administrators, and the several women who work as teachers' aides, there are also at least five men who work as school custodians, not in cleaning but in general supervision of the cleaning staff and the grounds. Even though patronage and connections may have helped them to get these positions, I have the impression that Yemenites are overrepresented in this job elsewhere as well, and that it is not fortuitous.

More important, perhaps, is the attitude toward school and conduct generally. Kiryat Eliahu's Yemenites set great store by *ḥinukh*, a term denoting education, but for them not so much in the sense of *learning* (*haskala*) but more in the sense of proper upbringing, knowing how to behave. They speak constantly of the need to give children a grasp of right and wrong and of proper behavior at home. They expect the school to complement and complete this process in conjunction with the home. They often complain about the behavior of "Israeli youth," saying that bad conduct results when parents neglect proper guidance at home (*ḥinukh ba-bayit*) and expect the schools to do it all.

In the context of the behavioral expectations of Israeli schools, the Yemenites of Kiryat Eliahu are considered rather good students. Even if they are no brighter than others, they are reasonably attentive and anxious to please, and rarely present serious behavioral problems, according to the testimony of numerous teachers, some of them Yemenite, some Ashkenazi and Moroccan. They are not a problem for the truant officer or the school social workers. Few Yemenites are found among their cases, and hardly any are found in the classes for difficult children and slow learners. They often express the belief that they are good students, some granting first place to the Ashkenazim—and some not.

In addition the discipline imposed by each father upon his sons to study and learn the Torah and the services, a practice derived from Yemen but continued today in Kiryat Eliahu, must have an effect in impressing upon boys, at least, the importance and seriousness of study and discipline. As Goitein notes, "the great efforts made by the Yemenites throughout their lives to master the biblical text and its Targum [translation in Aramaic] with precision not only rendered them excellent Hebraists, but had also a strong disciplinary effect on their whole mental frame."[24]

In an article comparing the school achievement of immigrant children in the United States, Michael Olneck and Marvin Lazerson contend that success and persistence in school require attitudinal and behavioral characteristics as well as intellectual ones. "They include the ability and willingness to obey and to follow the prescribed regimen, responsiveness to the school's reward system, facility with words and abstraction and the belief that completing school is important."[25] What is not conveyed through the teaching of the fathers at home is increasingly stressed by the young professional teachers, who are also mothers, fathers, siblings, aunts, uncles, and neighbors.

As might be expected, the teachers within the community are deeply concerned about the problems of education, and often speak about them. They appreciate the importance of the home environment and of early education and enriched cultural opportunities, and they are profoundly disturbed by what they perceive to be the shortcomings and weakness of the families and households that many of their students come from. Many of them teach in nursery and primary schools with children of Moroccan background and are quick to speak of the problems these children have. (They do *not* see the same problems with Yemenite children.) They are especially anxious about the education of their own children, filling their rooms with educational toys and books and attending to their schoolwork and school situation. The presence of such a large percentage of teachers within the community cannot fail to have an impact on the next generation.

In his book on education in an Israeli town, Arnold Lewis argues that the cultural deprivation which Israeli teachers believe their "Oriental" students suffer from is an illusion, and that the parents of these families are eager for their children to succeed in school.[26] Without engaging in a discussion of the wider implications and validity of his argument, I suggest that the awareness and capacity of these young Yemenite teacher-parents place them in a different cultural world from the parents Arnold Lewis discusses. Lewis shows his population defeated by an inflexible and insensitive educational system. The Yemenites of Kiryat Eliahu know how to use the system and even participate in the running of it.

In evaluating education in Yemen, based on his interviews with new immigrants in 1952, S. D. Goitein wrote, "There was a perfect partnership in thought and action between the parental home, the school and adult society. The place and value of learning in life were obvious to the boy from his first day at school. There was a connection between the work at school and the sphere of work in the world outside."[27] This connection was probably less clear in Kiryat Eliahu in the early years when young people had to move rapidly into factory labor and craft work, but it is evidently becoming more so again today, and the heritage from Yemen may still play some role.

The Family and the Sexes

It has been common for Israeli social scientists and government officials to view the pre-*aliya* Jewish communities of Asia and Africa as marked by strong extended families, "large patriarchal families of three or four generations."[28] Giora Yosephthal spoke of them as "societies that may be defined as authoritarian, that is, societies in which the source of authority is an unquestioned tradition handed down over the generations. Authority is concentrated in the person of the head of the clan, the Rabbi, the head of the family unit, the community elders . . . Most problems . . . are settled by authority; the father reigns supreme in his household."[29] The image is of a society in which older men dominate the young and women.

In fact, we lack detailed information on family structure and relations in Yemen. Yael Katzir maintains that the basic socieconomic unit in the southern Yemen region called al-Gades was the extended family household, ideally three generations in depth and patrifocal. It is not clear, however, how common this was ("The next most prevalent family form in al-Gades was the nuclear household") or how general in the rest of Yemen.[30]

Berreby takes quite a different view of the Yemenite family. Speaking of the characteristics of the Yemenite immigrants who came in 1949-50, he writes:

> This Jewish Yemenite family resembles more the conjugal family of the West than the extended patriarchal type of Oriental tradition. Even when the emotional ties remain very strong, the individual married adult is eager to found a new and distinct social unit (*cellule*), composed of the couple and its children. Even at the center of this small family, each one has only to observe the religious prescriptions which concern him, and of which the father is the arbiter, in order to be in line with the whole community. And for the rest, it is "Shalom alekh nafshi," each one for himself.[31]

Whatever may have been the case in Yemen, it is clear that the patriarchal family is not a reality in the Yemenite community of Kiryat Eliahu. Even if Berreby is wrong, and it was once more prevalent than now, its passing has not been very traumatic.

In Kiryat Eliahu Yemenite family life is based on the nuclear family in its own household. Although parents and their adult children usually live near each other in the same neighborhood, they do not live in the same apartments. Parents and grown children visit each other, show solicitude, and often help each other financially and in other ways, but the patriarchal extended family, with elders in authority, does not exist. Siblings, too, visit each other, and may help each other, but there is no such thing as a joint family. (In fact, I have been told that even in Yemenite communities where business enterprise is more common than it is in Kiryat Eliahu, brothers are most unlikely to be partners—in contrast, for example, to people of Iraqi origin.[32] Berdichevsky reports from his experience that "Perceptions of . . . the existence of *hamulot* [family clans] are exaggerated."[33]

The fragility of the patriarchal extended family, in those cases where it may have existed previously, is suggested by Katzir, who reports that "Within two or three years of resettlement all . . . households [in the *moshav* she studied] were operating on a nuclear family basis."[34] In any case it does not exist in Kiryat Eliahu, nor do people speak as though it once did.

Parent-Child Relations

Despite the reality of parent-child conflicts, which must exist in any society that has changed as this one has over the past thirty years, the extent of parent-child mutual respect and concern is very striking.[35] Nevertheless, in the past and today the young see their parents as old-fashioned. How could it be otherwise when the older generation lived until the age of twenty-five or thirty in a world as different from Israel as Yemen was in the 1930s and 1940s? Reciprocally, the elders cannot help but be *at least* ambivalent about all of the changes they have seen, about the lack of religiosity in Israeli society in general, and the many temptations for the youth to desecrate the sabbath, to mix the sexes, and to give themselves up to hedonistic pleasures. They came from a society which segregated the sexes to one which features mixed dancing, bikinis on the beaches, and revealing women's clothing. There are ample reasons for conflict, and it is undeniable that tensions and arguments have existed in the past and still do, though of course this varies from family to family.

On the other hand, the mutual respect and concern of parents and children are very marked in Yemenite families and apparently grow over time as the young people themselves grow older, establish families, and begin to have some of the same concerns as their parents did. At least they begin to understand their parents better. Percy Cohen noted this tendency in Sha'arayim in 1955-57: "young Yemenis *do* rebel against the older generation . . . but much of the force of this rebellion is spent by the time they reach the age of twenty-four or twenty-five, and possibly even a little earlier; this change is associated with marriage or preparation for it."[36] This seems to be the case today in Kiryat Eliahu as well. There is a common pattern of early rebellion, often quite mild, and then a "return" to the family and to the community and its values.

A number of commentators have suggested why Yemenite youth tend to respect their parents and return to at least some of their precepts. Mishael Caspi writes:

> Yemenite society in Israel still retains most of the traditions and the isolation that it had in Yemen, but from time to time it forsakes some in order not to create conflicts and tension. Under the influence of the modern society which surrounds it, Yemenite society often has difficulties in keeping its consecrated values either by ban or excommunication. [After discussing a verbal formula meant to bring wayward youth into line Caspi continues:] . . . the elders have been giving legitimacy to newly arising phenomena which they have investigated and analyzed in order to avoid conflict which might one day lead to to revolution.[37]

In a similar vein Berreby reported that when he asked Yemenite fathers whether they accepted the independent ways and the new mores of Israeli youth which their children were taking on, "the most frequent response was a proverb equivalent to, 'When in Rome, do as the Romans.' The most extreme response was made by a venerable rabbi, spiritual leader of a village of sixty-eight families: 'Here it is Eretz Yisrael! Our children will not know slavery; they must adopt the ways (*moeurs*) of their country.' The other extreme was represented by this response, 'The Sabras don't value anything; they are impudent, and respect neither religion nor their father. But I can do nothing about it.'"[38]

The pattern seems clear: Yemenite parents have recognized that in this new world they must yield to some extent, even on important matters, in the hope of retaining as much as possible of the family and mutual respect. (Phyllis Palgi found this to be the case in her experience as well. The crises she has described were not evident in Kiryat Eliahu in 1975-77.)[39] On several occasions I heard Yemenites explicitly compare their own approach to that of Moroccan elders, who, they believe, try desperately to keep control and end by alienating their children. It is possible that this perception is derived from the media or from the conventional wisdom of the social work and educational community, but it is significant that they accept this characterization of their own attitudes.

I spent several sabbaths with an observant man in his sixties whose high-school-age daughter was doing schoolwork, perhaps even writing, acts contrary to sabbath proscriptions. This must have displeased him, but he ignored it, although one day he quietly gave a brief but pointed lecture about respect, indicating his unhappiness at the fact that she sometimes laughed at him. On the other hand his older children, all of whom are successful, would sometimes come to visit on *shabbat* with their spouses. His sons and sons-in-law attended services with him and were generally respectful to him. And if the youngest daughter was not thoughtful and observant, perhaps there was some compensation in the fact that she was well-behaved and a serious student.

In a passage relevant to this point Berreby writes:

> Contrary to the orthodox Europeans, the Yemenite's intransigence and fanaticism [in the practice of religion] is exercised only with regard to himself and the members of his family. Also, it is necessary to note that he admits more easily than other religious people the estrangement of his children from strict observance. The conflicts which can originate from this subject between father and children are always resolved in favor of the latter; if not, the familial unit would be irremediably compromised; another proof of the exceptional cohesion of the Yemenite family.[40]

Indeed Yemenites and others not infrequently comment that, important as religion is to them, they are not "fanatics."

Regardless of the intergenerational conflicts, which both young and old complain about, there is no question that the Yemenite families of Kiryat Eliahu, as a rule, are firm and in good shape. If there were major difficulties in the early years (and I have no evidence that there were), those storms have been weathered, and it is not possible to speak of any general family crisis or breakdown. That this is so is confirmed by every type of social worker and specialist in town: public health nurses, teachers, school social workers, the truant officer, welfare officials, and those who work with the elderly. Examination of the files of these specialists leads to the same conclusion.

Yemenites hardly come to the notice of those who deal with social problems. Out of more than 200 families there are a few men whose drinking has caused family problems, but even in these families the children are generally obedient and successful. There were *at most* a half dozen actual or borderline delinquents in the Yemenite community in 1977—despite the fact that there is a center of delinquency and crime located just beyond the Yemenite *shkhuna*. (By 1981 one of these young men had married, moved to the Yemenite section of another town, and begun steady work at a well-paying trade.)

At the time I examined the files of the welfare department there were 116 cases involving old people whose problems needed attention by social workers. There was just one Yemenite among them. It is typical for Yemenites to be attentive to the needs of their aging parents. They visit them and advise them, and sons try to honor their fathers in the synagogue. (Young men sometimes claim that they keep the sabbath primarily for the sake of their parents.) When the parents are sick or hospitalized, they often take especially good care of them, visiting, perhaps arranging to have family members at their bedside constantly, bringing food, and trying to help care for the patient. (This does not always please the hospital staff.)

Beyond the immediate family, there is an attempt to maintain links with kin, many of whom live in other communities. There is a great deal of visiting, especially for the celebration of *mitsvot*: weddings, ritual circumcisions, visiting the sick, and comforting the bereaved.

The Status of Women

In Yemen the Jewish woman's place was in the home. The care of the home and of children, the preparation of food, and the feeding of family members—these were the primary tasks of the woman. Normally women did not work outside the home, and did not even go to market.[41] These were men's activities, as were those associated with the synagogue. They were not taught literacy or Torah, and were usually married by the time they were fourteen. Katzir has written at length about the subordinate status of women in al-Gades in Yemen,[42] and Rathjens and Brauer note the general pattern of separation of men and women in public activities.[43] On the other hand, Kafih claims that the man was not in fact a dictator or commander, and that, in San'a at least, women had considerable indirect influence, even though they lacked direct and open public prominence.[44]

Although once they arrived in Israel many women went to work outside the home and had to shop in the marketplaces and stores,[45] among the older women, especially those in their fifties and sixties, there is a marked tendency to stay out of public affairs. As was the case in Yemen, women are separated from men, not only in the synagogue, but on many social occasions. When there are guests in a house it is not unusual for the older women to remain out of sight. On occasions celebrated in the home it is usual for the older women to sit in separate rooms from the men. Interestingly, this does not seem to be the case with affairs held in hired halls such as weddings and some circumcisions. On these occasions husbands and wives usually sit together.

This does not mean, however, that the older women are silent if they feel they have something to say. They are not at all shy about speaking out and may come join the men or speak, unseen, from the other room. (I have often observed people speaking from one room to another in a quietly modulated conversational tone, and getting a similar response in return. This is quite characteristic.) This segregation is based on religious precepts and does not keep even the older women from voicing their views.[46] In fact older Yemenite women are known to engage in ribald humor on some occasions. Their oral poetry, produced originally in Yemen, can also be quite earthy and passionate.[47]

"Modern women," those in their forties and younger, may or may not accept the formal segregation of the occasions mentioned above, but are very often quite outspoken and have no hesitation in taking the lead in public gatherings. Moreover, women these days generally have at least equivalent, if not superior, education to men. When they are religiously observant, however, they accept the segregation of women in synagogue service and the fact that public worship is the responsibility of men. One group of very religious young women, under the influence of the Chabad Hassidic rabbi, has its own prayer services. They hold to the separation of the sexes even more firmly than the others—if that were possible. Synagogue and other public religious affairs thus remain the sphere of men, at least formally and publicly. Otherwise younger women show no sign of subordination to men, whatever may have been the case with their mothers and grandmothers.[48]

Notes

1. Yael Katzir reports on the rapid and apparently easy adoption of the practice of retail marketing of agricultural produce by the Yemenite women who settled in the *moshav* she calls Ramat Oranim. As she sees it, the women did this "to gain independent income so that they could achieve greater economic power in the household." While the women's industriousness and enterprise is notable, so is the fact that their husbands seemed to have raised no objection to their participation in the economy, their absence from the home when they were away selling, and the men's attendant loss of authority. (Katzir, p. 249) As an anonymous reviewer of this manuscript noted, "Many other Middle Eastern and North American women of the immigrant generation did not enter the labor force for years, if at all." Katzir, "The Effects of Resettlement on the Status and Role of Yemeni Jewish Women: The Case Of Ramat Oranim, Israel" (doctoral dissertation, University of California, Berkeley, 1976), pp. 154ff.

2. The concept of *ḥevra* is an important one in Israeli society. Meaning literally "society" or "association," it refers to informal groups that develop in schools, youth movements, and the army. It often includes friends who met in these places and who wish to stay in contact after marriage. The term "our crowd" is a good English approximation.

3. The Yemenites who arrived between 1948 and 1950 met many difficulties, but the social and political climate they encountered was more propitious for successful integration and mobility that it had been for the Yemenites who came earlier. By 1948 there was a Jewish government responsible for absorption, welfare, and nearly everything else. The *olim* from Yemen were only a small part of the sea of immigrants and gained from the ideology and the policies which were developed to deal with all the newcomers. By this time there was a greater sense of shared danger and of the need to integrate all equally. Kiryat Eliahu's Yemenites do not have the bitter memories of decades of opposition and struggle for recognition and equal conditions that the earlier comers often do.

4. See, for example, Norman Berdichevsky, "The Persistence of the Yemeni Quarter in an Israeli Town," *Ethnicity* 4:292-293, 305, 1977; Harold I. Greenberg, "Rosh Haayin—Neglect and Tradition," *Plural Societies* 11:71, 1980.

5. See Jean-Jacques Berreby, "De l'Intégration des Juifs Yéménites en Israel," *L'Année Sociologique*, 3rd series:127, 1956; Berdichevsky, "Persistence," p. 293.

6. S. N. Eisenstadt, *The Absorption of Immigrants* (London: Routledge & Kegan Paul, 1954), p. 115.

7. There has been some change in residential patterns since 1977. See the Postscript.

8. See Leslie Schwarz Perelman, "Something Old, Something New: The Domestic Side of Moroccan-Israeli Ethnicity" (doctoral dissertation, University of Wisconsin, Madison, 1983).

9. See Yael Katzir, "The Effects of Resettlement," p. 34.

10. *Ibid*, p. 237; see also Greenberg, "Rosh Haayin," p. 71.

11. See E. O. Laumann, *The Bonds of Pluralism* (New York: John Wiley, 1973).

12. Cf. Berreby, "De l'Intégration," p. 127.

13. *Statistical Abstract of Israel*, No. 31, 1980. (Jerusalem: Central Bureau of Statistics.)

14. See, for example, Moshe Lissak, *Social Mobility in Israeli Society* (Jerusalem: Israel Universities Press, 1969); Judah Matras, "Ethnic and Social Origin 'Dominance' in Occupational Attainment in Israel" (discussion paper for Brookdale Institute of Gerontology and Adult Human Development in Israel, Jerusalem, 1977); Judah Matras and Dov Weintraub, "Ethnic and Other Primordial Differentials in Intergenerational Mobility in Israel" (discussion paper for Brookdale Institute, Jerusalem, 1977); Sammy Smooha, *Israel: Pluralism and Conflict* (Berkeley: University of California Press, 1978).

15. Matras and Weintraub, "Ethnic and Other," pp. 42-43.

16. Vered Kraus, "Occupational Perceptions in Israel," *Megamot* 26: 283-294, 1981. [Hebrew]

17. Kraus's figures include all men between the ages of twenty-five and fifty-four. The comparable combined figure for Yemenite men of all ages would be 33.57.

18. See S. D. Goitein, "The Jews of Yemen," in A. J. Arberry, ed., *Religion in the Middle East* (Cambridge: Cambridge University Press, 1969); Yosef Kafih, *Jewish Life in Sanà* (Jerusalem: Ben-Zvi Institute, 1969). [Hebrew]

19. S. D. Goitein, "Jewish Education in Yemen as an Archetype of Traditional Jewish Education," in C. Frankenstein, ed., *Between Past and Future* (Jerusalem: Henrietta Szold Foundation, 1953), p. 135.

20. Goitein, "Jewish Education in Yemen," p. 232.

21. I have more up-to-date information on the education and subsequent careers of these students as of 1987. See Postscript—1987, Chapter 10.

22. Cf. Greenberg, "Rosh Haayin," p. 66.

23. Lisa Gilad, who studied the Yemenites of a smaller city in 1980-81, has this to say about *derekh erets*, which she calls "the primary value central to Judaism and the Yemeni world view of the organization of the family." "The first most important prescript of *Derech Eretz* is that certain religious practices such as daily prayers, dietary laws and *taharat hamishpacha* (purification of

the family) be followed. Secondly, it demands honour and respect for parents, neighbours, and strangers before the consideration of oneself." (See Lisa Gilad, "Changing Notions of Proper Conduct: The Case of Jewish Unmarried Yemeni Women in an Israeli New Town," *Cambridge Anthropology* 7:46, 1982.)

24. Goitein, "The Jews of Yemen," p. 232.

25. Michael R. Olneck and Marvin Lazerson, "The School Achievement of Immigrant Children, 1900-1930," *History of Education Quarterly* 14:472, 1974.

26. Arnold Lewis, *Power, Poverty and Education* (Ramat Gan: Turtledove, 1979).

27. Goitein, "Jewish Education in Yemen," p. 145.

28. Eisenstadt, *Absorption of Immigrants*, p. 93; see also Aharon F. Kleinberger, *Society, Schools and Progress in Israel* (Oxford: Pergamon Press, 1969), p. 50. Harvey Goldberg noted in 1972 that patrilineal descent groups of this sort were *not* characteristic for Tripolitanian Jews and in 1985 he suggested more generally that such descent groups were not common for most Jewish groups before their immigration to Israel. Goldberg, *Cave Dwellers and Citrus Growers: A Jewish Community in Libya and Israel* (Cambridge: Cambridge University Press, 1972), and "Historical and Cultural Dimensions of Ethnic Phenomena in Israel" in A. Weingrod, ed., *Studies in Israeli Ethnicity* (New York: Gordon and Breach, 1985) p. 188.

29. Ben Halpern and Shalom Wurm, eds., *The Life and Opinions of Giora Yosephthal* (New York: Schocken Books, 1966), p. 267.

30. See Katzir, "Effects of Resettlement," pp. 38-39; Goitein, "Portrait of a Yemenite Weavers' Village," *Jewish Social Studies* 17:20, 1955.

31. Berreby, "De l'Intégration," p. 111.

32. On the theme of fraternal conflict in Yemenite folklore, see A. Shenhar, "Fraternity in the Folktales of Yemenite Jewry," in Y. Yeshayahu and Y. Tobi, eds., *The Jews of Yemen* (Jerusalem: Ben-Zvi Institute, 1975). [Hebrew]

33. Berdichevsky, "Persistence," p. 307.

34. Katzir, "Effects of Resettlement," p. 164.

35. Lisa Gilad has dealt in detail with the problem of inter-generational attitudes and conflicts, in a different town, from the point of view of daughters and their mothers, emphasizing attitudes and behavior relating to sexual relations in particular. Gilad, "Contrasting Notions of Proper Conduct: Yemeni Jewish Mothers and Daughters in an Israeli Town," *Jewish Social Studies*, 45(1): 73-86, 1983.

36. Percy Cohen, "Alignments and Allegiances in the Community of Shaarayim in Israel," *Jewish Journal of Sociology* 4:38, 1962.

37. Mishael Caspi, Manuscript of a paper "Dedicated to Professor Joseph Silverman" (n.d.), pp. 30-31. It is interesting that one of the most frequent causes of conflict in Yemenite communities is the battle over the hour to begin morning prayer. The young rebels want to begin at 6:00 a.m. rather than at 4:00!

38. Berreby, "De l'Intégration," p. 148. For a discussion of a very similar attitude encountered among new immigrants from Yemen, see Goitein, "Jewish Education in Yemen," p. 123. See also Elihu Katz and Awraham Zloczower, "Ethnic Continuity in an Israeli Town," *Human Relations* 14:297, 1961. Recent testimony to the same attitude comes from Zion Mansour Ozeri who was born in an immigrant transit camp two years after his parents arrived from Yemen. Ozeri, *Yemenite Jews: A Photographic Essay* (New York: Schocken, 1985), p. xiii.

39. Phyllis Palgi, "Socio-Cultural Trends and Mental Health Problems in Israel" (report, Government of Israel Ministry of Health, Jerusalem, 1969), pp. 41-43.

40. Berreby, "De l'Intégration," p. 148. Lisa Gilad's article points in this direction, when she concludes "It seems, however, that despite their constant references to the evils of premarital sex, most of the women in this research set demonstrated a great deal of accomodation [sic] respecting their daughters' sexual conduct." As in Berreby, this suggests that there is an air of resignation on the part of mothers, in preference to risking an open conflict and irreconcilable differences. Gilad, "Contrasting Notions of Proper Conduct," p. 85.

41. See Kafiḥ, *Jewish Life*, p. 182. Brauer says that some women in the towns, especially widows and divorcées, had begun to work for wages during the Turkish occupation in San'a. They "hire themselves out for corn-grinding, for baking, for coffee sorting and even as domestic servants and nurses with the Turks." See Erich Brauer, "The Yemenite Jewish Woman," *The Jewish Review* 4:46, 1933.

42. Yael Katzir, "Preservation of Jewish Ethnic Identity in Yemen: Segregation and Integration as Boundary Maintenance Mechanisms," *Comparative Studies in Society and History* 24:264-279, 1982.

43. Carl Rathjens, *Jewish Domestic Architecture in San'a, Yemen*, Oriental Notes and Studies 7 (Jerusalem: Israel Oriental Society, 1957), pp. 33, 47; Brauer, "The Yemenite Jewish Woman," pp. 46-47.

44. Kafiḥ, *Jewish Life*, p. 182; see also Goitein, "Jewish Education in Yemen," pp. 125-128.

45. It is said that the women who worked in the homes of the more successful European Jews were often more influenced toward change in material and other aspects of domestic and family life than were their husbands, whose work gave them a more restricted, or at least a different, view of Israeli society. The women brought new ideas and needs home with them. In her 1976 dissertation, Yael Katzir develops this theme with reference to the Yemenite *moshav* she studied.

46. Cf. Goitein, "Portrait of a Yemenite Weavers' Village," p. 22; Katzir, "Effects of Resettlement," pp. 69-70.

47. See Mishael Maswari Caspi, *Daughters of Yemen* (Berkeley: University of California Press, 1985).

48. In discussing marriage with young couples in 1987 I found that some women believe that Yemenite men are too demanding of their wives, too much the boss. (For more on this, see the Postscript.)

Portion of Yemenite neighborhood showing original apartment blocks with added rooms, balconies, and front yards.

Vilot being built in the 1980s.

A *mori* with his pupils.

Retired men studying Talmud on a weekday afternoon.

The bride-to-be at her *ḥinna*, with women drumming and singing *ghane*.

Men of different generations dancing at *shabbat al-bid'*.

Singing and drumming at *shabbat al-bid'*.

Three brothers dancing at a wedding, 1987.

Bride-to-be at her *ḥinna*.

Placing *ḥinna* on the groom's hand. The groom is Ashkenazi, the bride Yemenite.

6

Religion and Social Life

Religion in Yemenite Life

In Yemen the Jews lived a life which was grounded in Jewish law and tradition. They knew no other way of life, save that of the religious Muslims who surrounded them, nor, from all indications, did they desire another one. They followed Jewish law both from their own desires and with the official sanction of the imams and of Muslim law.

Jewish boys and men were concerned with prayer and study from a very early age. Where conditions permitted the boys spent many hours, over a period of years, in study with a *mori* (religious teacher), and much time with their fathers in religious study. Part of each day as well as the *shabbat* was spent in prayer and study in the *beit knesset* (house of gathering, the synagogue). For men and women the time cycle was dictated by the Jewish calendar: six days of the week were "profane" and could be used for work or for the preparation for the seventh, the holy day, the sabbath. The whole year was measured with regard to the holy days and festivals mandated by the Torah and elaborated by the rabbis through the centuries. These, and the celebration of the events of the life cycle, broke up the mundane routine and gave meaning to life.[1]

Women did not study or regularly attend the *beit knesset*, but they were concerned with the maintenance of the dietary laws and proscriptions, and all the laws pertaining to the domestic and familial aspects of life. Jewish religious law touches every aspect of life, and the Jewish men and women of Yemen knew these laws and attempted to follow them—religiously. As Goitein points out, their occupations and the other conditions of their life permitted them to lead a life not dissimilar from that of the spirit of Talmudic times.[2]

It is ironic, therefore, that the return of the Jews from exile in Yemen has meant a confrontation, in the Land of Israel, with social, economic, and material conditions which make the maintenance of a Jewish life more difficult than it was in Yemen. In Israel the majority of the Jewish population is not observant of the Jewish religious laws and practices, and the temptations to abandon traditions are considerable, especially for the young. For this reason many people, including some Yemenites and social scientists, assume that religious tradition has, in fact, been largely abandoned by the Yemenite community. In Kiryat Eliahu this is definitely not the case.

The Yemenites of Kiryat Eliahu are outspokenly loyal to Israel, to the Jewish people, and to Judaism. The men and many women know the Torah and the other sacred writings, and both men and women know and follow the basic rules for practice and conduct. They accept these as correct, as God-given, and as a guide to life. They continue to try to live by them and to teach them to their children. They frequently refer to and quote from the holy books. The key elements include the observance of prayer and study, especially by men; the sanctification of the sabbath; the maintenance of the laws relating to diet and personal hygiene; and the celebration of holy days, festivals, and life cycle rituals.

It is impossible to say that everyone does exactly what he or she is supposed to; that each person believes with complete faith; or that some (especially the young) don't profane the sabbath behind closed doors or when they are away from home. The crucial point is that within the community these are the accepted and expected norms and behaviors.[3]

Synagogues

For the Yemenite men of Kiryat Eliahu the synagogue is the most important place after the home, and in Kiryat Eliahu as in the larger communities of Yemen there are quite a few of these institutions. Jewish public prayer does not require an ordained rabbi or any religious functionary as a leader. Thus any man who is ambitious enough or is feuding with others can start his own synagogue. He only needs to attract enough men to have at least ten adult males present for public worship services. Any group of men with sufficient desire and motivation can establish their own. It just requires access to some unused space, a building permit in order to add on to an existing structure, or sufficient funds to construct a new building.

There are six Yemenite synagogues in Kiryat Eliahu. Three of these were built by individuals who wanted to be leaders in their own right and felt that they had sufficient religious learning and the financial ability to undertake the project. They built extensions on to their apartments and then tried to attract family members, friends, and additional members who were dissatisfied with the major congregations.[4] Those who attend the smaller synagogues have more opportunity to lead prayers and read from the Torah, and it costs less for the honor than it does at the larger ones.[5] The small ones are not all well attended, however, and sometimes they have difficulty getting ten men together for the required *minyan* (quorum) for public prayer.

The three larger synagogues are each associated with one of the larger cities from which Kiryat Eliahu's Yemenites have come: San'a, Dhamar, and Amran. Although not all of the regular worshippers are from the appropriate city, each one has its core of loyal members who are. These synagogues are often referred to as the San'ani, the Dhamari, and the Amrani synagogues, even though they have other formal names. Each one of these seats more than 100 men and is filled every *shabbat* and on the major festivals and holy days.

The larger synagogues are run as public bodies, with elected committees for leadership. The committees, which also include a treasurer and perhaps other officers as well, are composed mainly of men in their forties who have some education and experience dealing with bureaucracy. All of them, of course, are also knowledgeable about Judaism. The older men sit in places of honor but leave the organization and business affairs of the synagogue to the younger men, their sons and nephews.

This community does not need special religious leaders for synagogue life.[6] All men have the necessary knowledge and skills to lead prayers or to read from the Torah, and there are many men with the voices, the presence, and the willingness to lead. There are too many sometimes because competition often leads to conflict. In fact this desire and ability to lead and direct services is what leads some men to start their own synagogues. One synagogue does, however, have an informal rabbi, or *mori*, a respected and learned man who can explain religious works, such as Aboab's *Menorat Ha-Ma'or* and Maimonides' *Mishne Torah*, with skill and understanding. Otherwise all synagogues function with a variety of volunteer and elected leadership. These include men who act as *gabbai*, collecting the donations and overseeing the affairs of the synagogue, and the *hazan* who directs the reading from the Torah, among other tasks. (The terms, definitions, and arrangements vary from one synagogue to another.)

Religious Education

In Yemen, wherever possible boys studied prayer and Torah with a teacher, or *mori*, who drilled them for hours, day after day, for years. "The syllabus and the school had one aim, namely to teach the child prayers, the reading from the Torah, the appropriate passages from the Prophets and their translation, and the Oral Law so as to enable the boys to follow the discourses which were a regular feature in Yemenite synagogues."[7] But not every community had a *mori*, and in any case the school was less important than the synagogue itself and the home.

From an early age the Yemenite boy went to the synagogue with his father. There he sat with his father or with other boys under the direction of adults. "The fact that he spent hours amidst a congregation whose members were studying and praying, implanted in the child a firm feeling of belonging to the community of Jews as a whole. . . ."[8]

In addition the home was a major source of religious instruction for the Yemenite Jewish boy. "In order to understand the position in Yemen, we must always bear in mind the fact that in this, as in all other spheres of life, the Yemenite obeyed the Jewish law literally: it is the father's duty to instruct his son in the Torah, a duty of which he cannot absolve himself by paying a fee for his son's instruction."[9] Whereas the *mori* taught the boys to recite and read, rarely was he an educator who explained things. "The child acquired his real understanding of things, as far as he attained it at all, from his father and not from his teacher. The father considered this an ancient tradition and a holy duty."[10]

The preparation for reading from the Torah is of particular importance. In Jewish tradition the Torah (the Five Books of Moses) is divided into fifty-four sections (*parasha*) which are to be read aloud, in public assembly, throughout the year. (Two are combined to make fifty-two.) Each sabbath has its own *parasha*, and each of these is in turn subdivided into seven sections, each of which is read by a different person. It is an honor as well as a *mitsva* (a meritorious deed or religious duty) to read from the Torah, and throughout the world each Saturday, in every Jewish community, men are called to read from the *parasha*.

In most Jewish communities throughout the world the actual reading of the words from the Torah is delegated to a special reader, or cantor, who has the skill and the training to read the portion without mistakes and to follow exactly the correct cantillation. The person who is honored by being called to the Torah usually reads only the blessings before and after the actual reading from the scroll. This is not the case among the Yemenites, because they believe that every man should be able to read for himself.[11] For this reason the Yemenite boy must learn to read correctly in order to take his place in the congregation.

In contrast to most other Jewish communities, the Yemenite boy need not to wait to read until he is *bar mitsvah*, at the age of thirteen, but may begin as soon as he is able. By the age of seven, and sometimes earlier, the Yemenite boys of Kiryat Eliahu start to read from the Torah in front of the congregation, reading not the blessings alone, but the whole section. The sixth section is traditionally reserved for these youngsters. Moreover, the Yemenites are the only group to retain the tradition of publicly reading the translation of the Hebrew Torah portion into Aramaic, as was the practice from about the fifth century C. E. This, too, is the duty and privilege of the Yemenite boy from the age of six or seven. As a reader chants his section of the *parasha*, he stops at the end of each verse to permit a boy, who stands near him, to read the same line in the Aramaic translation, the Targum Onkelos. This translation is read in a completely different cantillation from that of the Hebrew.

A father thus has to prepare his son for general prayers, for the reading of the Torah, and for the reading of the Onkelos, and he should try to impart understanding as well. By the time a young man is in his twenties, he can be a real virtuoso in the synagogue, if he has the voice and the presence required and has learned his lessons well. In addition to knowing the Yemenite tradition, he will have learned the Ashkenazi or Sephardi tradition in school and in the army, and therefore may be able to read and chant in all three traditions. This makes young Yemenites particularly welcome at Ashkenazi synagogues which are very likely to be short of cantors and readers. Several young Yemenite men in Kiryat Eliahu served on occasion as cantors for the Ashkenazi synagogue, and those who attend the mixed synagogue in town are all called upon to act as readers and cantors.

The tradition, both in Yemen and today, involves a close connection between learning and prayer and from an early age imparts a sense of relationship between belief, morality, education, discipline, music, and poetry. It also entails strong father-son and, more generally, all-male relationships. There is a whole social and cultural sphere of Torah and prayer, and of knowledge, skill, and music, in which all males participate. It is highly democratic and involves both solidarity and intense competition.

In Kiryat Eliahu today Yemenite boys and girls learn to read and write Hebrew in their regular school, where they also learn about Judaism and participate in prayer services. But it remains the father's duty to see to the proper teaching and preparation of his sons, and most take this obligation very seriously.

The school cannot properly and fully prepare a Yemenite boy for participation in the synagogue because in school they use the prayer traditions of the Ashkenazim or, sometimes, an attempted compromise between Sephardi and Ashkenazi called *nusah Yisraeli* or *nusah Yerushalmi*. Yemenite pronunciation and cantillation are different from any other tradition, and it is important to most Yemenite men that they be maintained. Yemenites want to be able to pray together with their sons and grandsons and have them read properly from the Torah in Yemenite synagogues. For this reason, and to fulfill the obligation to impart understanding, fathers work at home with their sons each week on the Torah portion.[10] And on the sabbath fathers and sons sit side by side, or opposite each other across a narrow table, so that the father can make sure that his son is concentrating and following the service. From time to time the father may lean over to ask his son to explain the meaning of some passage, or to explain one himself. The boys are expected to follow the service and the readings, marking the place with a quill or metal pointer. Sometimes a father finds it necessary to call attention with some physical reminder, but often he uses playful or affectionate physical contact. There is frequently a little candy for the younger children as well, to make the association with Torah a sweet one.

Shabbat

As it does for observant Jews all over the world, *shabbat* holds a central place in the life of Kiryat Eliahu's Yemenites. It is not just a day off from work, but a time of spiritual, familial, and social refreshment, a time for the restoring of the soul.

In Kiryat Eliahu *shabbat* is celebrated by the Yemenites in very much the manner Yosef Kafih describes for San'a before 1948.[13] According to Rabbi Kafih, in Yemen the preparations for the sabbath began on Wednesday as men began shopping for the appropriate foods and women began the preparation of flour for the *shabbat* breads and for pita and other special baked foods. Things are not so different in Kiryat Eliahu, for the foods must be bought and prepared and the home made clean and neat before the start of *shabbat* at sundown on Friday afternoon. No work can be done after that time until an hour or so after sundown on Saturday night. All food must be prepared in advance but can be left to keep warm in ovens which are already hot.

Especially in homes where the women have outside jobs there is a mad rush on Fridays to finish all the cleaning and cooking before the deadline. (Isaac Bashevis Singer's story, "Short Friday," portrays this same activity in Europe.) In Israel's Jewish communities most people stop working early on Friday. Life begins to quiet down and shops close as people go home for the sabbath. At home the observant shower or bathe and put on clean, good clothes. There is an air of expectation as the sacred is about to replace the profane. (The Hebrew weekdays are called *y'mei ḥol*, "profane days." *Ḥol*, "profane," is used in opposition to *kadosh*, "holy.") The woman of the house lights candles and says a blessing over them just before the official start of *shabbat*. The men and boys leave for the synagogue for *Kabbalat Shabbat* (Welcoming the Sabbath) and evening prayers.

While the men are at evening prayers, most women and girls stay at home to await their return. Some girls and very young boys may go to meet their fathers and brothers and walk home with them after services. The men and boys do not linger at the synagogue, but hurry home where the family waits to make *kiddush*, the "sanctification." This vital part of *shabbat* involves a series of short readings and blessings honoring the sabbath, recited over a cup of wine. After the men walk in the door and are greeted with the phrase *shabbat shalom*, "sabbath peace," the whole family gathers around the table and the burning candles. The father recites the blessings while holding the wine in his right hand; he drinks a bit and then passes the cup around to the other family members in order of age and status. He blesses the children individually and then, to honor his wife, he may recite the poem from Proverbs in praise of women, *Eshet Ḥayil* (often translated as "A Woman of Valor"):

A woman of valor who can find?
Her worth is far more than rubies
The heart of her husband trusts in her
And he has no lack of gain.
She does him good and not harm
All the days of her life.

The poem continues to outline the qualities and skills of such a capable and energetic woman, as well as the honor she brings to herself through her works.

After the blessing over bread ("Blessed art thou, Lord our God, King of the Universe, who bringest forth bread from the earth"), the family eats the sabbath evening meal. It is usual for them to sit for a while afterwards, eating fruit, nuts, and popcorn (food that Yemenites call *ja'ale*) and singing *shabbat* songs. Ideally they should also discuss religious subjects, especially the Torah portion for that week, explaining it, drawing moral lessons, or telling stories related to it. Guests may visit but generally *shabbat* evening is spent quietly at home with one's family. (This is the night that the nonreligious youth groups often hold meetings and activities, which makes it difficult or impossible for the religious to belong.)

At the Synagogue

The following morning men gather in the synagogue for sabbath services starting as early as 5:00 or 5:30. Not many come that early, but by 6:30 the three major synagogues are quite full of men and boys of all ages. The only age group which is underrepresented consists of those in their late teens and early twenties, although many youths will attend, particularly if a special event, such as a wedding, is to be celebrated.[14]

Although there are variations a general similarity is found in the layouts of the main synagogues. The old men sit on the chairs and benches along the walls near the ark containing the scrolls of the Torah. Also along the wall, perhaps on the opposite side, sit the members of the governing committee (*hanhala*), and near them are the men with children between the ages of six and fourteen. Wherever possible men are seated with narrow reading tables in front of them; some of the tables contain compartments which can hold the worshippers' books and prayer shawls (*tallit*), as well as other ritual paraphernalia. They may also contain some wrapped candies which the fathers give to their children from time to time.

Women are not required or expected to go to the synagogue regularly for services, although they certainly may do so. They attend primarily when there are celebrations as, for example, on the sabbaths before and after weddings, when a family donates a new Torah scroll to the synagogue, or when a young boy reads from the Torah for the first time. On such occasions a woman might join the bidding, in order to purchase an honor for a son or other near relative. Following orthodox Jewish practice the women are unseen by the men. They sit in separate galleries, sometimes in an upper balcony, hidden from view by curtains.[15]

The services usually last until 9:30, but they can be extended for an hour or two if there are special circumstances. When there is a special event such as a wedding, a *bar mitsvah*, or a *brit milah*, family members and special visitors are honored by being called to the Torah. The *parasha* may be broken into more than seven segments, and some sections are repeated in order to give many men a chance to be honored. On such occasions the celebrants usually supply cake, wine, and candy which is distributed among the congregation.

The services are not led by a rabbi. Various men play leading roles, but because everyone is familiar with the prayers and procedures, these roles are often limited to starting off a particular prayer or section of the service by saying the first word. Then everyone else begins to chant aloud, and the leader can no longer be heard.[16]

A more important task, however, is to designate which men should lead these prayers. In some congregations this honor and task of designating others falls to a particular official, the *gabbai*. In others it may be a man who has won a bid and will pay for the honor of directing the service. In the small, privately owned synagogues it is the owner who runs the show. In Kiryat Eliahu slang such a man is called the *mamluk* ("king"), from the word for the Turkish rulers.

The distribution of synagogue honors is a tricky business, filled with competition and potential conflict. It is frequently settled by auction, as men bid on the spot for the right to lead portions of the service or to read passages from the Torah portion and the *haftara*. (The *haftara* are readings from the Prophets or other books of the Bible that accompany the Torah portion each week.) When a man's son or daughter is getting married the following week, it is expected that he and his male kinsmen, his special friends and guests, and perhaps the father and brothers of the other marriage partner, will be given honors. A man should also have priority on the anniversary of the death of a parent. There are many other reasons why a man might be particularly anxious to read or lead on a given *shabbat*. In addition, guests and strangers should also be honored by being called up to read from the Torah.

With so many claimants, therefore, it is hardly surprising that conflicts arise, as men are either chosen by one central figure or bid against each other for the right to perform these *mitsvot*. Prices in the bidding go higher and those who care more or have the most money can win the day, but not without leaving hard feelings among the competitors and their supporters.[17]

In the words of one informant, "The *beit knesset* is the focus (*moked*), the central point of concern. Men talk of it all week; they pay for it; they fight over it. All take part; they aren't passive. Shlomo and Moshe and the others all know how to pray and read and lead, and they all want to show what they know and can do. All want to be the *mukh'wat*," the *hazan*, the man who stands in front of the Torah and points to each word, directing and perhaps correcting the actual reader.

The scene in the Yemenite synagogues of Kiryat Eliahu is one of concentration and interest as men and boys who know what they are doing actively lead and participate in the services. They appear to pray with *kavanah*, concentration and devotion, as a Jew is supposed to. As with the synagogues of other Jewish communities, however, this does not preclude some talking and even, on occasion, some verbal conflicts. The synagogue is the locus of the most important and regular joint activity and social event for the men of the community. As in Yemen, it is the center of attention and the primary setting for worship and devotion as well as camaraderie, display, competition, and conflict.

After Synagogue Services

On those special occasions when a joyous event (*simha*) is being celebrated, instead of going right home after services, most men and some women will join a procession (*zaf'a*). They accompany new grooms, or families that donated new Torah scrolls, or those about to have a *brit mila*, to their homes. They walk slowly and sing songs from the major Yemenite book of poetry, the *Diwan*. At the house the appropriate blessings are recited, cake and wine are distributed to the company, and rose water may be sprinkled over everyone. Then most people return to their own homes.

At home the family gathers once more for *kiddush* and for the second *shabbat* meal. Often this meal is accompanied by specially baked pita (of which there are a number of varieties), and two favorite baked goods, *kubane* (or *kubano*) and *jehnun*. *Kubane* and *jehnun* have a very special meaning for Yemenites. They stand for "Mom's cooking on *shabbat*," like *gefilte* fish for Ashkenazi Jews or hot apple pie for Yankees. After four or more hours in the synagogue this treat tastes just right. Rabbi Yosef Kafih writes, "Shabbat without *kubane* isn't *shabbat*," and my informants echo this sentiment.[18]

After the *shabbat* meal, which is usually eaten at one's own home or that of one's parents, it is time for rest and conversation and for visiting. In many homes the family sits around, sings *shabbat* songs and again discusses *divrei torah*. But after this it is time to visit friends, family, or people who are celebrating a *simha*. Early afternoon on the *shabbat* is also the time for *ja'ale*, to sit, snack, drink, talk, and sing Yemenite religious songs. By mid-afternoon most people go back home to rest. Sleep on *shabbat* afternoon is also considered a *mitsva*.

Late in the afternoon some men and fewer boys return to the synagogues for "lessons," discussions of Talmud (*Gemara*) or of Maimonides, or for reading of the scrolls of the Bible, *megillot*, appropriate for certain holidays. They read Ruth for Shavuoth, Song of Songs for Passover, and Ecclesiastes (Kohelet) during Succoth. The sessions on regular sabbaths, however, are not very well attended.

The sabbath then concludes with afternoon and evening prayers. The men and boys again return home, this time for a brief *havdala* ceremony. This ritual marks the end of the sabbath, the sacred day, and the beginning of the six days of the mundane week. After this people are free to go to parties, movies, dances, or any other Saturday night activity.

Other Religiously Mandated Public Observances

For those well acquainted with the practices of traditional Judaism the preceding will be very familiar. The only surprise may be the extent to which these rules and customs are still observed among the Yemenites of Kiryat Eliahu. Their observance of the rest of the *mitsvot* is equally strict and according to *halakha*, or traditional law. All of the major holy days (the Days of Awe—Rosh HaShana and Yom Kippur) and festivals (Passover, Succoth, and Shavuoth) and the Days of Commemoration (Purim, Hanukah and Tu B'Shvat) are celebrated in the prescribed manner. Similarly, ritual circumcision (*brit mila*) and mourning (*evel*) are carefully observed according to tradition—both according to Jewish law and with the addition of specific Yemenite customs.

Ja'ale

Ja'ale in the narrow sense refers to food, which might be rendered in current American English as "munchies." It consists of popcorn, sunflower and pumpkin seeds, nuts and roasted parched grain, pigeon peas, chick-peas, and fruit. In its wider sense, however, it refers to a major social activity of the Yemenites. *Ja'ale* also denotes a social gathering attended by any number of people who eat, talk, and sing certain songs. *Ja'ale* can be carried on after meals on *shabbat*, during holidays, or to celebrate weddings, *brit mila*, the birth of a child—indeed any sort of happy event. It is also appropriate at the time of mourning, when people gather to comfort the bereaved family.[19]

Ja'ale normally takes place within the home. Furniture and rugs are moved out of the way in one or more rooms, and tables and benches or chairs are moved in. (Here is another advantage of having little furniture and easily moved rugs.) Bowls of fruit and dishes of *ja'ale* food are set upon the table, as are bottles of wine, beer, *'arak* (home distilled liquor), and soda. Many men come with contributions of food and drink. Some bring favorite delicacies to eat and to share with others. Men join the crowd and are seated at available places. Women may have their own quiet get-together in another room but rarely join those at the table when old men are present.

As they partake of the different foods each man says aloud the appropriate blessing for each, blessing in turn those foods which grow on trees, those which grow directly on the ground, and the wine and other drinks. (These blessings are known to all observant Jews and are not distinctively Yemenite.)

After a while the men begin to sing songs from the *Diwan*, a collection of more than a thousand poems, about half of them written by Shalom Shabazi in the seventeenth century. These poems are primarily on religious themes and deal with the exile and coming redemption of the Jewish people and their relation to God. Many are concerned specifically with *shabbat*, with festivals, and with marriage, circumcision, and other events. These poems and the melodies which accompany them (called *nashid*) are the basis of much Yemenite art and creativity today. At *ja'ale* the singers usually sing the traditional melodies in preference to their modern adaptations. If a learned man or a particularly good speaker is present, he may be called upon to give a little talk (*divrei torah*) on an appropriate theme, explaining or discussing some aspect of Torah, law, or the *mitsva* which is being celebrated.

In the Yemenite *shkhuna* one can find a *ja'ale* on almost any *shabbat*; sometimes there are two or three or more going on simultaneously. They may attract as many as thirty to fifty men, or even more. Some men hardly ever miss one, while others are less sociable. It is above all an activity for older men, but middle-aged and younger men attend, too, and grandchildren often come and sit by their grandfathers for a while and listen and partake of the foods. Moreover, *ja'ale* has become a prominent activity when young couples get together, and in this case women and men are not segregated. *Ja'ale* is a major social activity and provides a frequent opportunity for the displaying of traditional values, knowledge, and culture. Zion Mansour Ozeri writes of the impact of *ja'ale* on him as a child. "It was a time of communal joy and celebration which succeeded in imparting to the children the strong feelings of kinship and warmth that were a part of our Yemenite Jewish community."[20]

Weddings and Marriage

Weddings in Yemen were apparently spectacular events involving as much as two weeks of celebration. Older people are often heard to lament the passing of those days, when they had the time to celebrate at such length. But families in Israel with sufficient desire and means can still produce quite a long and lavish event if the wedding couple will cooperate. An elaborate marriage may involve a special evening party for the bride (the *hinna*) and one for the groom (*bid'*); a celebration at the groom's synagogue and home on the *shabbat* before the wedding; the wedding itself; and several days of special meals (*se'udot mitsvah*) and *ja'ale*, culminating with celebrations on the following *shabbat* at the groom's home and synagogue.

It was typical for new Yemenite acquaintances to ask, when they learned of my interests, whether I had yet been to a *hinna* or a wedding. These are occasions for music and dance, for costuming and colorful ritual, and Yemenites are very proud of them.

Hinna is preeminently a party for the women. Although today there are various degrees of mixing of the sexes, in most cases the women spend at least part of the time in their own room, singing and dancing by themselves.

The *hinna* usually takes place in the home of the bride, about a week before the wedding. Once again the furniture is moved out of the way and room is made for lots of guests. At one end of the main room sits the bride-to-be, splendidly costumed in traditional dress. She wears embroidered robes, many pounds of metal jewelry, garlands of flowers, and a huge, elaborate headdress. (Later in the evening she will change to another less elaborate wedding costume.) Next to her sits the woman who owns the costume and has dressed her. Even in Yemen it was rare for a family to own its own wedding costume, and so there, as well as in Israel, it was rented from a woman who owned one.

The bride sits by a table containing candles, flowers, a fancy cake, and various sorts of greenery. Much of the time she merely sits, surrounded by her friends and women from her family. In the meantime the other women, led by good singers and drummers, sing and dance to a special genre of music, called *ghane*, whose lyrics are in Arabic. (Often a professional singer and drummer are hired for the evening.) These lively songs, which are not sung by the men, deal with life, love, and marriage in Yemen, from the woman's perspective. The women's songs " . . . are the very mirror of life, the reflection of their own roles in society," according to Mishael Caspi and Deborah Lipstadt. Their poetry expresses sadness at leaving their families, or fear of their unknown futures, or deals with the tensions of life under a mother-in-law's control. (It was common for girls to marry very young, and to go to live in the home of their husband's father and mother.)[21] The houses are packed with women, but everyone else joins in as well and the spirit is one of gaiety and celebration.

Around 11:00 p.m. a group of women come ululating and dancing into the room, carrying a pot of wet, gloppy, prepared henna dye, as well as shallow pans filled with elaborate symbolic items such as decorated eggs, glowing candles, and greenery. After dancing for a few minutes, the women bring the henna to the main table in order to daub it on the hand of the bride-to-be as a symbol of good fortune. Members of her immediate family then come to the table, one by one, and place some henna on her fingers and kiss her. The party continues until about midnight when, in deference to neighbors and in recognition of the need to work the following day, the affair ends.

Shabbat al-bid' offers a parallel occasion for the groom and his family and friends. It should take place on another night, but sometimes it may be on the same night, even in the same apartment in a different room. The groom is attired in a special elaborate robe and sits at a table similar to that of the bride-to-be. The men's music is normally derived from the

Diwan and is usually accompanied by drumming on an empty square metal cracker tin. The men's dances are also different from those of the women and are frequently danced with special vigor by old men, who put on an exciting show. With the *bid'* as with the *hinna*, women bring in a bowl of henna for daubing on the hand of the groom. Anyone else who wants to bear a red stain on the fingers or the hand for the next few weeks is free to dip in as well.

Later in the evening it is usual for younger people to dance the newer Yemenite circle and line dances. Using either old or new Yemenite melodies, perhaps playing tapes of the newer music, boys and girls, men and women, dance together. But throughout much of the evening the music and dance at *hinna* and *bid'* are the traditional ones described above.

It is said that twenty years ago relatively few Yemenite girls were willing to have a *hinna*. It seemed to some that the tradition was dying out. Today these celebrations are extremely popular. They are a source of great enjoyment and attract people of all ages. In Kiryat Eliahu, even in cases of mixed marriages, the non-Yemenite partners usually dress up and participate.

In the fifteen or so *hinna* and *bid'* I attended, I saw very few non-Yemenites. Although the crowds might consist of fifty to 100 people at each, there were rarely more than a few individuals who were not Yemenites. These were usually immediate neighbors, either specially invited or just curious. They never stayed very long. On the few occasions of mixed marriages it was only the parents and perhaps the siblings of the non-Yemenite partner who attended.

The weddings themselves conform to standard Israeli style and are held in hired halls in the big city. This is the event that is attended by non-Yemenite guests, who are most often fellow workers and friends from the army. The affair is catered, the food is usually Ashkenazi-Israeli (not to the taste of the Yemenites—nor the author), and the dress is "Western standard": wedding gown for the bride and formal dress for the groom.

The ceremony, in keeping with Jewish tradition, is a brief one. With the bride and groom standing under the marriage canopy (*hupa*), a rabbi reads the marriage contract (*ketuba*) and says the appropriate blessings (*sheva brakhot*). The bride and groom drink some wine, the groom breaks a glass under his foot (for good luck), and they are married. Then comes the food and the music and dance, as in any modern wedding.

The music, however, is likely to be mostly Yemenite. Whereas some years ago a young couple might have been embarrassed by this, and would have wanted ballroom dancing (*salonim*), today the Yemenite music and dance greatly outweigh the other kind. Sometimes there are two orchestras, one that comes with the hall and plays *salonim*, and the other a Yemenite group hired by the wedding party. There is much more enthusiasm for the latter.[22]

In the days following the wedding there will be celebrations at home and at the synagogue, as noted above. These days not many families have the time and money for several days of elaborate meals, feeding many guests, but they will certainly mark the event at the synagogue on the following *shabbat*, and have a few ceremonial meals (*se'udot mitsvah*) and *ja'ale*.

It is important to note that weddings, like circumcisions and mourning, are *mitsvot*. In the Jewish religion a *mitsva* is something that people are commanded to do by God. The word carries both the sense of obligation and of "good deed." It is a *mitsva* to participate in these events. Thus they are open to all who will come, and it is right for people to attend. This is especially true of those activities such as the *brit mila*, the *bid'* and *hinna*, and certainly the comforting of the bereaved, which are held at home, within the community. These cost little, and the visitor may even come with a basket of food and drink to contribute to the event. Weddings held in halls, however, are by invitation. Despite the fact that at a wedding hall each guest must be paid for by the family, crowds of over 100 may be invited to the weddings as well.

Comforting the Bereaved

According to Jewish law the members of the family of a person who has died must remain in their house for seven days and do no work during that mourning period. It is a *mitsva* for others to aid them and visit them during this period of confinement and bereavement.

This *mitsva* is practiced assiduously by Yemenites in Kiryat Eliahu, as neighbors, relatives, friends and *landslayt*[19] from all over the country come to comfort and be with the mourners (*avelim*). Some people aid the family by cooking or bringing food and by taking care of the other comforters. Others bring food and drink or contribute money in order to help reduce the costs of properly receiving the scores, even hundreds, of people who may come during the seven days. Members of one or more synagogues hold their daily prayers in the house of the mourners so that there can be a *minyan* for the men of the family to say the mourners' prayer, *kaddish*.

In addition, people will eat and have *ja'ale* at the mourners' homes. Rabbis and other learned men come to discuss *divrei torah*, reading from Maimonides and other authoritative sources on the subject of death and mourning, and talking about the deceased. When the customs are followed a great many people attend, there is much activity, and a great deal of food and drink will be consumed.

As one might expect when so many people are brought together in a small space, the scene can become quite hectic, and I have heard younger Yemenites complain of the expense, the work, the lack of order, the noise, and the party atmosphere that can result. But several who had been mourners themselves told me that they realized how important it was, how good it was to feel that so many people cared and to see how many friends and relatives they and their family have. They may explicitly contrast this to the situation among the Ashkenazim, whom they think are more likely to have smaller gatherings and an atmosphere of heavy sadness. While noting the expense, the noise, and the problems of this institution, these young people (in their late twenties and thirties) returned to the theme of the importance of the social occasion through which the living receive support, see how many people care, and remember the dead. They recognized it as an important institution for the support of the living, who receive from it a sense of sharing and belonging at a difficult time.

Said one well-educated young woman, "When my grandfather died it was very sad. But I must tell you that from the *evel* I got such a feeling of belonging. First of all, people came from all over; not just from here, but from Tel Aviv and all over. Then when they came bringing baskets of food and drink, and the neighbors shared the cooking and all helped out and participated, it gave me a great sense of togetherness."

It is clearly a time of reunion, of remembering, and perhaps of renewal as well. It is a time of vulnerability, when young people who have strayed from religious practice and the community are brought together with that community. They spend the week directed by the religiously mandated requirement to sit and be comforted, and to say the *kaddish* regularly in case of the death of parents. This practice tends to be taken very seriously by Jews throughout the world, even, very often, by the nonreligious. It undoubtedly plays a role in the "return" of the young among the Yemenites.

Conclusions

For 1,500 years Judaism was the element that separated Yemen's Jews from its Arabs, but linked them with the rest of world Jewry, no matter how remote. It is paradoxical that today in Kiryat Eliahu the practice of Judaism is a major ethnic boundary marker between the Yemenites and their Jewish neighbors and fellow citizens. On the one hand it differentiates them; on the other it results in an intensification of interaction and sentiment within the group.

To begin with, the orthodoxy of the Yemenites separates them to some degree from their more numerous nonobservant neighbors. It directs their children to the smaller religious schools, leads their men to mark their distinctiveness with the *kipa* and perhaps with beards and side-locks, and limits their ability to socialize with the nonreligious on Friday nights and Saturdays. These same restrictions apply to observant Jews of any other ethnic group as well, but there are other distinctive elements which separate Yemenites from religious Moroccans, Tunisians, Europeans, and others, but tie them closely to their fellow ethnics.

As we have seen, despite the commonalities of Jewish worship among all groups, the apparent minutiae—the melodies, the cantillation, the accent of liturgical Hebrew, the differences in style and attitude—are major forces for the separation from others and the intensification of relations within the group. Indeed these minor differences loom so large that Yemenite communities are themselves seriously split between the followers of two distinct Yemenite prayer traditions: the *shami* and the *baladi*, whose differences are discerned only by insiders. They loom large to the practitioners, however. It may be that the divisions based on the *shami/baladi* distinction or on city and district of origin will fade, if not disappear entirely in the next generation, as similar ones have for most European Jews in the United States. But the distinction between Yemenites and others will probably not disappear, at least as long as their religious observance continues. The ties within and the boundaries without are too strong and meaningful.

The maintenance of *shabbat* means that the whole community remains within itself one day of each week—the only day off from work. Members of the community renew their ties and heighten their interaction with other Yemenites in the synagogues, visiting parents, relatives, and friends.   They may not drive to the beach or go touring with unobservant friends but must depend upon their community for companionship and relaxation.   Nor is this necessarily seen as deprivation, although there are surely some, especially among the young, who view it this way. The observance of *shabbat* is among the very highest values of Judaism, derived from the Ten Commandments given by God on Mt. Sinai. Not only does the celebration of *shabbat* fulfill the commandment, it also brings rest, peace, study of Torah, sociability, and the renewal of ties with family and friends. It is a time to see and be seen, to perform at synagogue and *ja'ale*, and perhaps to help insure one's place in "the world to come" (*olam ha-ba*). It is, in sum, a time of intensive interaction in the context of the highest shared values of the community.

Finally, the religiously mandated life cycle ceremonials are celebrated in a distinctively Yemenite way. *Ḥinna*, *bid'*, *zaf'a*, and *ja'ale* all involve music, poetry, and perhaps costumes, food, and dance. Above all they call for the lively participation of large crowds. All of these reinforce the sense that there is something special about being Yemenite and a member of the community. It is a sociable community and there is always something doing that brings groups of Yemenites together *as* Yemenites. There are a few people who are not happy to join the crowd if they can avoid it. At the other extreme there are those who can always be counted upon to show up at any affair, perhaps taking a leading role in cooking and serving or singing and dancing. But most members of the community seem to spend a good deal of time at these activities *that are almost wholly ethnically homogeneous*.

Yemenites in Kiryat Eliahu and elsewhere in the country are very aware of their life cycle celebrations and they are proud of the way they celebrate them. They are proud not merely of their faithfulness to the traditions, and of their artistic creativity, but also of the idea that they are capable both of holding to the laws and practices of Judaism and of having a good time while doing it.

Notes

1. Compare the discussion of life among the Ḥasidim in Jerome R. Mintz, *Legends of the Hasidim* (Chicago: University of Chicago Press, 1968), p. 50. It should be understood that much of the religious life that is described in this chapter, especially with regard to the synagogue, the *shabbat*, and the life-cycle celebrations, could apply to any traditional Jewish community. Many of the traditions, practices, and proscriptions are mandated by Jewish rabbinic law and would be equally true of practice in Morocco and Tunisia, Russia and Poland, or Iraq and Germany. The practices and dynamics of Yemenite synagogue life show strong resemblances to those described, for example, by Samuel Heilman for an orthodox Ashkenazi *shul* in an American city. Yemenite religious practice has certain distinctive emphases, as well as a rich overlay of custom, activity, poetry, and music. Today it is above all their observance of these traditions that distinguishes them from most of their neighbors and intensifies their own social and cultural life.

2. S. D. Goitein, "The Jews of Yemen," in A. J. Arberry, *Religion in the Middle East* (Cambridge: Cambridge University Press, 1969), pp. 226-229.

3. A primary symbolic indicator of religiosity among Jews is the skullcap (*kipa* in Hebrew, *yarmulke* in Yiddish) worn by orthodox men at all times. The population of Kiryat Eliahu as a whole is not especially religious, so the *kipa* is not worn by that many men—certainly not more than a quarter of them. But virtually all Yemenite men of Kiryat Eliahu wear the skullcap when they are in town. At most a handful of young men in their late teens and twenties can be seen without them. Some young men remove their skullcaps when they are away in the army or at work outside the city. The reasons for removing them may be either the fear that secular people will be prejudiced against them (especially in the military), or the embarrassment of young men among their secular peers. This was more likely in the 1970s than the 1980s, however, for there is a new assertiveness on the part of the orthodox at present.

4. By 1987 schisms in the established congregations had resulted in the establishment of three more Yemenite synagogues. In addition, young men who had moved to the other side of town organized one of their own. See Postscript.

5. It is a common practice with the Yemenites, as in many other Jewish communities, to auction off the tasks which bring honor, such as leading various sections of the services and reading the set sections of the Torah portion for each *shabbat*. The funds thus collected help pay for synagogue expenses.

6. Cf. Samuel C. Heilman, *Synagogue Life: A Study in Symbolic Interaction* (Chicago: University of Chicago Press, 1973), p. 87ff.

7. See S. D. Goitein, "Jewish Education in Yemen as an Archetype of Traditional Jewish Education," in C. Frankenstein, ed., *Between Past and Future* (Jerusalem: Henrietta Szold Foundation, 1953), p. 117.

8. *Ibid*, p. 118.

9. *Ibid*, p. 118.

10. *Ibid*, p. 120.

11. There is a role for a special reader, a *ḥazan*, who stands in front of the scroll, points out the places to begin and end, corrects mistakes, and blesses the reader and his family afterward.

12. As in Yemen, the training a father gives his son may be supplemented by regular lessons with a *mori*. In the mid-1970s Kiryat Eliahu had no active *mori*, but by 1981 one of the synagogues had established a *talmud torah*, a small religious school in which an old man drilled students in Torah and prayer. By 1987 there were several *mori* teaching.

13. Yosef Kafiḥ, *Jewish Life in Sanā* (Jerusalem: Ben-Zvi Institute, 1969), pp. 3-9. [Hebrew]

14. The late teens and early twenties are apparently a time of rebellion among Yemenite men, and this accounts for their underrepresentation. As we shall see, there is also a pattern of return later in life.

15. As Samuel Heilman notes, the separation of the sexes in the synagogue "evolves from a religious principle which demands that men and women approach divine otherness in separate and different ways." Observant Yemenite women accept this principle as well. Their religious responsibilities are fulfilled in the home and with the family. What Heilman says of the Ashkenazi women of his congregation in "Sprawl City" is equally true of the Yemenite women of Kiryat Eliahu: "Her domain is simply not the shul (synagogue); her turf is her home." (See Heilman, *Synagogue Life*, pp. 71, 72.)

16. On the *ḥazan* and *shaliaḥ tsibur* in orthodox Ashkenazi congregations, see Heilman, *Synagogue Life*, p. 87.

17. For a detailed picture of the same phenomenon among American orthodox Jews, see Heilman, *Synagogue Life*, p. 74ff.

18. Kafiḥ, *Jewish Life*, p. 8.

19. See Y. Kafiḥ, "What is the Eating of Ja'ale?" in Y. Tobi, ed., *Legacy of the Jews of Yemen: Studies and Researches* (Jerusalem: Bo'i Teman, 1976), p. 53ff. [Hebrew]

20. Zion Mansour Ozeri, *Yemenite Jews: A Photographic Essay* (New York: Schocken, 1985), p. xiii.

21. Caspi and Lipstadt, p. 4, in Mishael Maswari Caspi, *Daughters of Yemen* (Berkeley: University of California Press, 1985); also Yeḥiel Adaqi and Uri Sharvit, *A Treasury of Jewish Yemenite Chants* (Jerusalem: The Israel Institute for Sacred Music, 1981). [Hebrew]

22. In the summer of 1987 I attended a wedding in a hall, with people I had known well ten years earlier. The women were much more fashionably dressed than would have been the case a decade before, an indication both of increased wealth and the coming of age of the Israeli-born cohort, more style-conscious than their immigrant elders. At the same time, there was no *salon*

dancing at all. The band played only Yemenite music, and there was vigorous and enthusiastic dancing, especially by younger men and women, and many older women.

23. I have used the Yiddish term here for want of a reasonable English equivalent. *Landslayt* (*landsman*, sing.) refers to people who come from the same town or district in the old country.

7

Identity, Values, and Attitudes

The Yemenites of Kiryat Eliahu are a very self-aware people. They have a powerful sense of who they are and where they have come from. They are proud of their history and culture and have a feeling of being special, even different, and for the most part they evaluate their ethnic group positively, though not without some criticisms and reservations.

As might be expected, however, it was sometimes very difficult for young Yemenites to accept the differences between their parents' culture and that of the new society around them. To some extent it still is. Their parents were not only "old-fashioned," as parents so often are, but "primitive" as well. They knew they had come from a "backward" country and were seen by others as primitive, and there were young people who were deeply embarrassed by this. It is clear that some people, especially those in their thirties, still have feelings of ambivalence and embarrassment in the face of these cultural contrasts.[1] On the whole, however, the early crisis has passed and it is not really acceptable to admit these feelings or to attempt to flee one's identity as a Yemenite.

Here is the testimony of one well-educated woman of thirty, who held a relatively high position in the educational system.

> When I was in school everything led one to the feeling that what was Ashkenazi was good: the holiday customs, the teachers—all led one to believe that their ways, even blue eyes, were good and that our own ways were *busha* (embarrassing, shameful). But by the age of twenty I began to understand that "You will never be like them," and to understand that "This is mine." And soon I understood this and became proud of what is mine, what is Teymani (Yemenite). Day by day I am more and more myself. I want to preserve the culture (*tarbut*), the songs and the poetry. I don't want these things to disappear. I don't want to be something else.

To a great extent the Yemenites of Kiryat Eliahu, as those elsewhere in Israel, accept the image of themselves at the time of their *aliya*, as simple, unsophisticated people, who had never seen airplanes or traffic lights, who stood agape before the wonders of the modern world and reacted in amusing ways. There is a genre of jokes Yemenites tell about themselves, based on their naivete (and their frugality) when they first came. They enjoy stories in the heavy Yemenite dialect of the newcomer, making fun of their earlier attitudes and misunderstandings.

This simplicity and naivete of the Yemenites is also seen as goodness and moral strength, however, and may stand either explicitly or implicitly in contrast to the behavior of those they feel tricked or cheated them.[2] Although largely ignorant of the modern world, they were honest, religiously observant, home-loving, and hard-working. As a leading Yemenite political figure put it before an audience of his countrymen, "We didn't have doctors and we didn't know engineering, but we knew how to get along without narcotics, and we knew how to teach our children to behave." This is said in the light of what Yemenites view as the troubling modern problems of the breakdown of families, the growth of secularism and misconduct in the young, the spread of a youth drug culture, and the general loss of values in the wider community of Israel, all of which were being widely decried in the mid-1970s.

It is interesting to compare the situation in Kiryat Eliahu in 1977 with that described by Elihu Katz and Awraham Zloczower for the Yemenites of Sha'arayim (Rehovot) in the 1950s. They concluded that

> Yemenite culture is a familistic culture, emphasizing the inter-dependence of family members and the authority of age. It is a culture in which achievement in the instrumental sphere is not a primary value, though it is beginning to take root among the young. It is a culture which emphasizes (religious) learning and religio-national loyalty. Evaluating themselves in these terms—particularly with respect to familial, religious, and national loyalties—the Yemenites do not perceive themselves as wanting, and this self-respect (though it is not unmixed with feelings of inferiority) contributes substantially to the picture [of intergenerational continuity in attitudes and behavior] presented here.[3]

The only significant difference between their findings and mine is that in the 1970s, as they had apparently anticipated, the young became more concerned with instrumental achievement. Today those who are educated and have succeeded in their work see that they can be the equal, in all spheres of activity, of people of any ethnic background. Nevertheless the standards of evaluation stressed above are still of basic importance.

Kiryat Eliahu's Yemenites often speak of *arakhim*, the modern Hebrew word for "values." Just as they talk of *derekh erets* ("proper conduct") and *orekh haim* ("mode of life")—concepts derived from Jewish tradition—and of *hinukh* ("education," "upbringing"), so they speak of those elements which they consider to be basic to their own attitudes and behavior. For this they may use the term *arakhim*. They are, of course, influenced in this usage by newspapers, radio, and television, as well as by the education courses that many younger people have taken, and the seminars they have attended. Israelis generally spend a good deal of time discussing and analyzing their society, and it is difficult to find a naive informant, unaware of the words of commentators and analysts, perhaps learned second- or third-hand in conversations with others.

Not only are these people influenced by general analyses of Israeli society, but more particularly they are aware of the way their own ethnic group is viewed and compared to others. All these elements enter into the image that Yemenites have of themselves, but this in itself does not render the image less interesting or valid, or even less of a guide for behavior.

Twenty years ago Katz and Zloczower wrote that the image of the Yemenite in Israel portrays him "as hard-working, self-respecting, accepting of his (lesser) place in the status system, well educated in Jewish faith and practice, traditional in his behavior, and strongly identified with family, group, and the Jewish people."[4] What is more, they report that they found, contrary to their prior expectations, that "this picture of Yemenite life," although suffering "as do all stereotypes, from gross oversimplification," was not an unreasonable characterization of the situation.[5]

The Image of the Yemenites

For no other Israeli Jewish group does there exist anything like the developed, detailed, and positive image which has grown up about the Yemenites. That image is encountered over and over again in the popular press; it finds its way into the scholarly literature, and is frequently heard from people in conversation. Yochanan Peres reports that in a survey carried out in the late 1960s the Ashkenazim praised the Yemenites as "Full of the joy of life; lovers of work; simple and nice; warm-hearted; strong and healthy," among other traits.[6] These and other positive characteristics comprise the stereotype of the Yemenite in Israeli society.

Many of the terms stress niceness, cheerfulness, diligence, enjoyment of life, and the willingness or ability to endure hardships and poverty without complaint. Still another is encompassed by the term *tsanu'a* (modesty), which has a similar range of meanings in Hebrew and English. It can mean humble and retiring, or unassuming, but it may also refer to modesty of ornamentation and dress, and lack of ostentation. (It has the additional connotation of sexual modesty.) The words *adin* (delicate) and *adinut* (delicacy) are also used by Yemenites and others in connection with their culture.

As we saw in Chapter 3, the elements of the Yemenite image were noticed a century ago. Yafa Berlovitz demonstrates that Ashkenazi writers depicted Yemenites in these terms as early as the 1880s. They were seen as living in poverty and wretchedness and yet having an internal life of purity, propriety, and modesty.[7] They were seen as optimistic, full of faith, and mystical, but also as lovers of work, the exemplars of the "conquest of labor."[8] They maintained their self-respect despite their low economic and social position.

There is a remarkable degree of agreement between the Yemenites themselves and outsiders who comment upon Yemenite behavior. In addition to the references in the literature, the casual comments of friends, and the responses of non-Yemenite informants to questions about that group, I have results of a survey question asked of high school students in Kiryat Eliahu. Although only about fifty out of 150 students were willing to answer the question which asked about ethnic attributes, those who did, who came from a variety of ethnic backgrounds, stressed the same range of positive qualities as those just cited.[9] The same cluster of traits were not attributed to any other groups. Although many aspects of this characterization of the Yemenites as a people are completely subjective and probably impossible to verify, the degree of concurrence is in itself impressive. I argue, in addition, that the image, or stereotype, has certain behavioral implications. I suggest that it is not merely a supposed description of observed behavior, but that it may also serve Yemenites as a guide to, and measure of, their behavior.

The terms used in the preceding characterizations of Yemenites implied positive evaluations. Given the relativity of values it is possible that some readers might question how positive some of these (e.g. diligent, quiet) are, but it seems safe to assume that they were intended as positive by those who use them. Despite occasional negative evaluations (Moroccans are likely to call Yemenites "stingy"), in Kiryat Eliahu, as in Israel generally, the overwhelming impression one receives of the Yemenite reputation is a favorable one. And Yemenites themselves join in this positive evaluation, although not without criticisms of their own, based on their inside knowledge of their people and society.

The question arises, shouldn't any ethnic group be pleased to be evaluated in such approving terms? Shouldn't we expect the members of any such group to think well of themselves and to choose flattering labels to describe themselves? Assuming that the answer is "yes," that still leaves open the question of which adjectives and adverbs to choose. What traits from the wide range of human behavior should be selected? Some people might consider as positive such characterizations as shrewd, quick-witted, generous to a fault, ambitious, brave, tough, sophisticated, and quick to defend his honor. But these are not the ones usually applied to Yemenites as a category of people. This is not the way they see themselves or that others see them. Flattering or not, the terms noted above are the ones that the Yemenites themselves have chosen to emphasize and that others seem to see reflected in their behavior. In contrast, here are some positive and negative traits attributed to Moroccans in the same survey of high school students: proud, know how to receive guests well, love children, jumpy, touchy (*atsbanim—* nervous, irritable), full of energy, hot-tempered.

Yemenites do indeed see themselves as generally quiet, well-behaved, cheerful, nice, and simple in the sense of honest and straightforward, as well as diligent, religious, and frugal. In contrast they often portray Ashkenazim as cold, closed, and snobbish, but Moroccans as showy, hot-blooded, and perhaps prone to aggressive behavior. Those Yemenites who know Indian Jews consider them far more quiet than themselves; in fact they see them as passive (*adashim*). Some Yemenites even consider their people's gentle behavior and uncomplaining attitudes as a handicap. Because they are pleasant and uncomplaining they can be ignored and exploited, according to this perspective. Invariably they contrast the behavior of the Moroccans, whom they see as aggressive, clamoring loudly, either organizing or turning to aggressive behavior in order to get what they want from society.

Are Yemenites all so nice? Obviously not. As any people they display a range of personality types and therefore include grumps, back-biters, shirkers, manipulators, fakers, and more than their share of envious people. But it also seems to me that they do try, in general, to project an image of pleasantness, especially to outsiders. They try to seem friendly, cheerful, hospitable, uncomplaining, and hard-working. I cannot say how deep these traits may be in their psyches, but I can say that these are frequently encountered elements of the Yemenite persona. These are important aspects of the "typical" Yemenite "presentation of self in everyday life."[10]

These aspects of the Yemenite image are the elements in a sort of implicit code in terms of which the Yemenites of Kiryat Eliahu evaluate behavior, their own and others'. Again, not every Yemenite could always be reverent, thrifty, cheerful, obedient, helpful, industrious, modest, and content. Rather these are widely shared ideas and attitudes, and they can be manifested and observed in a wide range of contexts, in speech and action. Furthermore, insofar as people act in terms of these values there may be implications in terms of the results of this behavior.

Attitude Toward Work

In a narrative which S. D. Goitein collected from a Yemenite newly arrived in Palestine in 1929, the speaker says,

> [In Yemen] the barber is very much despised by the Muslims; no Muslim would ever give his daughter to a barber or a barber-surgeon [who applies leeches] or a tanner. These only marry among themselves. If one Muslim calls another a barber, he can be haled into court. We Jews don't despise anyone for his profession; with us baths are heated by burning dried dung, not only cow dung, but also— by your leave—what is taken from outhouses [it is mixed with cow dung]; don't think that the people whose job this is are thought less of than anyone else on that account. "Aristocracy" with us means only that someone is descended from an unsullied family and can support himself by his own work.[11]

Compare the Talmudic dictum, "Flay a carcass in the street and earn a wage and say not, 'I am a great man and degrading work is not for me.'"[12] An article in the *Encyclopaedia Judaica* points out that the

Talmud enjoined work both for economic independence and against the dangers of idleness. In fact, for many Talmudic rabbis, the ideal was to combine the study of Torah with the pursuit of a worldly occupation, especially skilled artisanry.

This attitude toward work also prevailed in Yemen, where knowledge of the Talmud was extensive and where, as Goitein has said, life was lived very much as in Talmudic times.[13] According to Mishael Caspi, "The three most important tasks of a man in this society . . . are to build a house, feed his family, and pray to God, the King of the Universe."[14] A man's occupation was not of central importance in his self-esteem or status. It was not a matter for honor and shame. And this attitude has played its role in Israel as well.

From the time they arrived in Jerusalem in the 1880s through the early decades of the twentieth century when they were sought after for work in agriculture, the Yemenites established a reputation as hard workers, willing to undertake difficult and menial work and to do it responsibly, probably even cheerfully. In the early 1950s Jean-Jacques Berreby wrote, "Enterprising and pressed to provide for himself, the Yemenite accepts with good grace any kind of task. His eagerness for work, and his natural liveliness has gained him the liking, at first condescending but then more and more respectful, of his fellows and superiors."[15]

When they arrived in Israel in 1949-50, most Yemenite men old enough to work were employed as unskilled laborers, some of them in garbage and sanitation work. Women took jobs as housemaids. They established their reputation as diligent and uncomplaining workers; many men moved into skilled work and some became foremen. Nevertheless, there are still quite a few older people who continue to work as cleaning women or in sanitation, and it is not a source of shame for them—or for their children. On the contrary, younger people often speak with pride of how their parents worked at the jobs in order to give their children opportunities. Even today young women who are successful students will sometimes fill in when their mothers are unable to come to work, and men who have other jobs by day may moonlight by cleaning up public halls after weddings or other events. One of the most respected elders in the community, the unofficial rabbi of one of the synagogues, continues to work in sanitation although he is quite old and has four successful children. Some years ago he was offered a salaried position as a rabbi but modestly turned it down, at least partly because of the traditional Yemenite belief that it is not meritorious to live from the performance of religious functions.

By no means are the Yemenites the only ones to work in cleaning and garbage collection in Israel. These days far fewer Yemenites are involved in such work, and there are others hired to do it. It is my observation, shared by others, that the Yemenites have an attitude of acceptance of menial labor, seeing it as work which must be done in society and as a valid way to earn money. This is not so typical of other groups. It is not at all uncommon to hear others complain loudly and often about menial labor, or to turn a custodial job into a platform for visibility and the expression of discontent. Yemenites, however, apparently feel that a job done well and without complaint may bring rewards in the form of reputation, acceptance, and possible future advancement. From the instrumental point of view, they recognize the potential in good performance of even the lowliest work.[16]

I do not recall ever hearing an older Yemenite complain about the work he or others had to do in road building or afforestation during the early years. Yemenites are much more likely to be proud of the progress that they and the state have made since those days, rather than resentful of the fact that they had to do such work.[17] In contrast to the attitude of the Yemenites, it seems clear both from my own observations and from the literature that many Moroccan Jews, in particular, look upon the downward mobility they experienced upon arrival in Israel as shameful and traumatic. Not only do the adults who went through it complain, but so do their children. For example, Erez Bitton writes, "When [my father] arrived here, he'd never done any physical work, and suddenly he was taken to clean toilets, to do very dirty work. That pains me; the type of work and the fact that there wasn't enough work . . . I remember his face when he worked on the railroad, lifted tracks. . . ."[18] I did not encounter the same sense of shock and outrage from Yemenites.

Yochanan Peres notes that the 1948-50 Yemenite immigrants "adapted easily compared with members of other ethnic groups to the assignments given to them in the framework of the program for the development and dispersal of the population."[19] Those Yemenites who came to Israel at that time, as those who came in prestate days, are well aware of injustice and discrimination, and they have some resentments, as well as appreciation and satisfaction at having returned to the Holy Land. But the resentment seems to be directed at any unfairness and discrimination they perceived, not at the nature of the work itself.

The Yemenite value for economic independence and against idleness or living from the community is manifest in Kiryat Eliahu. Living in a section of the city where a number of families are supported wholly or in large measure by welfare, the Yemenites do not see this as a respectable alternative to working at a job. [20] Even men who are quite old continue to work, and one exception, a man in his sixties, is pitied. People feel there is something wrong with him. Even those few men who have drinking problems and make life difficult for their wives and children continue to work well and responsibly and to provide for their families—although not as well as they could were they sober.

One Yemenite man, in his early seventies, left Kiryat Eliahu recently in order to realize his lifelong dream of living in Jerusalem. He sold his little grocery store, from which he had a decent if modest living, and was willing to try working as a street cleaner. He found it hard on his legs at his age, however, and he was able to start a small business using skills he had learned as a teenager in Yemen. But he considered street cleaning a reasonable way to earn his daily bread, and took it for granted that he would work rather than live on old-age insurance.

Among the older generation and the middle-aged the subject of work and occupation rarely arises in general conversation. Seldom did I hear about the work a person did, and information was hardly ever volunteered. People were not identified by their occupation, even if it was a relatively high-status one, and men of the older generation are still evaluated in terms of how they support their families, raise their children (in Torah and *derekh erets*), and keep the traditions, rather than in terms of the work that they do. Neither is it usual to hear comments about people's wealth, although there are occasional hints about the numbers of apartments that someone owns or the value of the jewelry a woman has in a bank vault.

It is very clear that these people were not content to see themselves as a permanent caste of hewers of wood and drawers of water. Not in the Land of Israel at any rate. As we have seen, the upward mobility of the young has been marked, and even many older men moved up to more skilled, more responsible, and better paying work. While there is general pride in their reputation as uncomplaining, responsible, diligent workers, there is resentment by some against the Ashkenazim who, they believe, only saw them as fit for this sort of work, at least at first. And I have heard young people say such things as, "Certainly they like us. We are suckers, *frayerim*, working hard and not complaining." But they, too, see this as an outstanding trait of the ethnic group. Yemenites are, on the whole, proud of it and of the moral qualities it implies. There is, at least in the older generation, a general recognition of the constraints and difficulties of the early days, and of their own lack of education and skills for the new economy they had entered in 1949. These limitations no longer apply, and many in the younger generation see no limits to their own goals.

This does not mean, however, that they will—or we should—assume that those who choose skilled trades such as welding, metallurgy, diamond cutting, and mechanical or electrical work are selling themselves short. There is, as we have noted, a positive value for working with one's hands, supported not only by the Talmud and by their heritage as craftsmen in Yemen, but by Zionist ideology as well. To many Israelis this ideology seems old-fashioned in light of the new technological, economic, and political realities, but many Yemenites— and many old Labor Zionists—still think that there is ennoblement in the work of one's hands. Manual labor, building and creating, which pays relatively well, was still seen, in the 1970s, as an honorable career choice in preference to occupations deemed more prestigious in other social circles.

It is too early to predict the fate of the Yemenite work ethic in the rapidly diversifying educational and occupational context in which the younger generation lives. As we note in the section on marriage, education and socioeconomic status seem to be having the predictable effect in directing marriage choices. The development of a new Yemenite residential section, starting with young, better-educated people with higher occupational status is another such indication. Those of similar education and status seek out each other's company. This is a natural and expected development. But there is no question that over the past thirty years attitudes toward work brought from Yemen have played an important role in Kiryat Eliahu, and we must assume that it will continue to have implications for the future. There are still rewards for diligence, responsibility, and a good reputation.

Histapkut B'mu'at: Frugality and Contentment with Little

The term *histapkut b'mu'at* is often applied to the Yemenites by themselves and by others. It refers to their supposed characteristic of being willing to accept difficult material conditions and scarcity without complaint and even cheerfully. The image this conjures up for many Israelis is that of a simple old man with long side-curls and a beard, or a simple cleaning lady wearing embroidered trousers under her skirt, her head covered in a kerchief, responding to the question "How are you?" with the phrase "God be praised" (*barukh ha-shem*). Even though their house is barely furnished and they have so little, yet they thank and praise God and go cheerfully about their business. It is an image cherished by many Yemenites as well as their admirers within Israel.

One evening, before an audience of several thousand Yemenites at an ethnic festival in Jerusalem, Yisrael Yeshayahu (a Yemenite who was then Speaker of the Knesset) explained the matter as follows: "It is not that Yemenites are so simple that they don't want the same things that other people do. But they know how to do without, if need be. They don't blame others for their troubles, and yell and shout, but work to improve their situation." His words were very much appreciated by the audience. However, the importance of this trait is not merely that Yemenites know how to suffer cheerfully.

As we noted earlier, Yemenites tend not to furnish their homes with the wallpaper, carpets, drapes, furniture, paintings, and knick-knacks that so many other Israelis favor. The same is true of clothing and women's fashions. Even on the most formal occasions Yemenites are likely to be dressed quite simply, though in clean clothes. Yemenite women don't go to beauty salons for fancy and expensive hair styles, although these abound in Israel today. Nor do they wear the latest fashion in shoes or other items of dress. Once again the contrast with Moroccans is strong. For many Moroccans modish dress is as important as a house well and fully furnished. I understand that people of Iraqi origin are often extremely concerned with high-quality goods and are willing to pay for fine things. Indeed the Israel of the 1970s was marked by a consumer orientation which horrified old socialists whose Zionist dream was of a very different place. While Yemenites are certainly not unaffected by this "revolution," in Kiryat Eliahu, at least, they were far less involved with it.[21]

Members of other ethnic groups, especially Moroccans, are wont to call Yemenites *kamtsanim*, tight-fisted, stingy people. In a 1977 theatrical production, *Kriza* (Crisis), which was based on the problems and complaints of African and Asian Jews in Israel, a Moroccan or Iraqi man complains that after years of struggling to get a license to open a *kiosk* (small streetcorner stand), he was finally given a place in a Yemenite neighborhood. The audience understood that this meant he wouldn't do much business.

Today, at least, the Yemenite tendency to do without and to control consumption is not a product of poverty. Though in the past they may have had no choice, today the Yemenites of Kiryat Eliahu are a relatively affluent part of the population. On the other hand, it has been often noted that people on welfare in Israel may nevertheless manage to furnish their homes very well indeed. This contrast was put very clearly in the following statement from a nineteen-year-old Yemenite girl who was working in Tiveria (Tiberias) for the welfare department while spending a year in National Service (*Sherut Le'umi*). Speaking of her Moroccan clients who were on welfare, she said, "They have lots of men, strong men, able to work, but they go to the welfare office and are supported by welfare (*sa'ad*) rather than work. But they have such stereo sets—like we wouldn't dream of buying. In every house a stereo set. And the salon furniture! What luxury, magnificence (*pe'er*)! Every few months they change their furniture! Not like among us. And yet their children go barefoot! I know, because I have to visit their homes for my work."[22]

As this quotation suggests, Yemenites of Kiryat Eliahu frequently compare their own attitudes and behavior to that which they think typifies the Moroccans. This is especially true with respect to the values and priorities involved in work and welfare, consumption and expenditure. They believe that the contrast between these two groups are marked and important. Not only do they feel that Moroccans often turn to welfare rather than work, they also perceive them as conspicuous consumers, wasting their money on showy furnishings, clothing, fancy *bar mitsvahs* and weddings, and expensive food.

To the Yemenites of Kiryat Eliahu, fancy wallpaper (*tapetim*), a house filled with expensive furnishings and accessories, elaborate hairdoes and platform shoes, all stand for the externals of modernity (*hitsonim* is the word they use) and almost seem to betoken a loss of values. Young Yemenites will say, "They have learned only the externals, while we understand what is really involved in becoming modern, in *modernizatsia*."

Nowadays Yemenites are very likely to claim that they are like everyone else in Israel, and want the same things. In 1982, when I revisited a young couple I had known five years earlier, the wife told me, "Today all that *histapkut b'mu'at* has changed and now everyone,

from all the *eydot*, strives for *luxus* (luxuries) and automobiles." I
persisted in my questioning.

"Are the Yemenites the same as all others now?" I asked.

"Well, not like the Moroccans," she answered. "They want good
food, good clothes, a salon full of new furniture, and wallpaper (even
textured wallpaper, like corduroy!). But their apartments? It doesn't
matter to them (*lo ikhpat la' hem*); and their children—beneath all
criticism."

I asked her to spell out the differences, and I used the term *seder
adifut*, order of preferences. She then continued, "First, for us there
is the apartment. In our old place we had iron cots, but we weren't
embarrassed; not at all. Later we got a nice sofa, but before that came
the washing machine. We had no oven at first, but it came later, as
did the TV. It is a waste to buy salon furniture for 100,000 lira [worth
about $700 at that time] when there are young children. They just mess
it up. So we'll wait until later. Instead we want more rooms for the
children to sleep and study—not for *luxus*. Later will come the table
and chairs and sofa and the fancy kitchen cabinets and the oven and
television and the car. First we are concerned to own a satisfactory
apartment, and about the children." (I was surprised to find wallpaper
in their living room, but not to hear that it had been put put up by the
previous owners, who were Ashkenazi. It was gone by my next visit a
year later.)

Despite the undoubted truth of my friend's claim that young
Yemenites, like everyone else, want nice and useful things, I believe
that her subsequent words still indicate an attitude of mind and a
set of priorities and standards that suggest that the old patterns are
being updated rather than abandoned. Even in the 1980s the material
conditions of the Yemenites both in Kiryat Eliahu and elsewhere in
Israel reveal a distinctive esthetic, certain preferences, and a measure of
frugality.

The Rewards of Thrift

The control of consumption is not only consistent with what we
have read about the manner in which Yemenites hid their well-being
in Yemen; it also has the effect of encouraging saving, and thus the
accumulation of wealth. Often, as we have seen, this takes the form
of the acquisition of apartments, which are an excellent investment in
Israel. Berreby saw, in 1954, that "the Yemenites like to capitalize

the fruit of their labor in the form of real estate. Most prefer to deprive themselves of the rewards of current consumption in order to economize with a view to future ownership, at least of their homes. It is significant to see, among long-term residents who are owners of one or several houses, families living very miserly. A great number of immigrants are already home-owners, in part or totally, of dwellings assigned by hire-purchase."[23] This was only four or five years after the penniless newcomers had arrived!

Further evidence of the instrumental importance of Yemenite "contentment with little" comes from a study of poverty in Israel based on 1963 data. According to Jack Habib and his associates, if poverty were measured in terms of income, the Yemenites showed the highest rate of poverty of any ethnic group.[24] These groups were listed as coming from Iran-Iraq; Yemen-Aden; Morocco-Tunisia-Algeria; the rest of Asia-Africa; the Balkans; and Western Europe and the Americas. When measures of wealth were introduced, however, the Yemenite rate of poverty was much lower; it came closer to that of groups from the Balkans and to Europeans, while those from Iran-Iraq and North Africa appeared far poorer.[25] (Wealth was measured in terms of savings, stocks, imputed value of owner-occupied dwellings, and durable goods.) The authors noted that "Our results seem to support the reputation [Yemenites] have established as a particularly industrious and thrifty group."[26] It is regrettable that we have no comparable figures for the current situation, now that most Yemenites have been in the country for almost forty years.

Histapkut b' mu' at, contentment with little, is more than just an ability to endure hardships cheerfully, thus establishing a nice reputation while relieving the guilt of those who have more. It apparently helps to survive on little in hard times and, when conditions improve, to save and to invest for the future. Yemenites know how to budget and save. This is again consistent with the observations of Habib and Berreby, and with the stereotype.

Working hard and cheerfully, living modestly and not complaining, gives the Yemenites a good reputation. Peres, for example, attributes the popularity of the Yemenites among Europeans to the willingness of the Yemenites to work hard "and to identify with Israeli society without demanding a full portion of its resource."[27] But diligent work and intelligent saving and investment also have paid off economically. It is generally the case that Kiryat Eliahu's Yemenites present themselves as friendly, pleasant, hard working, modest, religiously observant, and peaceable. (The general public is unaware of their synagogue feuds, which are not very violent in any case.) Yemenites are by no means simple, however, and they know quite well what is required to get along in their new world. They are alert, sensitive, aware, and successful. Where they differ from the Egyptian Jews, for example, who also know how to succeed quietly in the world, is that the Yemenites have a very visible heritage and "culture," of which they are very proud, and which they continue to maintain and develop. We shall discuss this aspect in the next chapter.

Leadership, Politics, and Envy

Despite the closeness of the Yemenite community, it is not characterized by strong leadership or organization. It is a highly egalitarian and decentralized community. Unlike some Yemenite communities, it has no organized performing group or any other overall community-wide activity. In the past few years one of the synagogues has apparently managed to organize its own after-school religious instruction for boys and a mutual aid society, but the level of such activity is evidently much lower than some people would like.

As a general rule Kiryat Eliahu's Yemenites are suspicious of politicians and organizers. This is an attitude which apparently is shared by Yemenites throughout the country.[28] In part this is certainly a reaction to their experiences in Israel as the various political parties vied for their support, made promises to them, and recruited members of the community. But there is another source for this suspicion, and that is pervasive envy, jealousy, and competition.

Perhaps envy and competition might be expected in such a close-knit community which is so involved in religious observance and the carrying out of the religious laws, practices, ceremonies, and good deeds (*mitsvot*). One man, who is married to a Yemenite, explained the phenomenon this way. "It is written, 'Run to do *mitsvot*.' The Yemenites want to say, 'I'm first,' so they compete and fight among themselves for the honor." The primary arena of the competition is, of course, the synagogue, where most men are capable of leading, and no hierarchy is needed. It is here that one is most likely to witness disagreements and outbursts of anger. Feuds within and between synagogues have gone on for years in Kiryat Eliahu, as they did in

Yemen before *aliya*. But jealousy, envy (*kin' a*), and begrudging ill will (*ayn tsara*) arise in many contexts, especially between families, which may see each other as competitors. There is a pervasive undertone of suspicion about the motives of others and perhaps a begrudging attitude toward those who succeed. In the words of one informant, discussing a nearby community, "If someone wants to do this or that, others think that there must be something in it for him. 'He must have "interests." Why should I help him?"' This suspicion of the motives of others may be an additional deterrent which keeps people from going into business, and perhaps it reinforces the value against material display.

Regardless of these leveling attitudes, members of the community continue to work, save, study, and get ahead. They may, however, have the effect of limiting certain activities that depend upon the support and patronage of the community, such as political leadership and shopkeeping. This said, it must be reiterated that the Yemenites are not without influence in Kiryat Eliahu. By 1987 three of the thirteen members of the city council were Yemenites, one each representing the Labor Party, the Likud, and the National Religious Party. One of these was the deputy mayor. Another Yemenite holds a useful administrative position in the municipality. The "Sephardi" chief rabbi is a Yemenite. (As is true of the country as a whole, the city has a dual chief rabbinate.) The Yemenite community knows what is going on and has connections in the city.

Social Relations and Ethnicity

Throughout their lives the Yemenites of Kiryat Eliahu must interact with Jews of other ethnic origins. They interact with others in the neighborhood, at school, in the places they do their shopping, on the job, in the army, and in all public institutions other than their synagogues. Their fellow students and teachers (and their students, if they are teachers), their army buddies, coworkers, bosses, shopkeepers, and neighbors come from many different backgrounds. They know how to live in this heterogeneous world and how to succeed in it; this is particularly true of the young and Israeli-born. Nevertheless, off the job, in the neighborhood, out of school, and out of the army, most Yemenites have their most frequent, regular, and socially intimate relations with other Yemenites.

This is true not only of the important ritual and religious activities discussed above, but also in informal friendships, visiting, leisure-time activity, and general social interaction. With few exceptions, Yemenites of Kiryat Eliahu visited with, talked with, and were friends with other Yemenites. When people left Kiryat Eliahu to travel or to visit, it was very often to attend a *simḥa* or to spend *shabbat* at the home of kinsfolk or with other Yemenite friends or *landslayt*. Sometimes they went to attend a Yemenite activity such as a folklore show, or the celebrations of holidays organized by Yemenite cultural or political organizations.

Even though they are by no means segregated from others, Yemenites exercise a clear pattern of choice in intimate social relations, that is, those where the interaction is not dictated by the necessarily heterogeneous context of the school, workplace, or military unit.[29]

Marriage

Of a sample of 114 couples with children in school in 1977, 85 percent are endogamous Yemenite marriages, and 15 percent (eighteen) are marriages of Yemenites to Jews of other ethnic origins. This is just slightly more than Judah Matras reports for Yemenite intermarriage based on the 1961 census.[30] (No pattern of preferences is apparent in these "mixed marriages.") Most of the couples too old to have children in school are, of course, endogamous, since they married before, or shortly after, *aliya*.

More recently, however, during 1976 and 1977, eleven of twenty marriages listed in the rabbi's register show Yemenites marrying non-Yemenites. The answer to this apparent change lies, I believe, in the area of socioeconomic status. There is a "marriage squeeze," a lack of appropriate partners which forces some people to "marry out." The eight Yemenite men who married non-Yemenite women (four Moroccan, two Ashkenazi, one Turkish, and one Tunisian) were all relatively low-status workers, skilled and semiskilled, without much education. In general, women seek marriage partners who are older than they, and younger Yemenite women in the Kiryat Eliahu marriage pool are generally better educated than the men two to three years older. Some have gone to teacher's seminary, if not beyond, and we may presume that they are looking for men with better prospects, and with education and interests more in keeping with their own.[31] I have heard it said that the young women complain that there are not enough Yemenite men for them. Possibly it is not only demography, but socioeconomic status as well, which determines availability in these cases.[32] As for the Yemenite women in this sample, two come from one of the most problematical Yemenite families in town, and the third is not from Kiryat Eliahu but comes from a *moshav* some miles away.[33]

The incidence of intermarriage found in these years seems, therefore, to point to a situation where the status of the younger women is higher than that of the older men, thus forcing some men and some women to look beyond the ethnic group (or, alternatively, beyond the community) for marriage. I believe that we are dealing with what Milton Gordon has termed *ethclass*[34], the confluence of ethnicity and class, and that there is some temporary lack of fit here between the sexes on the dimension of socioeconomic status.

Intermarriage does not necessarily mean that a couple leaves the Yemenite community, however, especially when the Yemenite partner is a man. If they continue to live in the neighborhood, as do most of the twenty-nine couples noted here, the father takes his sons to the synagogue with him and sends his children to the religious school. This has the effect of keeping them at least partially within the Yemenite community, particularly in those cases where the Yemenite family is large and solid, and the other partner's family small or weak.

In Israel the rate of intermarriage between Jews of different countries of origin has been increasing. Most demographic studies focus primarily on those marriages between people from different continents of origin (African-Asian to European-American). That rate now stands at about 24 percent, which may be quite high in comparative worldwide perpsective for marriage between partners from such different backgrounds. But there are few data and studies dealing with within-country and within-continent endogamy and exogamy. There is evidently no study that discusses the implications, results, and impacts of intermarriage.[35]

Jewish-Jewish intermarriage in Israel is a complicated matter, and in the absence of any detailed studies only speculation is possible. On the one hand there is a very strong value which sees all Jews as brethren (*kol Yisrael haverim*) and as one people (*am Yisrael am ehad*). Many point with pride to the steadily growing rate of intermarriage. On the other hand, marrying out means a lack of continuity and, reciprocally, an intrusion, bringing into a family someone who cannot do things in the expected and approved manner. It also involves questions of status and of ethnic loyalty.

The adjustments of the partners to a mixed marriage, and those of their respective families, can be even more difficult than the normal ones that newly married people face. This may be particularly true in the Yemenite community with its distinctive ways and strong sense of identity and heritage. An initial consideration for Kiryat Eliahu's Yemenites is religion. Will the in-marrying partner be as religious as the family would like? If the husband is the non-Yemenite partner, the grandsons will not be brought up in the Yemenite prayer traditions. The Yemenite father is likely to be disappointed because he would have looked forward to the honors in the in-laws' synagogue, the distinctive celebrations, and the *ja'ale*. If the wife is not a Yemenite, how will she be able to cook and bake all the Yemenite foods, both those eaten daily and the special *shabbat* and holiday dishes? (Much of the food that Yemenites eat is still quite distinctively their own.) The relations between Yemenite wives and their mothers-in-law have traditionally posed difficulties, [36] and these differences cannot make them any easier. In fact it is said that even the intermarriage between San'ani and Dhamari Yemenites causes problems!

Finally, a marriage to an Ashkenazi partner may be seen by other Yemenites as social climbing, an attempt to leave behind one's fellow Yemenites and family, and it may thus be considered something of a betrayal. Berdichevsky observed that a Yemenite politician in Sha'arayim had suffered a precipitous decline in popularity when he moved out of the Yemenite neighborhood "in order to 'live among the snobs'" near the Weizmann Institute in Reḥovot. [37] Out-marriage could have a similar effect. Perhaps it is not accidental that Yemenites, along with Jews from Kurdistan, "retain strong patterns of in-marriage in both the immigrant and the first born-in-Israel generations." [38]

Student Responses to a Survey

In 1977 we asked 150 high school students in the two schools in Kiryat Eliahu to answer a large number of questions on a seven-page schedule. None of the eighty students in the secular high school was Yemenite, but there were ten Yemenites among the seventy students in the religious school. There were four girls and three boys in the eleventh grade and one girl and two boys in the tenth grade. Although this is a very small sample indeed, their responses were interesting.

In the first place, on the whole their answers were the fullest and the most seriously considered of any ethnic group in either school. Whereas others often left many questions unanswered or showed impatience, this was not true of the Yemenite students. They took the exercise very seriously and never indicated hostility to questions about ethnicity, as many other students did. (Some students wrote regarding specific ethnic groups, "They are all OK" or "All are Jews.") What is more, Yemenite students gave by far the fullest consideration to questions about their own *eyda* and their feelings toward it. The only comparable attention came from several Tunisian students whose families came from the island of Jerba.[39] Moroccan students, the largest group by far, had a wide variety of reactions to the questions, but few, if any, compared in completeness with those of the Yemenite students, while many failed to answer at all.

Half of the Yemenite students claimed that they would raise their own children very differently from the way that they were raised. While five of ten said that they would raise their children more or less the same way, the other five all said "very differently" or "completely differently." This indication of dissatisfaction is interesting in a number of ways. (1) teenage rebellion has often been reported by Yemenite men in their thirties, who now say they have "returned" to an appreciation of their parents and traditions;[40] (2) the rebellion is directed at the behavior or attitudes of specific parents and not at the ethnic group and its values and behavior. (The latter were generally treated sympathetically elsewhere in the questionnaire.); and (3) two of the five who expressed dissatisfaction with their upbringing came from families with problem fathers who drink and then come home and fight with their families. Along with "primitivity" and lack of freedom, these two students complained of fights, shouting, smoking, drinking *'arak*, and chewing *gat* (*qat*), a plant with stimulant properties that was important in Yemen and is grown and chewed by some Yemenites. They were thus confirming the values in their negative reaction to their own upbringing.

A third student complained of too much religion, which might have been expected, but turned out to be unique in the group. A fourth came from a family that might be considered one of the "best," with a "modern" mother who was quite ambitious for her children. This student felt restricted and denied things that were current but in "good taste." The rebellion, as articulated by these students, would seem on inspection not so serious.

The students were asked to discuss both the negative and positive aspects of their ethnic groups. On the positive side, in addition to the expression of appreciation for Yemenite art, music, dance, literature, folklore, and the observance of the sabbath and of weddings and *ḥinna*, there were comments referring to behavior and values. Yemenites were said to be characterized by good heart, good behavior, mutual aid, and neighborly relations. Supposedly, they "relate to all with warmth" (this from a student who said he was raised badly), and "the older, more religious, are faithful, close to one another, full of life" (from another student who claimed to be unhappy).

Four respondents spoke of the negative aspects of Yemenites: that they fight in synagogue; that they quarrel and shout (from one of the children of the drinkers); that they don't yield or concede; that they are prejudiced and have a generally poor attitude toward women; and that "they like to talk behind the back."

Turning to the total sample of respondents, we find once again that the Yemenites stood out in the way they were evaluated by others. They were among the three most frequently discussed groups, and they were almost invariably evaluated in positive terms. The other two groups which stood out were the Moroccans and the Georgians (*Gruzinim*), but they were generally seen in a more negative light. Thus only three groups seemed to have much visibility for outsiders: Moroccans, Georgians, and Yemenites, and of these only the Yemenites had a positive image.

The results of the survey, modest as they are, seem to underline certain general points about Yemenites in Israel: (1) they are notable for their visibility to the general population; (2) others tend to think well of them; and (3) they are very aware of their own group and its characteristics, real or imputed.[41]

Notes

1. Zion Mansour Ozeri testifies, "Only after we grew up did we come to appreciate their inner strength and patience, their sincere and intense religiosity, and most of all, their forebearance under duress. Only after we matured did we realize that we could be proud of the integrity our parents represented." *Yemenite Jews: A Photographic Essay* (New York: Schocken, 1985), p. xiv.

2. Many Yemenites say that they had jewelry, costumes, and manuscripts that they were forced to leave behind at the airstrip in Aden, or that were

taken from them in Israel. Even more tragic is the case of the Yemenite babies who were taken away, ostensibly for hospital care, and never seen again. This occurred during the time the Yemenites lived in the immigrant reception camps. It is firmly believed that these babies were given to Ashkenazi families that had lost their children in the Holocaust. These old wounds and resentments welled up and were readily discussed in the climate of interethnic tension of 1981-82. By 1987 these tensions had subsided.

3. Elihu Katz and Awraham Zloczower, "Ethnic Continuity in an Israeli Town," *Human Relations* 14:306, 1961.

4. *Ibid*, p. 294.

5. Katz and Zloczower were investigating reports of social disorganization and adolescent rebellion among Yemenites in Rehovot. Thus their conclusion is phrased in terms of the problem: they found the positive image, which they describe, as coming "closer to the facts we have to report concerning the second generation than does the competing image," that is, of breakdown and rebellion.

6. Yochanan Peres, *Ethnic Relations in Israel* (Tel Aviv: Tel Aviv University Press, 1976), p. 55. [Hebrew]

7. Yafa Berlovitz, "The Image of the Yemenite in the Literature of the First *Aliyot,*" *Pe'amim* 10:82, 1981. [Hebrew] See also Haya Hoffman, "'Kfar HaShiloah,' a Saga of Yemenite Immigration by Israel Zarhi," in Shalom Seri, ed., *Se'i Yona: Yemenite Jews in Israel* (Tel Aviv: Am Oved, 1983), pp. 113-127. [Hebrew]

8. Berlovitz, "The Image," pp. 100-101.

9. Some of the students who wouldn't answer questions about ethnic characteristics or ranking wrote comments such as "they are all Israelis" or "all Jews." They apparently did not consider this a proper question, and implied that they recognized no differences among these groups. I must assume, in light of the commonly known stereotypes of Yemenites, Moroccans, Georgians, Romanians, in particular, that this is, in part, an expression of the ideology of the unity of the Jews and Israelis. And perhaps to *some* extent, in the school setting, these students really did not distinguish among their classmates in this way.

10. Cf. Erving Goffman, *The Presentation of Self in Everyday Life* (Garden City, N. Y.: Doubleday/Anchor Books, 1959).

11. S. D. Goitein, *From the Land of Sheba: Tales of the Jews of Yemen* (New York: Schocken Books, 1973), pp. 36-37.

12. *Encyclopaedia Judaica*, Vol. 10 (Jerusalem: Keter, 1972), p. 1321.

13. See Goitein, *Land of Sheba*, pp. 58-60. Cf. Barry Kosmin, "Exclusion and Opportunity: Traditions of Work Amongst British Jews," in Sandra Wallman, ed., *Ethnicity at Work* (London: Macmillan, 1979), pp. 38-39.

14. Mishael Caspi, Manuscript of a paper "Dedicated to Professor Joseph Silverman" (Jerusalem, n.d.), p. 30.

15. Jean-Jacques Berreby, "De l'Intégration des Juifs Yéménites en Israel," *L'Année Sociologique*, 3rd series: 127, 1956.

16. In a recent testimonial to this attitude, a university student told me in 1987: "I learned from my grandmother—a self-made woman—that it doesn't matter what you do: do it well and thoroughly. In the army I was responsible for religious affairs in my unit. It isn't an important or prestigeful position but I wanted to make it more important, so I organized all sorts of activities that brought people closer to the tradition, and I learned."

17. The same student volunteered the following story: "In San'a my grandmother used to see the richest Jew in Yemen. He was a fat man, and he would just sit and eat, surrounded by his servants. She could see him walking with his entourage to the Turkish bath. Then she met him after they had come to Israel. He was wearing simple Israeli clothes, with a hoe over his shoulder, going to work. She asked him, 'How do you feel doing this, after your old life?' He answered, 'I feel happy (*m'ushar*). I am working on the roads; I am doing something.'"

18. Kenneth Brown, "Words of an Other Israeli Poet: Erez Bitton," *MERA Forum* 5(4):14, 1982. See also S. N. Eisenstadt, *The Absorption of Immigrants* (London: Routledge & Kegan Paul, 1954), pp. 116, 120-121.

19. Peres, *Ethnic Relations*, p. 55.

20. For details on welfare see footnote 5 in Chapter 8.

21. Cf. Yael Katzir, "The Effects of Resettlement on the Status and Role of Yemeni Jewish Women: The Case of Ramat Oranim, Israel" (doctoral dissertation, University of California, Berkeley, 1976), p. 237. By 1987 women in their forties and younger were certainly more fashion-conscious than their elders, but I believe the contrast still holds, relative, for example, to Iraqis, Moroccans and others. It certainly does in housing and furnishings.

22. Here and elsewhere invidious distinctions have been made between the Yemenites and the Moroccans, apparently to the disadvantage of the latter. This is a problem on many levels. It sounds like a confirmation of Israeli stereotypes; it is ethnocentric, preferring one set of values to another, and it is an overgeneralization which is very unfair to those many Moroccans who do not conform to these supposed patterns. There is no place here to discuss the vast topic of Moroccans in Israel, and in any case the variations among them are great and pitifully little research has been carried out on key questions. In justification of the statements made about them, however, I believe I have reported what Yemenites feel to be true. These ideas play a role in Yemenite perceptions and attitudes. The variations among Moroccans in Israel are far wider than those among the Yemenites; they are probably greater than among any other Jewish group. Moroccans came with widely varying degrees of education, sophistication, skills, and economic well-being. They came from different cultural country-of-origin traditions as well. Some had been involved with French culture and education; others had lived in

traditional and fairly sophisticated cities, like Meknes and Fez, while some came from highland villages in remote parts of the Atlas Mountains. Some have remained highly religious, while others have left the practice of the religion behind. Thus simple generalizations about Moroccan Jews in Israel are not merely perilous, but practically impossible. In any case, despite some excellent studies of Moroccan *moshavim*, there are no studies which try to deal with the wider question of Moroccan Israeli culture and society. (On Moroccan *moshavim*, see Moshe Shokeid, *The Dual Heritage: Immigrants from the Atlas Mountains in an Israeli Village*, Manchester University Press, 1971; and Alex Weingrod, *Reluctant Pioneers: Village Development in Israel*, Cornell University Press, 1966.) One recent exception is Leslie Schwarz Perelman, "Something Old, Something New: The Domestic Side of Moroccan-Israeli Ethnicity" (doctoral dissertation, University of Wisconsin, Madison, 1983). This study of a relatively successful Moroccan community in a small Israeli city confirms the perception that household furnishings, decorations, appliances, and conspicuously generous hospitality play a major role in the aspirations and self-image of many Moroccan Israelis.

23. Berreby, "De l'Intégration," p. 127.

24. Jack Habib, Meir Kohn, and Robert Lerman, "The Effect on Poverty Status in Israel of Considering Wealth and Variability of Income," *Review of Income and Wealth* (series 23) 1:17-38, 1977.

25. *Ibid*, p. 26.

26. *Ibid*, p. 26.

27. Peres, *Ethnic Relations*, p. 55.

28. See Percy Cohen, "Alignments and Allegiances in the Community of Shaarayim in Israel," *Jewish Journal of Sociology* 4:31, 1962.

29. Cf. Katz and Zloczower, "Ethnic Continuity," pp. 313-316. See Postscript for the situation in 1987.

30. Judah Matras, "On Changing Matchmaking, Marriage, and Fertility in Israel: Some Findings, Problems, and Hypotheses," *American Journal of Sociology* 79:364-388, 1973.

31. Cf. Katzir, "The Effects of Resettlement," p. 219.

32. Cf. Matras, "Changing Matchmaking," p. 365; Yochanan Peres and Ruth Schrift, "Intermarriage and Ethnic Relations: A Comparative Study," *Ethnic and Racial Studies* 1:448, 1978.

33. There has been much more out-marriage in the decade since these data were collected and the five years since this was written. Rather than introduce anachronism and confusion into the discussion here, the topic is updated in the Postscript.

34. Milton M. Gordon, *Assimilation in American Life: The Role of Race, Religion, and National Origins* (New York: Oxford University Press, 1964), p. 51.

35. One recent exception is Sherry Rosen, "Intermarriage and the 'Blending of Exiles' in Israel," *Research in Race and Ethnic Relations* 3:79-101, 1982.

36. Cf. Katzir, "The Effects of Resettlement," p. 71ff.

37. Norman Berdichevsky, "The Persistence of the Yemeni Quarter in an Israeli Town," *Ethnicity* 4:302, 1977.

38. Matras, "Changing Matchmaking," p. 374. See also Eliezer Ben-Rafael, *The Emergence of Ethnicity* (Westport, Ct.: Greenwood Pres, 1982). pp. 85-86.

39. Cf. Shlomo Deshen, "Political Ethnicity and Cultural Ethnicity in Israel During the 1960s," in Abner Cohen, ed., *Urban Ethnicity* (London: Tavistock, 1974). Deshen's findings would lead us to expect this.

40. See Cohen, p. 38.

41. In contrast, Judith Goldstein notes that "The Iranians are not necessarily included in the stereotype of Oriental Jews, nor do they have an elaborated category of their own in non-Iranian eyes." They do, however, see themselves in terms of "some shared understanding of what an Iranian is and does . . . Thus in relation to Moroccans, Iranians might see themselves as hardworking and thrifty; in relation to Ashkenazim, as having a strong family life and high moral standard among unmarried girls . . . ." "The Rise of Iranian Ethnicity in Israel," *The Jerusalem Quarterly*, #29, Fall 1983, pp. 49, 43-44.

8

The Yemenites Beyond Kiryat Eliahu

Our study to this point has dealt primarily with the Yemenites of just one community, with an occasional glance at supporting material derived from a few others. The question naturally arises as to how typical or representative this Yemenite community is of those around the country. To what extent are the patterns delineated here idiosyncratic and accidental or the result of the conditions in this city? How true is this as a picture of the 165,000 Yemenites who live throughout Israel?

Unfortunately we do not have many published studies of Israeli Yemenite communities. There are several papers and one dissertation based on the Sha'arayim-Marmorek section of Reḥovot, but most of these were completed in the 1950s.[1] Yael Katzir's dissertation offers a picture of some aspects of life on a Yemenite *moshav* in the Jerusalem Corridor.[2] Lisa Gilad has recently published a book about the Yemenite women of a large town.[3] Apart from more general writing by Berreby and by Patai[4] there is virtually nothing available, so much of what follows will have to be based on my own less thorough acquaintance with a number of Yemenite *moshavim* and urban communities, and on the few existing studies.

Kiryat Eliahu is clearly not "typical" in any narrow sense. There is too much variation and complexity in the overall picture for this. It is, however, a representative case within the range of variation in Yemenite life: it is not the "best" and not the "worst," not the most "traditional" and close-knit, and not the least integrated.

There are at least twenty-two urban Yemenite communities larger than Kiryat Eliahu. Aside from the 18,000 Yemenites in Tel Aviv, the 12,000 in the all-Yemenite town of Rosh Ha'Ayin, and the 10,000 in Petaḥ Tikva (near Rosh Ha'Ayin), there are five or more cities with more than 5,000 Yemenites: Jerusalem, Rishon LeTsion, Ramat Gan, Ḥolon, Reḥovot, and Netanya. With its 1,200 people of Yemeni origin,

Kiryat Eliahu occupies a middle ground between the larger cities and the smaller towns and *moshavim*, which average about 500.

If we consider the degree to which the members of the community are integrated within the general society of the city and country, those of Kiryat Eliahu are probably as integrated as the members of any *community* can be. Elsewhere there may be individual families living in relative isolation from any wider ethnic community, but for those who are part of larger and rather cohesive communities, few can have any more opportunities than those of Kiryat Eliahu to participate fully in the wider, non-Yemenite, society. Whereas the people of Rosh Ha'Ayin and the *moshavim* live most of their lives in the company of other Yemenites (in school, in work, and in the community), in Kiryat Eliahu they are usually in the minority in these other settings. The ethnically homogeneous contexts are those which they create for themselves: the synagogue, the celebrations, and informal gatherings and friendships within the community and beyond, with kin and other Yemenites. Thus we cannot attribute the closeness of Kiryat Eliahu's Yemenite community to lack of choice, imposed upon them by the residential or institutional setting.

Because Kiryat Eliahu is relatively distant from the centers of Yemenite population, which are located in the Tel Aviv conurbation, its Yemenites are not in a position to participate as fully in Yemenite social and cultural life as those near the center. From this point of view they are actually more isolated from other Yemenites than many other communities. But this is only a relative isolation, and their networks keep them in connection with Yemenites all over the country.

In terms of economic and social well-being and status, once again we can place Kiryat Eliahu somewhere in the middle of the spectrum. On the one hand, it is an economically secure and unproblematic community within a city which lies quite close to the national average on many social indicators.[5] The city does not share the problems of some of the development towns or of the urban poverty areas, nor is the Yemenite community marked by the social ills which are said to trouble Rosh Ha'Ayin and a few other Yemenite communities. On the other hand, Kiryat Eliahu's Yemenite community does not contain the number of successful or prestigious people, or the leaders and institutions, that some of the others have. Cities such as Jerusalem, Tel Aviv, Netanya, Holon, Herzliya, and Petah Tikva offer more political, economic, and educational opportunities, and they either attract or produce more successful and sophisticated people. In this way, too, Kiryat Eliahu's Yemenite community may be reasonably characterized as lying in about the middle of the range of variation. In the following pages I shall suggest that the social and cultural patterns encountered among Kiryat Eliahu's Yemenites are similarly representative of the national scene.

Yemenite Settlement, Residence, and Community

Today Israel's Yemenites are heavily concentrated in the center of the country, with 38 percent or more in the greater Tel Aviv area. This zone includes, in addition to Tel Aviv itself, the cities of Bnei Brak, Ramat Gan, Holon, and Bat Yam in an inner ring, and Ra'anana, Herzliya, Petah Tikva, Kiryat Ono, Yehud, and smaller communities in an outer ring.[6] If we extend the ring to a radius of 35 miles, it would account for just over 90 percent of the total Yemenite population. Such a circle would also include the cities and towns of Jerusalem, Rosh Ha'Ayin, Netanya, Kfar Saba, Rehovot, Nes Tsiona, Ashkelon, Rishon LeTsion, and Hadera, and would take in most of the important smaller towns and a good percentage of the Yemenite *moshavim*. Yemenites, however, are poorly represented in the north and south of the country. For example, less than 2 percent of the Yemenite population lives in the Haifa conurbation, although 12 percent of Israel's Jewish population is located there.

Yemenites are to be found in relatively large numbers in approximately ninety different locations. According to figures from the 1972 census, almost 89,000, or 57 percent, live in twenty-four different cities, while a little over 42,000 (27 percent) live in smaller urban settlements, of which perhaps twenty to twenty-five have substantial Yemenite populations. About 80 percent are settled in the older, more veteran urban settlements, but they are very poorly represented in the newer development towns established in the mid-1950s. In fact, of seventeen new towns in 1961, only four had any numbers of Yemenites at all (averaging seventy-five per town), while the other thirteen had a total of seventy-nine! This picture had not changed by 1972.

Yemenites are, however, well represented in the new agricultural villages. There are fifty-three such *moshavim*, thirty-five of them wholly composed of Yemenites, and eighteen with small minorities of people from other ethnic groups. In 1972 almost 18,000 Yemenites lived in these villages with populations ranging from about 400 to 600. With more than 15 percent of their population living in rural locations, they

are among the most rural of Jewish groups, compared, for example, to
7.5 percent for the Moroccans and 5.7 percent for the Iraqis.

There is a clear tendency for Yemenites everywhere to cluster in
distinctive ethnic enclaves such as that in Kiryat Eliahu. Berreby wrote
of the situation in 1954 that "70 to 75 percent of the new immigration
is set in a Yemenite milieu. More than 50 percent remains in a milieu
of new Yemenite immigrants, 20 to 25 percent in the milieu of earlier
Yemenite residents."[7] It would be surprising if this figure were not closer
to 80 or 90 percent today. This is not to say that such a large percentage
lives in homogeneous communities (as do the 12 percent living on the
moshavim), but that, as those in Kiryat Eliahu, they live in relatively
compact neighborhoods where they comprise a heavy percentage of the
population. Such neighborhoods may contain several hundred to several
thousand Yemenites, numerous Yemenite synagogues, and a distinct
identity as a Yemenite neighborhood or community. There may be
more than one Yemenite *shkhuna* in a city. In fact, 14,000 of Tel Aviv's
18,000 Yemenites live in two such communities.

Ethnic concentration is a widespread and common phenomenon in
complex societies, including Israel.[8] Furthermore, residence in Israel,
as elsewhere, is affected by such things as government settlement and
housing policies, the housing market, the availability of mortgages,
opportunities for work and for children's education, and considerations
of social and economic status. Granted these other factors, the settlement
pattern of Yemenites can best be explained by their strong preferences—
the value for living within their own ethnic group and the apparent
desire for a particular type of housing, neighborhood, and residential
landscape.[9]

A typical Yemenite neighborhood in a city or town usually consists
either of rows of two-story apartment blocks, just like those of the
Kiryat Eliahu *shkhuna*, or of detached houses (*vilot*). These houses
are frequently small, but very often have been remodeled and added
on to. They may have gardens, perhaps planted with *gat*, spices, and
aromatic plants. In and around the house and gardens there are likely to
be small sheds and possibly concrete building blocks, sand, and gravel
for building the next addition. As in Kiryat Eliahu, the open spaces
will generally be quite barren, and the neighborhood will most likely
have few shops, no cafes or restaurants, but a profusion of synagogues.
Sha'arayim-Marmorek has forty, while Rosh Ha'Ayin was said, as of

1970, to have 12,000 people and "66 synagogues, but not a single coffee house"! [10]

Neighborhoods like these can be seen, for example, in the Ben-Tsion section of Netanya, Neve Amal in Herzliya, Sha'ariya in Petah Tikva, in Neve Haim and Nahaliel in Hadera, in Sha'arayim-Marmorek in Rehovot, and in the whole town of Rosh Ha'Ayin. The *moshavim* and the few nonagricultural villages present a very similar pattern of homes, gardens, and synagogues in a more rural setting. In some cases even the urban neighborhoods manage to look very rural. In all of these the Yemenite predilection for low housing (not more than two stories) and for *vilot* and gardens is manifest.

It may be objected that almost anyone in Israel might want a "villa," but the question is, at what price? The Yemenites are willing to pay for the small, poor, unfashionable housing which others are abandoning in favor of "better" housing and neighborhoods. Many Yemenites prefer to acquire a little, old place, live in it as it is for a while, and gradually build it into something much nicer and larger as conditions permit, rather than to buy a more fashionable and newer apartment in a four- or eight-story apartment house. [11] Yemenites often express dislike for such buildings, as well as a positive preference for living near the ground. Harold Greenberg reports resistance to the building of apartment houses in Rosh Ha'Ayin. [12]

Some of these communities have their roots in prestate days, as far back as the first decade of this century. These include Sha'arayim (Rehovot), Nahaliel (Hadera), Kerem HaTeymanim in Tel Aviv, and the somewhat more recent Ben-Tsion (Netanya). [13] Many others are located in the typical housing of the 1950-51 crash building program, as is the case in Kiryat Eliahu.

These quarters are distinguished socially as well as demographically and physically. They are the centers of religious worship in the Yemenite manner, and of the rituals, ceremonies, and celebrations of the Yemenite communities. The homogeneous Yemenite *moshavim*, of course, cannot help but be the locus of intense Yemenite social and cultural life.

The Yemenite preference for settlement in their own quarters has been evident since the first immigrants came to Jerusalem 100 years ago. The clearest expression of this in the literature comes from the Sha'arayim section of Rehovot, where loyalty to the community has been noted as a major theme. Although Sha'arayim was long a neglected neighborhood, and one with a bad reputation in the outside world, Katz and Zloczower found that "Yemenites perceive 'their' neighborhood as a meaningful social context," in contrast to the Ashkenazim in their study.[14] They also report that "loyalty to the neighborhood among the Yemenite men is striking indeed," and that whereas "the Ashkenazim state that they would refuse [to leave] because of attachment to their family or their friends . . . the Yemenites in addition . . . emphasize their attachment to the 'place.' It is not only family, not only friends, but the entire social structure which ties the Yemenites."[15] Twenty years later Norman Berdichevsky discovered the same attachment to place in Sha'arayim as had his predecessors. When studying Rehovot and Sha'arayim he found that "Only in Sha'arayim were there answers [to a questionnaire] demonstrating a vocal expression of local patriotism and sense of elan . . . ."[16]

The case of Rosh Ha'Ayin offers an interesting comparison to Sha'arayim. Its roots go back no further than 1949, when it began as a reception camp for Yemenites arriving "On Wings of Eagles." Nevertheless it has grown steadily despite its poor reputation as a troubled community. More significantly, in a study of social indicators, Rosh Ha'Ayin ranked sixty-second out of sixty-four cities and towns in the rate of out-migration! Although it also ranked last of the sixty-four cities in *in-migration*, during the 1970s it was consistently among the lowest three in loss of population through out-migration. (The rate varied from 14.9 to 24.1 per thousand against 90 to 150 per thousand at the other end of the scale.) Even more striking, when the authors combined various measures in order to produce a factor analysis, they found that on the dimension called "*lack* of community identity" Rosh Ha'Ayin ranked *last* of the sixty-four communities.[17]

Lest it be thought that the low out-migration rate is due to an inability to move, it should be noted that many of the towns and cities with the highest out-migration rates are the poorest and least desirable communities, such as Or Akiva, Bet Shemesh, Dimona, and Yeruham. These cities and towns rate higher (worse) on the factors of dependency and poverty than Rosh Ha'Ayin, so the low rate of out-migration from Rosh Ha'Ayin cannot be simply explained in this way. It would be more reasonable, and in keeping with the comparative evidence, to attribute part of the reason to the positive attraction, the loyalty to the community, despite the disadvantages and shortcomings of the town.[18]

The creation of Yemenite neighborhoods and communities is an ongoing process. There are, for example, two different sections at the outskirts of the city of Hadera that are currently undergoing a transformation from communities primarily of Ashkenazim to partly Yemenite ones. These are areas of small, one-story unattached houses, evidently built by Europeans, especially postwar refugees with reparations money from Germany. Now their children are grown and have moved on to other places, perhaps to more prestigious areas, and the old sell out or die. Yemenites have started buying these homes and, as one man expressed it, "One draws the next," and a process of ethnic succession develops.

These quiet neighborhoods, away from the central city, with their little houses on small plots of land and room for expansion, suit the desires, needs, and values of the Yemenites very well. They acquire the houses and begin to add more rooms. And they start a synagogue. The first Yemenite synagogue recently opened in one of these sections and numbers among its young congregation teachers, clerks, a building contractor, factory and skilled workers, and a member of the Egged bus cooperative (usually a lucrative position).[19]

Other values may lead to the creation of new Yemenite communities in different settings. The desire to live in Jerusalem had led some, who could afford it, to move into a newly developing area in that city, Givat Mordekhai. This is a district with relatively well-off religious Jews from many ethnic groups. The Yemenite population there has grown rapidly to about fifty families in recent years, including a dozen families from Kiryat Eliahu, and they have begun to create their own networks and institutions side by side with those of the Ashkenazim and "Sephardim." In general the educational and occupational level of the young here is quite high.

Although a very large percentage of Israel's Yemenites live within heavily Yemenite districts, such as that of Kiryat Eliahu, those who live in cities and towns without such concentrations are not necessarily lacking in connections to other Yemenites. Although it was previously uncommon for Yemenites to live in the newer development towns, in recent years some younger Yemenites have been attracted to these places for work as teachers, clerks, bureaucrats, and skilled workers. Whereas at first they may be quite isolated, gradually, as more come to the town it becomes possible to draw together.

An example of this process comes from Arad, a town established in 1961, which had grown to 11,000 by 1979. Despite the isolation of the first Yemenite settlers in time they were able to establish a synagogue and a dance group. The 120 resident families now maintain an active and self-conscious religious and social life. Although they are still dispersed throughout the town, a number of families now live in one district of *vilot*.

For individual Yemenites, as for anyone else in Israel, the choice of residence after they leave the homes of their parents depends on many factors. These are complex decisions involving considerations of ability to buy housing, location of work, relations with families, attitudes toward education, religiosity, esthetics, neighbors, and friends. I know families that have moved to more religious communities and to ones with better religious schools for their children. The evidence strongly suggests that for Yemenites the pull of the ethnic group itself, with all that this implies for social and religious life and values, is quite powerful. We might go a step further and argue that coresidence with fellow Yemenites implies the acceptance of certain associated values, in addition to the appreciation of the ease of interaction which common ethnic background permits.

Religion and Community

Kiryat Eliahu's Yemenite community is religiously observant, but here, too, there is a range of variation among Yemenite communities throughout the country. At one end of the continuum of observance there are Yemenite *moshavim* where *shabbat* can be even more strictly controlled because cars cannot enter the village, and the only outsiders will probably be other observant guests. And some Yemenite neighborhoods are located in such religious communities as Bnei Brak or the Givat Mordekhai section of Jerusalem.

At the other end of the continuum there are communities whose members are less universally observant, where some percentage of the youth, at least, do not observe *shabbat* as religious Jews should and spend little time in the synagogue. Yemenites often attribute the loss of religiosity in certain communities to policies of the labor movement and the secular socialist parties during the early stages of settlement when these new communities were most dependent on their aid. Where their influence was predominant, the children and youth were encouraged to become "modern" and secular, and were even discouraged from religious observance. There must be some truth to this claim, but to what extent is not clear. On the other hand, it is not certain that influence by the religious parties necessarily guarantees religiosity among the young.

In some communities soccer has become a passion of the young and the middle-aged, and since league football is played on the sabbath throughout Israel (it is the only nonworking day), players, managers, coaches, and fans must break the sabbath to play, attend, or even to listen to the matches on radio. In some communities there are teams which are largely Yemenite, such as Shimshon from Kerem HaTeymanim in Tel Aviv, Bnei Yehuda from Shkhunat HaTikva in Tel Aviv, and the two teams from Reḥovot, HaPoel Marmorek and Maccabi Sha'arayim. (This is a departure from the regular pattern of league football in Israel, for other teams do not usually have such a specific ethnic connection.)

Even in these communities, of course, there are many observant people. In addition it is often noted that young men may first go to synagogue with their fathers and brothers in the morning, and break the sabbath—by attendance at ball games, smoking, driving, and listening to the radio, stereo, or tape machine—only afterwards, perhaps when away from their parents. It also seems true that many young men and women begin to become more observant again as they get older, marry, and have children themselves. If the degree of religious observance of the Kiryat Eliahu community is not universal among the nation's Yemenite communities, it is still clear that the Yemenites remain the most observant of Israel's Jewish ethnic groups.[20]

As in Kiryat Eliahu, the institution of the synagogue is of great importance for all Yemenite communities and is at the center of much group and community life. Rather than just one synagogue per community, there are usually many. Depending upon the size of the community and the extent of the factions and feuds within it there may be three or a dozen, or even scores, as in Rosh Ha'Ayin. Arad so far has only one because of the newness and smallness of the community, but the normal situation is for new, small synagogues to be established as men strive to honor their fathers, act on their ambitions to be leaders, or find that a synagogue feud has gone beyond any chance of reconciliation. Such feuds may be the result of personal conflicts and ambitions or may involve disagreement over prayer traditions. It is difficult for adherents of the two traditions (*baladi* and *shami*) to coexist in the same synagogue, but demography and other conditions may force them to do so, as in Arad. In Kiryat Arba, the new religious Jewish settlement on the West Bank near Hebron, the Yemenites have at least one *baladi* and one *shami* synagogue already.)

While the average Yemenite synagogue is likely to be fairly small, and to serve only a small group or faction, there is also a trend for some to try to gain larger congregations, construct larger buildings, and attempt to make these centers suitable for a wider range of activities, in a manner not unlike many American Jewish congregations. To some extent these groups seem to be based on, or to compete with, the community center movement, organizing activities specifically for the Yemenite community. The leaders of one synagogue in Kiryat Eliahu would like to see such a development, but their efforts are far behind those of some other communities.

One synagogue in Netanya is in the process of physical and organizational expansion, and although its leader has not been able to convince everyone in the community to join his project, he is making his synagogue into an active center. There are daily study sessions in Torah and Talmud for older men; basic education courses for older women; religious instruction, under a *mori*, for boys; a dance and folklore group with instruction by professionals; a children's chorus; and craft groups. The leader hopes to build an auditorium, as well as a more complete facility for old people, where they can spend their days. Such centers are undoubtedly on the rise as there is a general expansion of organization and activity in Yemenite communities all over Israel.

Less formally, Yemenites in all communities are held together through the observance of the same festivals and holy days, and the same celebrations of the life cycle. These are, of course, basic to the Jewish tradition, but they are generally commemorated with greater faithfulness, and in their own particular way, by the Yemenites. *Ja'ale, hinna,* and the music, poetry, customs, and symbols associated with them are found wherever there are Yemenites. There may be minor local differences in extent or style, but a Yemenite can feel at home anywhere in the country among other Yemenites celebrating these *mitsvot* and *smahot*. These are basic to the identity of Israel's Yemenites and are central to the organization of Yemenite ethnicity at the national level.

Savings, Consumption, Display, and *Histapkut B'mu'at*

As we have seen, frugality and the apparent uncomplaining acceptance of material scarcity have long been considered outstanding Yemenite traits. These characteristics were a part of their reputation at the turn of the century and have been used over and over in literature and stereotype. I have also argued that there is considerable reality to such traits, at least in the context of Kiryat Eliahu. Can the same be said for the Yemenites in Israel more generally?

The use of the phrase *histapkut b'mu'at* today may be greeted with cynicism, irony, or hostility, especially on the part of the young and middle-aged. In the 1980s, particularly after the elections of 1981 with their well-publicized interethnic tensions, it became quite common for Yemenites to see these presumed characteristics, as well as the Yemenite devotion to work, in a critical light. It may be considered, at best, a sign of Yemenite naivete when they first arrived, or, at worst, as the basis for the Ashkenazi establishment to grant little to the Yemenites while expecting much from them. The response these days is usually "The Yemenites are just like everyone else. They want *luxus*; they want everything that others have."

The economic and technological climate of the late seventies seemed to lend credence to this claim. The combination of a staggering inflation rate and government policies encouraging the purchase of appliances and durable goods not only permitted the purchase of items once only dreamt of, but made it almost the only sensible domestic economic policy. These days Israelis of all backgrounds are acquiring automobiles, color television sets and video tape recorders, and are buying newer refrigerators, washing machines, and stereo sets. All over the country families are building small mansions, individually designed little dream palaces, by participating in a government-sponsored plan called *Bnei Beitkha*, "build your house." And the Yemenites are participating in this boom in consumption and building along with the rest of Israel's Jewish and Arab citizens, as can readily be seen in some Yemenite *moshavim* and villages where land exists for building. In fact it is a tribute to the effectiveness of their past frugality that so many Yemenite *workers* can now build such large *vilot*.

Despite these developments, however, and even though we recognize that Yemenites want material well-being like everyone else, we may still detect distinctive Yemenite patterns due to their esthetics, standards of evaluation, and priorities (*seder adifut*).

It is my observation and belief that the preferences expressed by the young Kiryat Eliahu couple in Chapter 7 are quite widely found throughout Israel. Certainly people would like cars, stereo sets, nice clothes, and modern appliances, but in what order and at what cost? I believe that the evidence suggests a high priority for neighborhood;

"suitable" housing; children's environment and conditions (which may include television); and religion. There is a much lower priority for furniture and decoration (indeed a preference for a certain openness and "underfurnishing") and for clothing and fashion. This can be observed in homes all over the country. Carefully decorated and furnished living rooms are the exception, although for Ashkenazim and for Moroccans of similar socioeconomic status they are the rule. And bright wallpaper has been practically tabooed. But concern for children's rooms, as well as home ownership itself, is paramount.

The following example may serve as an illustration of the attitudes and standards of evaluation. When doing fieldwork in 1975-77, I knew an upwardly mobile couple who had moved from the Yemenite neighborhood to a "better" part of Kiryat Eliahu. Their neighbors included many Ashkenazim, and even some doctors and other professionals, who served as very significant others for this couple. Their apartment was unusual in its careful decoration and furnishings. They were extremely sensitive to the material as well as the behavioral context in which they found themselves.

In 1982 I visited them again, this time in another city, where they lived in a higher-status neighborhood, but one with a relatively large Yemenite population. It is now the successful *Yemenites* who serve as their reference group, and the woman of the couple explained how her outlook has been affected. "In Kiryat Eliahu I was concerned with material things, but not here. I am not ashamed now to have old furnishings. Of course a washing machine and television are different. One needs them. But here we have things from Kiryat Eliahu which are ten years old. It doesn't bother me." My informant is extremely sensitive to social nuances and status and had adjusted her standards to that of the surrounding community of relatively well-educated, more successful, higher-status Yemenites. In doing so she was able to *lower* the priority she gave to material things. (They do not lack money for furnishings.)

Once more I must add a qualification. There *must* be *some* Yemenites who take on the evaluation and priorities of their non-Yemenite neighbors and coworkers, as the people just cited seem to have done previously. They might then attach more importance to investment in furnishings, clothing, and fashion. There are also parents who feel strongly that their children should have all those things that their own families were too poor to provide, and thus buy a great deal for them.

(A friend calls today's teenagers *ha-dor shel shefa*, "the generation of plenty"—even of superfluity.) We are dealing with a complex and dynamic process. Nevertheless I believe that the generalizations made above have a certain predictive validity. The furnishing of Yemenite homes is far more likely to be as I have described than not, even among the "middle-class" in the late 1980s.

Occupation, Work, and Status

It is difficult to speak authoritatively about the range and percentages of Yemenite occupations today because no published material on this is available. Estimates, therefore, must remain impressionistic, based on the people encountered and the appraisals of informants. If we consider those who today are in their forties or younger (that is, those who were born in Israel or who immigrated when still young enough to attend school), it seems once again as though Kiryat Eliahu is reasonably representative of the general picture.

An obvious exception to this is that portion of the Yemenites, perhaps 10 percent, who live on *moshavim* and derive their livelihood primarily from agriculture. Except for farming and agricultural labor (more common in the older generation than among the young), the leading occupations include skilled workers (electricians, metalworkers, mechanics, carpenters, and workers in the building trades); factory workers; office workers, secretaries, clerks, bookkeepers, and accountants; bureaucrats, managers, and workers in local and national government, business firms, and organizations; nurses, social workers, teachers, and other educators, religious workers (scribes, rabbis, and ritual slaughterers); technicians and engineers; career military personnel; artists and artisans, including musicians, jewelers, and diamond workers. [21]

If some communities have a larger proportion of drivers and semiskilled factory workers, others have a larger share of professionals, semiprofessionals, and higher-ranking government workers. In some areas more Yemenites work for town and regional governments or for the Histadrut and its enterprises, or business firms, than is the case in Kiryat Eliahu. Elsewhere, as in Kiryat Eliahu, the trend to postsecondary education and training is increasing rapidly.

As in Kiryat Eliahu, shopkeeping is not a common enterprise. There are entrepreneurs associated with agriculture, and contractors and others in the building trades and artisanry who have set up their own firms. Some shops deal in materials such as metals, wood, and plastics. There are jewelers with their own shops. In some areas, and especially in the Kerem HaTeymanim section of Tel Aviv, there are Yemenite restaurants. These cater widely to non-Yemenite Israelis and to tourists, but some may also serve as meeting places for Yemenite youth, as in Rehovot. This, however, is not very widespread. The operation of *felafel* stands is another activity for some Yemenites, especially for older men. In the last few years special Yemenite pita, called *m'lawah*, has become popular and is increasingly served along with other foods, or at specialized stands and restaurants.

It is my impression, on the whole, that selling is very underrepresented as an economic pursuit. As one knowledgeable Yemenite leader put it, "The Yemenites aren't a trading people." This is surely due, in part, to the general suspicion and low evaluation of businessmen, shopkeepers, and entrepreneurs. (Another acquaintance commented, "Fifty percent will sell *you*.") But it is probably also influenced by a preference for security over risk. This is something Yemenites sometimes point out themselves. Many prefer steady employment as salaried employees in large firms to seeking higher profits and status by striking out on their own or looking for more prestigious work. Large corporations, and especially Histadrut enterprises, offer steady work, regular salary, fringe benefits, and *kvi'ut*—permanence. Many young Yemenites work in defense plants which offer all of these benefits plus the attraction that the worker need not—indeed should not—reveal what specific job he has. If it is one of low status, it is sufficient for him to say "I work for the defense industry."

Just as in Kiryat Eliahu, teaching and education are a major occupational niche for Yemenites all over the country. Yemenites are not only well represented in the ranks of teachers, above all in the religious school system, but increasingly they are rising to higher levels in educational administration, from vice-principals and principals to inspectors, program and department heads. They are to be found on the faculties of teachers' seminaries, and one, Miriam Glazer-Ta'asa, became the deputy minister of education in the last Likud government.

As it did for the Irish in the United States, religious education offers a particularly fertile field for Yemenite work and advancement. With their religious background and their involvement with education they are well suited for success within the system.

Attitudes Toward Work and Status

It seems clear that the attitudes toward work discussed in Chapter 7 played an important role for the older generation of Yemenites throughout Israel. To what extent are they still important?

During the past few years a certain cynicism has developed as many Yemenites complain of how their people were exploited because of their hard-working and uncomplaining nature. Nevertheless there is still a pride in their dedication to working for a living, and working responsibly and well. Although Yemenites and outsiders speak of how the older generation worked hard, reliably, and without complaint, the values still play their role, though perhaps in modified forms.

For one thing, work is still preferred to idleness and living from the community, and thus relatively few Yemenites remain unemployed and dependent upon welfare. There are evidently a few communities where some members of the younger generation, in their late teens, seem to be departing from this value, to the consternation of their elders and the social workers. These are considered atypical exceptions, however, although some people worry that such tendencies could be increasing. On the other hand, it could be that the fears are exaggerated, an overreaction to the previously noted teenage rebellion.

The attitude that work itself is important and that a person's status depends not on the type of work, but on how he or she carries it out still seems to play a role. Yemenites are conscious of the line from Psalm 128: "When you eat of the labor of your hands happy shall you be and it shall be well with you." Or they could cite the Talmud: "He who enjoys the work of his hands is greater than the man who fears heaven." Such an attitude may help justify the acceptance of a somewhat lower status in the secure but not very prestigious jobs in industry and the skilled trades noted above. But it is also clear that the spirit of artisanry still exists in the community. There are young Yemenites who choose skilled hand work in technical, artistic, or practical fields out of a sense of pride in their skill or artistry and a recognition of the values involved.

I have heard a number of middle-aged Yemenite men decry the fact that fewer and fewer Israeli Jews engage in manual and skilled labor these days. They regret the apparent turning away from an appreciation of the importance of such work. In this they are close in spirit to some of the early socialist Zionists who spoke of the nobility of manual labor and of the need for the Jewish people in their own land to perform all types of work. The source of this attitude for most of these Yemenites, however, is religious rather than secular socialist. One such man, himself a fairly high-ranking city bureaucrat, attempted to direct his own sons toward skilled labor rather than higher education. (He was only temporarily successful, and all three are continuing with one or another form of education.) It is clear, in summary, that while pride in work and workmanship is still present, many young people want to climb higher on the ladder of status and economic success than the previous generation, and even their older siblings.

Moshavim

More than 18,000 Yemenites live as smallholders in *moshavim*, agricultural village communities. Only the Moroccans, numbering over 20,000, contribute more people to this type of agricultural settlement. (There are more than 130,000 people living on *moshavim*, but only about 90,000 on *kibbutsim*.) About 11.6 percent of all Yemenites live on *moshavim*, a figure matched only by the 13.8 percent of Libyan Jews.

The *moshav* was first developed in Palestine in 1921 as a form of pioneering settlement. In contrast to the collective ideals and structures of the *kibbuts*, the *moshav* is a cooperative community whose production units are individual households, each working a smallholding. While the land is owned by the nation and is nonalienable, each family was given an equitable portion of land (usually consisting of several plots of different kinds of land), along with water resources and capital equipment. All the families were expected to cooperate in various ways and to participate in marketing and buying cooperatives.[22] Each family had its own house and outbuildings, as well as barns, chicken coops, and sheds.

Immediately after the establishment of the state in 1948 it appeared that the *moshav* form of settlement would be more attractive to the new immigrants than the *kibbuts*, and 251 were established between 1949 and 1958. Most of the Yemenite *moshavim* were established between 1949 and 1952, and most Yemenite farm families received their allotments and settled in at that time. (Interestingly, quite a few young Yemenites have tried *kibbuts* life, but given it up. Only 714 Yemenites were members of *kibbutsim* in 1972.)[23]

Thirty-five of these Yemenite villages, whose populations usually range from 400 to 600, are ethnically homogeneous. There are eighteen others which contain two or more populations from different countries, but initial attempts to integrate families of different origins were not successful and soon gave way to the pattern of homogeneity. Although people from *moshavim* have many occasions to leave the *moshav* and meet others—in some primary and all secondary schools, when shopping or selling, in the army, and when doing off-farm work—much of their lives are spent within these tight communities.[24]

It was very difficult for the settlers at first. They had to learn a new way of life (few had been farmers before), adjust to the Israeli economic system, pioneer new farms on land that had to be reclaimed, and cope with austerity, poor material conditions, and sometimes terrorist raids.[25] By the the mid-1970s, however, most of the *moshavim* had become reasonably well established, especially with the development of such branches of the agricultural economy as poultry, flower, and dairy farming. With technologically advanced methods of production and efficient marketing it was possible to earn a good living. By the mid-1970s the problem was not keeping people on the farm, but finding farm plots and housing for the children of the *moshav*. Although many of the children had chosen careers off the farm, some still wanted to live in the communities, while others were interested in farming, both because of the economic rewards and an appreciation for the way of life and its values. However, only one person could succeed in each family, forcing the rest into other work.

In 1969 I drove around dozens of *moshavim*, with populations from all the ethnic groups, and noticed many signs of expenditure on improved housing, additional rooms, new porches, and exterior decoration. But many houses seemed, from the outside, to be unimproved and clearly showed their original one-room, 30-square-meter origins.

By 1981 there had been a spectacular change in housing on *moshavim*. As in the rest of Israel, a housing boom was underway. There is considerable freedom to expand because houses are detached, single family structures, unlike the apartment houses in Kiryat Eliahu and other urban settlements which were built at the same time. As well as adding on rooms or fancy porches, many families have built whole new houses or added a second floor and then built around the old house in such a way as to completely enclose and hide it. Often the designs are quite distinctive and imaginative. While there is still unimproved housing on almost any *moshav*, the general housing picture has changed considerably and mirrors the prosperity of the *moshav*, as well as the growing material well-being and rising expectations of the country as a whole.

Housing, as we have seen, is something in which Yemenites will invest. But while many of these new and expanded houses are quite large, there is still a tendency toward simplicity of decoration, light furnishings, and open spaces.

One particularly remarkable example may serve as an illustration. On one *moshav*, a man and his wife, who have worked and saved for years, recently built a two-story house of 240 square meters. This is a very large house by Israeli standards. Although it is furnished with things of good quality, and the kitchen is fully equipped with appliances, the house has a very open and almost empty feel to it. As usual the furniture is pushed to the walls, leaving wide open spaces in the center of the rooms. This house, however, has two special rooms. One is a study room for the couple's children, set up with a series of carrels along the walls. The other is a music room that contains musical instruments and a brand new organ for one of the children. The parents perform in Yemenite and other folkdance groups and are very aware of music education.

Occupation

The majority of young people cannot become farmers but must seek their fortunes elsewhere, even though they may live on the *moshav*. (This is true on all *moshavim*, not merely those of Yemenites.) I do not know of any studies that indicate where these young people are going, or what sort of work they seek. Yael Katzir's monograph indicates that the favored off-farm work for women was teaching (more common in the earlier period), and secretarial work (engaged in by twenty-three of forty-two working women in her sample). For thirty-nine men, some of whom would inherit farms, the off-farm work included skilled labor (18), unskilled (17), semiskilled (9), clerical (4), and professional (1).[26] It is hard to evaluate these figures because Katzir speaks elsewhere of some of the younger men becoming teachers and agricultural extension workers and instructors, but these seem not to be included in the table. In any case the tendency to seek work in skilled labor or teaching, or within the bureaucracy seems clear. In addition three men and two women were continuing their studies in universities.

Apparently the number of teachers, professionals, and continuing students at Katzir's *moshav* was limited compared to those at other *moshavim*. Some show a much higher rate of status achievement. At several nearby *moshavim* I met and learned of more university students, social workers, teachers, and managers. A number of young men had taken courses in *moshav* management, under the auspices of the Moshav Movement, and gone on to work in the administration of *moshavim*, as well as in the marketing and buying organizations of the Movement. As in Kiryat Eliahu, one encounters families with several sons and daughters in education, with younger ones continuing for university degrees. The youth of some *moshavim* seem to have particularly high aspirations and achievements, while others clearly do not. From the economic point of view these communities are successful today; their members are relatively well off and have learned how to deal effectively with the institutional machinery that affects their lives. This is in sharp contrast to the predictions of Gilbert Kushner, who suggested that these "administered communities" would always be dependent and their people passive.[27] The Yemenites of the *moshavim* of the Jerusalem Corridor, for example, play a leading role in the economic, political, and cultural affairs of the Matei Yehuda region.

Although most of the Yemenite *moshavim* were doing well economically in the 1970s, it cannot be expected that fifty-three separate communities, distributed throughout two-thirds the length of the country, will not vary to some extent with regard to their social lives. Some *moshavim* are beset by persistent factionalism;[28] others have no such problem. In some communities the young are said to be quite rebellious and disrespectful of their parents. In others, despite factionalism, the aspirations and achievements of the youth are considerable. The apparent self-confidence, assurance, and sophistication of the young of the Matei Yehuda *moshavim* are not necessarily shared by the youth of all other *moshavim*. In general, however, these are bastions of "Yemeniteness" and ethnic awareness.

Many Yemenite villages have signs outside their entrances announcing that the community is religious and that driving is forbidden within it on the sabbath. Even where this is not the case, however, the synagogues are prominent and vital institutions. They may lose some of the youth for a while, as is true in Kiryat Eliahu as well, but they continue to be significant for the older men and those with young sons.

Family remains important, and kin and ethnic ties are maintained beyond the *moshav* and throughout the country. Katzir notes that this is important for both men and women for instrumental reasons, especially to maintain connections for the marriages of their sons and daughters to other Yemenites. Both want to retain these links, and in doing so travel all over the country, visiting, and attending *smaḥot* and *avelim* (mourning). This visiting is a most important and prominent characteristic, and the seven-day mourning period may attract hundreds of relatives and *landslayt* from all over the country, and especially large groups from the *moshavim*. These people travel readily and know the country and its Yemenite communities.

For many Yemenites the *moshavim* seem to be repositories of the old ways. Of course they are changing, too, but they are said to be great places for celebrations. In these homogeneous communities of several hundred, Yemenites can be unself-consciously observant of all the *mitsvot* and the practices brought from their homeland. Weddings and *ḥinna* are thought to be celebrated with special zest. Very large numbers of guests can come because the expense is relatively low. The food is cooked at home (they slaughter and butcher their own animals), and no hall need be hired. (There are, of course, some *moshav* people who prefer to rent a hall.)

Whatever problems there may be within the *moshavim*, they remain oases of Yemenite tradition and culture. Quite a few have their own dance and performance groups. They represent little homogeneous islands whose inhabitants cannot help but be aware of who they are and where they have come from.

The Negative Image

Kiryat Eliahu's Yemenite population has been presented here as a successful one. That is, given the conditions they encountered, and their situation and prospects at the time of their arrival thirty years ago, they have risen in material well-being, status, education, political ability, and influence, while retaining the religiosity and family and community life which means so much to them. I have also suggested that this community is no exception, but is probably close to the norm in terms of its status and success. And yet there is also a contrary image of Yemenite communities in the Israeli public consciousness, a much more negative one.

Although the Yemenites as a whole have a positive reputation, a less pleasant picture is conjured up by mention of such communities as Shkhunat HaTikva, Kerem HaTeymanim, Rosh Ha'Ayin, or Sha'arayim.

These have unsavory reputations as backward places, with crime, poverty, alienation, and hot-blooded youth at odds with their religious parents and with society at large, ready to lash out with riots and other attacks. Any disturbances in these communities are seized upon by the press and are followed up by exposés. No matter how unrealistic and inflated, these reports leave a vivid impression of social pathology in the minds of many Israelis.

It is undeniable that Yemenite communities vary with regard to individual and group achievement, well-being, satisfaction, morale, and cohesion. They differ according to their locations, histories, neighbors, demographic characteristics, and opportunity structures, and thus also with respect to the well-being of their residents. Nevertheless it seems clear that the dismal and frightening picture of these communities is at least overdrawn, if not quite inaccurate. The bad reputations have been compounded from a few incidents, some historical factors (which no longer obtain), ethnocentrism (including fear of the unfamiliar), and press exposés based on extreme cases. As Emanual Marx points out in an article about the HaTikva quarter, these are examples of "stigmatized communities."[29] (He adapts Erving Goffman's arguments about stigmatized individuals.) Even their own inhabitants often have a low opinion of them, and thus reinforce the attitudes of outsiders. Once established, on whatever basis, the reputation hangs on.

Sha'arayim-Marmorek presents a good case of a Yemenite community which was once stigmatized, and may still be by some Israelis. This community was first settled in 1909 by Yemenite immigrants who began to work as laborers on the farms and as domestics in the homes of Ashkenazi smallholder farmers who had established themselves in the Reḥovot area several years earlier.[30] Throughout the succeeding decades, and well into the 1950s, the Sha'arayim-Marmorek community had complex and touchy relations with the rest of Reḥovot. To a great extent the community was independent of the larger city and remained in political and ecological isolation until 1948. They did not pay taxes to Reḥovot, and they maintained their own educational system and other institutions and facilities.[31] They lacked many services, however, and their children had a lower standard of education.[32] Despite their desire for this independence, there was considerable resentment of the Ashkenazim.[33]

By the 1940s the Ashkenazim, for their part, had come to see the Yemenite quarter as "an urban slum and a hotbed of social unrest."[34] Aside from the lack of services and the appearance of the place, there were constant quarrels and even a significant ideological political difference. Many Yemenites supported the nonsocialist militant Revisionist Party (the forerunner of today's Herut and Likud), and young Yemenites joined and fought with their underground army, the Irgun Tsvai Leumi (EZL). This added to the image of militancy and confrontation and caused further conflicts with those who strongly supported the socialist labor movement.

An atmosphere of misunderstanding, alienation, and confrontation continued and was heightened in the early years after the establishment of the state. This came to a head in 1954 when there were clashes between Yemenite youths who belonged to a street gang and members of a socialist youth group, which culminated in the stabbing death of an Ashkenazi boy by a "psychologically disturbed Yemenite youth."[35] This event spread Sha'arayim's name all over the country and deepened the stigma. As Berdichevsky points out,

> The daily press and topical journals held up Sha'arayim to the light of public scrutiny as a test case of Israel's failure to achieve social integration across communal lines. Much of the reporting was however quite shallow in its characterization of Sha'arayim as a "poverty" area and "urban slum." . . . Descriptions of Sha'arayim were based on quick visual perceptions of reporters who spent a day in the neighborhood. A rash of ill founded rumors reported "knifings" in a half a dozen different locations within a week following the incident in Sha'arayim. These proved to be evidence of the existence of an Ashkenazi hysteria and deeply held stereotypes of "primitive Yemenites," Moroccans and Sephardim in general. One newspaper ridiculously compared Sha'arayim to Chicago of the 1920s.[36]

The reality, of course, was far different from the press's version. It was this event that brought Katz and Zloczower and their colleagues to Sha'arayim to conduct the study cited previously. As we have seen, they did not find an urban slum or a hotbed of social unrest, but a hard-working community, with considerable intergenerational understanding and continuity, whose people conform more closely to the positive image of the Yemenites. Since 1961 relations have become much smoother, and Sha'arayim-Marmorek has now been integrated into the city of Rehovot. Some Yemenites must resent the old insults and injuries, but these seem to be largely behind them.

In a similar way the press and ethnocentrism seem to have worked to stigmatize other communities, such as the HaTikva section of Tel Aviv. Israelis react to the name "HaTikva" as though it were one large den of thieves, addicts, and undeserving poor.

Like Sha'arayim, HaTikva, had a historical involvement with the EZL underground (the main street of the quarter is called "EZL"), and there have been episodes of rowdy behavior and vandalism after some football games involving the local soccer team, Bnei Yehuda. (Football games in Sha'arayim-Marmorek have also sometimes erupted in fights.)[37] Moreover, HaTikva apparently is the home of some criminal gangs, gambling rings, drug dealers, and thugs. Nevertheless, its reputation for evil and poverty far exceeds the reality. According to Emanuel Marx, "The Hatikva Quarter is not a typical slum area," despite its numerous social problems.[38] Not only is there "no dire poverty," but it is quite a close-knit, safe community. "Most of the residents are strongly attached to a small network of neighborhood links, which involve a considerable amount of sociability and of mutual assistance when the occasion demands."[39] In other words, while there are certainly those with problems, most people live quite normal lives within the quarter. Furthermore, although it has a reputation as a Yemenite community, in fact only 17 percent of its residents are Yemenites. They are outnumbered by Iraqi and Persian Jews, and many other groups are represented. (Similarly, Kerem HaTeymanim, though bearing the name "Yemenites' Vineyard," is composed of members of several ethnic groups, of which Yemenites constitute only a quarter.)

Part of the image of the Yemenite as an urban slum-dweller, whose children have gone bad and take part in rioting and criminal activities, derives from the peculiar histories of these communities, compounded by a muckraking, overanxious and superficial press, and an ethnocentric fear of the unknown. Part is also due to the mistaken belief that the Tel Aviv quarters are primarily Yemenite.

If the primary source of the "social pathology" image of the Yemenites is found in these veteran districts, there are also some communities, established after the state, which have poor local or national reputations. In particular there is concern about an apparent lack of achievement, a tendency on the part of teenagers and older youth to depart from, and even scoff at, the values of their elders. This is said to be true especially with regard to work, study, and service in the military. They may show lack of respect for their parents and become problems at home and in the community. Though serious delinquency is not common, there is worry about the development of a youth culture of rowdy, cynical, and uncooperative individuals, quite different from their parents.

The outstanding example is Rosh Ha'Ayin, an all-Yemenite city of 12,000, looking very much like the smaller neighborhoods described earlier.   It has only one small shopping center and lacks many facilities and services. Its local government has long been unstable and ineffectual. According to the *Social Profile of Cities and Towns in Israel*, a relatively large percentage of the population belongs to large families, with four or more children (it ranks tenth out of sixty-four towns); it has a fairly high dependency ratio (ranking about eleventh); it is in fifteenth place with respect to families receiving some kind of financial assistance from the Ministry of Social Welfare, and in *fourth* place with respect to children placed in institutions, including boarding schools.

On top of all this, Rosh Ha'Ayin youth have been known to complain loudly about the lack of things to do in town, and have even had occasional but well-publicized clashes with the police. One apparently trivial fracas occurred in 1976, causing great consternation and press coverage for a few days.

Thus Rosh Ha'Ayin has its stigma, both within the Yemenite community and beyond. Its horrors are exaggerated and its assets and charms unknown. Consider, for example, the town's reputation for a high incidence of crime and delinquency. According to Harold Greenberg, even its own residents believe this,[40] although the *Social Profile* shows that Rosh Ha'Ayin's crime rate is 63rd out of 64, while on the combined factor for delinquency it ranked 54th! It is incredible that this city should have any reputation for delinquency at all.

Rosh Ha'Ayin is a sort of Yemenite cultural capital, the home of rabbis and teachers, musicians and artists and artisans. It is a place that holds to its religion, where children can learn Yemenite religious, folklore, and artistic traditions. Its community center caters to the needs of Yemenites young and old, and the high school contains a small museum of Yemenite history and culture. Some of its people have achieved status and position in the wider Israeli context, but, there are also many simple working people, not very well educated and not well organized. Some Yemenites would say that this condition is due to the homogeneity and relative isolation of the city and its people. In other words, Rosh Ha'Ayin may be simply too socially and culturally inbred. (Fanny Raphael reports that this is what the town's young people said from the beginning.)[41] But this does not mean that it is a deeply troubled place, as the stereotypes and exaggerations of outsiders imply.

It may be worthwhile to consider some of Rosh Ha'Ayin's problems in the light of our findings about the Yemenites of Kiryat Eliahu and elsewhere. Harold Greenberg, who worked as supervisor of social workers in Rosh Ha'Ayin in 1977-78, writes that the residents of this city "have been victims of studied neglect or worse for thirty years."[42] I am in no position to evaluate the question of governmental policies, its "studied neglect or worse," but at the risk of "blaming the victims," some of the negative features Greenberg points to seem to fit very well with characteristics we have noted earlier but not considered necessarily "bad."

1. Greenberg complains about the layout of the town, because "each small house was set on its own plot for gardening." "The main outcome of this error, however, is the barren space between houses, enabling the residents to add on to their homes, and the low density of population, making it difficult to get around town."[43] To Greenberg this seems like neglect and error, but it is precisely the layout that many Yemenites prefer! In fact, as the author points out, "Attempts at apartment house construction have met [resistance] since residents invariably prefer individual houses."[44]

2. The author notes that "one can see everywhere evidence of the ostentatious expansion of houses. Typically, rooms are added on to the original boxlike homes as resources become available. On every street one sees houses with odd additions tacked onto older sections in various stages of completion." This certainly agrees with the pattern of building we have observed in all Yemenite communities. But Greenberg apparently considers these homeowners to be improvident, for he adds, "After investing so much in the construction of new cavernous rooms the family's resources may be so depleted that they cannot at all be furnished."[45] In other words, the Yemenite preference for "underfurnishing" is taken by Greenberg as the inability to afford the things that he, with his Euro-American expectations and sensibilities, feels to be essential.

3. There have been constant local political problems in Rosh Ha'Ayin, due to persistent factionalism and accusations of corruption. These have hampered the development of the town. Greenberg points out

that in the late 1970s outside agencies had set about to improve local services. "There [is] now a new community center, improved bus service, medical care, social services, etc. There is still a widespread feeling among many who try sincerely to help, however, that their efforts are frustrated by the lack of partners in the form of local leaders and initiative."[46]

4. There is unwillingness to contribute money to secular causes and for organizations and the community. As Greenberg remarks, "municipal taxes are extremely low and even these residents widely neglect to pay with impunity."[47] This is borne out by the *Social Profile*. Rosh Ha'Ayin ranked *last* in income from local taxes per person in 1972 and 1973.

5. Rosh Ha'Ayin is notorious for its lack of shops, entertainment, and services. One might think that a small city of 12,000 would offer a reasonable opportunity for shopkeepers and entrepreneurs, but as Greenberg notes, the small number of existing shops and groceries are poorly patronized. People prefer to shop in Petaḥ Tikva, four kilometers away, where many of them work. This seems in keeping with our observation about the suspicion of businessmen and the unwillingness to engage in shopkeeping and entrepreneurial activity. If local youth are so upset about the lack of a movie theater in town, we must wonder why no local entrepreneur has started one there.

6. Rosh Ha'Ayin ranks among the leading communities in the rate of children placed in educational institutions. Greenberg makes clear that these are children living in "superior residential high schools."[48] He seems critical of this because the children are removed from the home and taught by Ashkenazim. But he also underlines what we noted in Kiryat Eliahu, that parents *want* their children to go to what they regard as superior religious schools. They even turn to the Ministry of Welfare for the funds to pay for tuition. Many are sent away to school "because the parents prefer this to their being exposed to the dangers of crime, drugs and prostitution which are widely felt to threaten the town's youth."[49] This means, however, that the "attractive" local high school has fewer than 300 students, primarily those who failed to get into the better ones.[50]

It is clear that Rosh Ha'Ayin does have problems. It does lack services, it does have some crime and delinquency, and it does have its share of large families in need of aid from welfare. It also has a stigma; it is considered backward by some of its own residents, by other Yemenites, and by outsiders. But its problems have been blown up out of proportion, as were those of the other communities we have discussed, by ethnocentrism, superficial judgments, and the impact of journalists following the occasional scandals and teenage fights.

Finally, we may consider the case of a large village of 2,000 which some people consider a "miniature Rosh Ha'Ayin."[51] This homogeneous Yemenite community was apparently also long neglected. Surrounded by largely Ashkenazi *kibbutsim* and *moshavim*, they were politically weak and lacked physical and social facilities. Also like Rosh Ha'Ayin, they had factions and weak leadership. They were not able to assert themselves within the regional council. They resented the neighboring communities and believed that they were being short-changed; and probably they were. (One perspective, a minority one, argues that they failed to take advantage of available opportunities, or to make ones for themselves, due to their own organizational weakness.) The town developed a reputation as a troubled community, with social problems and growing alienation of the youth.

In reality the older generation, as everywhere else in Israel, worked hard, usually at the same range of laboring and skilled work as elsewhere. They saved their money, maintained their synagogues, and lived, until recently, in small but decent houses. Some of the next generation, those now in their thirties and forties, moved on to more varied and prestigious occupations, such as teaching, nursing, medicine, dentistry, and the military, while others left school earlier and went into factory or skilled work. Despite the neglect of facilities and services, as well as the resentment of their neighbors, they were good citizens, hard workers, and good savers.

By the late 1970s, however, it was felt that the atmosphere was changing, and there was concern about the younger generation, those in their late teens and early twenties. There were signs of increasing "youth culture": young people were rebelling against their elders, were not religious, were not studying or working, and perhaps were even trying to avoid military service. Their main concern seemed to be for night life and excitement. And this together with the lack of development and the old resentments combined to give the community a troubled look.

By 1982, however, the atmosphere seemed to have changed. The community became independent of the regional council, got more dynamic and orderly leadership, and requested and received increased financial and technical aid from the government. They began to build new public facilities, paved and put curbs on the streets, built athletic facilities and playgrounds, and planned a swimming pool, community center, and theater. The government provided the budget to hire specialists to lead a wide range of activities for people of all ages. Pride began to replace resentment, and activity replaced passivity.

While building was going on in the public sector, a private building boom was occurring as well. Because the community has unused space, it has been possible for many people to build large villas from the ground up, while others continue to add extensions to their houses. Families are putting money into the community, people are anxious to live there, and the stigma seems to be fading. While there are still social problems, such as alcoholism among some middle-aged men, relations with the young seem much improved, and there is a much more optimistic air about the place. Once again it seems as though the problems were exaggerated, or at least were more readily remedied than was originally thought possible. At its core the community was solid.

Political Position and Influence

Although there have long been prominent Yemenite politicians on the national scene (most notably Yisrael Yeshayahu and Yisrael Kessar),[52] until recently Yemenites were not well represented in municipal or national party politics and government. In 1975-77 I was aware of only a few influential Yemenites. By 1983 there seemed to have been a remarkable change.

At that time there were at least fifteen Yemenites serving as heads of municipal or regional councils, and another half dozen as vice-chairmen. Others serve as chairmen or secretaries of powerful local workers' councils. More and more Yemenites are being appointed to posts in government ministries and departments, especially in the Ministry of Education. I am convinced that this is a definite trend, one that is only just beginning. Some would say that it is due to the new policies of affirmative action, and especially to the efforts of the ruling Likud party to promote members of the African and Asian communities. But this can be only a partial explanation because Yemenites comprise only a relatively small percentage of that population, and many of the positions I have mentioned are elective posts.

In Chapter 7 I suggested that leadership in Yemenite communities is often weak because of the widespread attitudes of envy and the strong egalitarianism. As one Yemenite politician once put it, "For us each family is a *va'ad* [council] and within it there are four or five or six *va'adot* [committees]." When this is combined with an intense community life, large families and family ties, and the feuds and factions which grow out of synagogue life, it is not easy for a Yemenite to play a role as a leader of his own people. Neighbors and associates often have the attitude, "Who is he to think he is so good? I knew him when . . .,"—as Cassius felt about Caesar. Others may suspect their motives and wonder "What's in it for him?"

When a Yemenite moves out into the wider political arena, however, he or she is not faced with the same constraints. I suspect that this is what is happening these days, as Yemenites in their thirties and forties, perhaps born in Yemen but educated in Israel, are becoming more frequently involved in nonethnic institutions and organizations—parties, student and *moshav* organizations, workers' councils, municipal and regional governments and their working committees—and are succeeding both as elected and appointed officials. In addition more and more are rising through their work as bureaucrats and organizers in many different settings. It is a rapidly growing trend.

The Maintenance and Development of the Yemenite Heritage

The Yemenite Arts in Palestine and Israel

Yemenites and their arts have long played a disproportionately large role in Israel and, before that, in the prestate Jewish community. From the beginning of this century, musicians, writers, and artists of all sorts sought "authentic" Palestinian and Jewish sources and styles appropriate to this revival of the Jewish people in what Herzl called their "old-new land."[53] The Yemenites provided that inspiration for quite a few Jewish artists of European origin. In their midst they discovered a rich tradition of crafts, poetry, music, dance, and costume, all rooted in the Middle East and in Judaism. And they found a talented group of Yemenite performers and creators with whom to work.

The Yemenites brought with them from South Arabia arts and music that were distinctively Jewish in their themes and inspiration, but were very exotic to the Europeans and seemed to represent a continuity from ancient Middle Eastern Jewish traditions. "This applied to their speech and pronunciation, dress, art, melodies and dances. It was no wonder that in the State of Israel many sought the elements of an original culture in the areas of song, dance, and art (goldsmithery and embroidery) from among this group."[54]

In 1906, Boris Schatz, a painter and sculptor who had recently arrived from Europe, established the Bezalel School of Art in order to create a national Jewish style of arts and crafts, utilizing Near Eastern motifs and European techniques.[55] Jerusalem's Yemenite Jews figured prominently at this early period because they had their own well-developed arts of jewelry-making, embroidery, and weaving. (A popular history book contains a picture of Yemenite artisans at work in Bezalel, with the caption: "Yemenites at Bezalel; artists, hard-working, and frugal— without ideology.")[56] Much jewelry and craft work that is accepted as "Israeli" had its origins in Yemenite arts and crafts. Beginning in the 1920s, various organizations, such as Shani and later Maskit and WIZO, strove to encourage, develop, and market fashions and handicrafts, and Yemenites with their designs and skills played, and continue to play, an important role in their success.

From the 1920s until today Yemenite music and musicians have had a powerful influence on Israeli and Palestinian Jewish music. One reason for the success of this syncretism may be that Yemenite Jewish music is more compatible with European music than are other Middle Eastern musical traditions.[57] In any case the first major impact occurred during the 1920s when Brakha Tsfira, a Jerusalem-born Yemenite woman, became "the first national folk singer" of the Palestinian Jewish community.[58] She created and sang music based on Yemenite and other Near Eastern sources, usually in collaboration with European-born musicians and composers, whom she influenced in turn. This new hybrid music made no attempt to stay close to the original traditions, but aimed to produce something original and acceptable to the newly developing Jewish community. Radio and recordings spread this new music to Jewish communities in the diaspora as well. In later years Shoshana Damari became equally prominent as a symbol of Israel's new national music culture. Today there are many Yemenite singers, both men and women, capable of creating and singing a wide range of new Israeli music.

In the field of dance, in 1925 a Russian Jewish ballet dancer, Rina Nikova, found her inspiration for the creation of a "Biblical Ballet" (later called "Yemenite Ballet") in the music and dance of the Yemenites. She worked with Yemenite dancers to create this dance company which performed throughout the 1930s.[59] One of the first dancers from this group, Rachel Nadav, created some of the first Israeli folkdances in the 1930s using Yemenite dance materials. And when the folkdance movement really became organized in the 1940s, other Yemenites figured prominently in the creation of dances using Yemenite music, poetry, themes, and dance movements. Sara Levi-Tannai, who later founded the Inbal dance company, was one of those who played a major role. Inbal itself was Israel's first and perhaps still most widely known dance group. It was composed originally of Yemenite dancers and developed Yemenite music, dance, and themes for performance. [60]

Through all of these art forms the traditions of the Yemenites became part of the developing artistic culture of Israel, and certainly played a role in Yemenite self-esteem and gave them an important reputation as proud, creative people. This creativity has not stopped, and Yemenite composers, musicians, choreographers, and artists continue to contribute to the national scene through the adaptation of their artistic materials for a nationwide audience. But the early developments were essentially adaptations in which Yemenites (and Europeans) modified their arts for a wider, largely European-derived audience. (It is not without significance that both Sara Levi-Tannai and Brakha Tsfira were orphaned and were brought up in institutions and foster families where they participated in Ashkenazi culture from early ages.) Today, however, there is increasing emphasis upon and development of Yemenite music, dance, and performance of a "purer" sort, largely for the benefit of the Yemenite community itself, as well as for anyone else willing to listen and watch. It is these arts we shall consider next. [61]

Music. Music plays a powerful role in Yemenite Jewish life, both traditionally, within the community, and in the Yemenite image as it is seen in the wider society of Israel. This music, in its traditional forms, can be divided into three major categories. [62] The first type, normally practiced only by men, has its locus in the synagogue and is based upon the prayer traditions and the reading of the Torah and other holy texts. Although some of this material today finds its way into the general Israeli musical culture via Yemenite composers who adapt religious texts for religious song festivals and the general market, its primary purpose is for worship and learning in the synagogue.

As we noted before, the religiosity and religious knowledge of the Yemenite men and their egalitarian and participatory approach, as well as their early instruction in various cantillations and prayer traditions in school and the army, lead not a few men to become virtuosi. They are frequently capable of acting as cantors for synagogues of other ethnic groups as well as their own. In any case the synagogue remains an excellent training ground for young men, as it was in the United States for Jewish cantors who also became opera stars—or even "Jazz Singers."

A second type of music, also sung by men, is based on the texts of the *diwan*. This includes both the songs sung around the table at *ja'ale* (*nashid*) and longer and more elaborate songs accompanied by drum or empty cracker tin. Men may dance to this music, which is used for *shabbat al-bid'* and at weddings, and can be adapted for stage performances. The themes are sacred ones or are related to the life cycle. They tell of love for Zion, *shabbat*, marriage, and the holidays.

The third genre of Yemenite music is composed and performed by Yemenite women. This *ghane* music is accompanied by drum or *sahen*, a round metal tray struck with another metal object. It is also meant to be danced to. The women create their own poetry for the lyrics, rather than using written texts. They sing about love, marriage, and everyday affairs. There are other unaccompanied women's songs, not meant for dancing, which deal with love, troubles, laments, and mourning.[63] *Ghane* music has also become the basis for some modernized and popularized Yemenite music. In any case women are enthusiastic singers and are most likely to be the ones who will start group singing when a crowd is gathered, as, for instance, on a trip in a chartered bus. Above all, the *hinna* is the women's show, and they take over the music and dance.

In Israel today all of these types of music flourish and are known in every Yemenite community. Males and females of all ages participate in ways appropriate to their status. In addition, sex and age lines are now being crossed more often, and the lines between the genres are becoming less clear as men and women participate together in secular settings. They dance together, and they create new adaptations of Yemenite music for Israel's various musical markets. On the one hand there is a search by some for "authenticity," to retain and transmit the "original" traditions. On the other there is continuing adaptation and modernization, both for the community itself and for the wider music-consuming public.

Whereas the earlier syncretism was with European musical culture, the current one seems to involve a closer rapport with Mediterranean music, especially Greek and North African styles. In any case Israel's current music scene is filled with Yemenite composers, singers, and musicians, writing songs, as well as performing and recording them.

Young boys and girls can be seen performing on stage like seasoned professionals. There are many popular Yemenite singers, some known throughout the country, like Yigal Bashan, Boaz Shar'abi, Yitshar Cohen, Ofra Ḥaza, Ofira Gluska, and Zohar Argov, and others known primarily within the Yemenite community, like Yosef Tsabri, Tsion Golan, Tsadok Tsubeyri, Aharon Amram, Uri Shevaḥ, Gila Bushari, Ḥaim Moshe and Mikhael Sinwani. The youngsters emulate them. [64]

Dance. There are also several Yemenite dance styles, most easily categorized as women's, men's, and the newer forms for popular mixed dancing. These can be observed within any community on the appropriate occasions, but they have also been developed for performance by dance groups. Throughout the country it seems that wherever the population of a community is large enough and has leadership, attempts are made to form Yemenite performance groups. These groups may be called upon to perform on television, at folklore festivals, or at cultural centers and schools. They may even be fortunate enough to be invited to make foreign tours. Dressed in a variety of traditional costumes, accompanied by singers and drummers, they perform dances built around themes or stories related to the lives of the Jews in Yemen. These include weddings, *shabbat* observance, the work or lives of women, the love of God and Zion, and even social problems such as those of the wife in a polygynous marriage.

The development of these and other ethnic dance groups was aided by the efforts of the European-born choreographer and folkdance exponent, Gurit Kadmon. She and others had the dances filmed in the 1950s and offered advice on the adaptation of traditional dances for performances before audiences in theaters and on stage.

Just as music is flourishing today, so is Yemenite dance, at all levels and in all contexts. Yemenite youth are increasingly interested in their dance traditions and participation in them. Whereas, I am told, fifteen or twenty years ago these seemed old-fashioned, even embarrassing, and young people preferred *salon* dancing at weddings, now they seem to resent anything but Yemenite dancing. Young people are learning more complex dances and older people, too, often seem to be just waiting for a chance to start dancing where circumstances permit.

Thus both in formal and informal contexts and in traditional and modern settings, dance, like music, is flourishing. It is increasingly being supported by funds and encouragement from government sources and by educational and community institutions, and it is enthusiastically engaged in by young and old alike. If there was a "crisis" in the 1950s and 1960s during which these things were devalued, that crisis has passed, and we are currently in an era of enthusiastic support and participation. The extent of this enthusiasm is very striking and should not be underestimated.

Literature and History. There have long been Yemenites who produced works of religious scholarship, historical accounts, descriptions of life in Yemen, poetry and, more recently, fiction and fictionalized history. The way was led by rabbis early in the century, but they were joined by individuals with secular educations (including Avraham and Mordekhai Tabib, Shim'on Greidi, Ratson HaLevi, Yisrael Yeshayahu, Moshe, Yosef and Ḥaim Tsadok, and Shlomo Tivoni) and by teachers, such as N. B. Gamlieli and Ezra Cohen, who felt the need to record the life and times and the literature of their people.[65] Leading scholars of the older generation include Rabbi Yosef Kafiḥ, and Rabbi Shalom Gamliel.

In this area, too, there is rapid expansion, as more and more works are being published and as a new generation of academically trained Yemenite scholars is establishing itself. Yehuda Ratzaby, Yosef Tobi, Mishael Maswari Caspi, Yehuda Nini, Aviva Klein-Franke, Bat-Tsion Klorman-Eraqi, Dina Greitzer, Nitsa Druyan, and a number of other younger scholars in history and literature represent a new wave of writers who are building on and adding to the work of an older generation that was largely self-taught. In these areas, too, interest in the Yemenite heritage is great and growing.

The Organization of Yemenite Cultural, Social, and Political Activities

While most Yemenite artistic and cultural activity takes place in the family, synagogue, and community, national organizations have been formed that support and are devoted to the maintenance and development of Yemenite culture and society. Over the decades there have been several such organizations, some completely independent, others attached to political parties or the Histadrut. Today the two leading independent Yemenite associations are the *Aguda* (Association for Society and Culture in Israel) and *Afikim*.

Afikim, whose motto proclaims that it is dedicated to "spiritual and social revival, to the defense of rights, and to *mizug galuyot*, the fusion of the communities" publishes a periodical devoted to these topics, as well as to Yemenite community affairs, discussions of literature and history, and original poetry. In addition they support the publication of books on these subjects.

The *Aguda l'Tipuah Hevra v'Tarbut b'Arets* aims to achieve similar goals: "(1) Revival of the Yemenite Jewish cultural heritage; (2) Fostering fundamental cultural and artistic values; (3) Fostering friendship and good will in people; (4) Concern and support for the needy; (5) Encouragement and aid for needy students; (6) Discovery of spiritual and artistic creativity." Under the leadership of Ovadiah Ben-Shalom the organization encourages and organizes cultural activities, celebrations, seminars, and a constant round of weekend get-togethers, aimed particularly at young and middle-aged married couples.

On these weekends a number of rooms in a hotel or *kibbuts* guest-house resort are reserved for Friday night through Saturday night. Forty to sixty participants spend the sabbath together, at prayer and at meals, singing, holding *ja'ale* sessions, perhaps listening to speakers or participating in discussions, and just visiting and relaxing. When the *shabbat* is over there will be well known Yemenite entertainers, music, and dancing.[66]

The Aguda works to honor and publicize Yemenites and Yemenite culture, and serves as a clearinghouse to aid the organization of activities. Anyone can turn to the Aguda to find singers, artists, performing groups, and writers. They can help arrange events and festivities. They planned celebrations for the 70th anniversary of Kerem Ha-Teymanim in Tel Aviv, and for the 50th of the Ben-Tsion section of Netanya. On Independence Day in 1976 the Aguda arranged an outing attended by about 10,000 people, many of whom stayed for more than one day. Yemenites from all over the country came to a forest near Hadera, set up tents, ate, talked, visited, smoked *narghila*, chewed *gat*, sang, and danced. They were of all ages; whole families and groups from communities came. Those who were near enough to the stage to see and hear were treated to a parade of nationally prominent and lesser known musicians, entertainers, and politicians. (In many respects this resembled the big Moroccan Jewish *mimouna* celebration which takes place each year on the day after Passover.)

In Israel today the Yemenite heritage is being celebrated and is flourishing at all levels: national, regional, and local. Aside from the regular or spontaneous celebrations and events within communities there is a constant round of activities throughout the country. There are conferences (in 1981-82 the 100th anniversary of the first *aliya* was recalled with several conferences); elaborate shows presenting Yemenite music, dance, and costuming; and other celebrations of the kind noted above. Sometimes these are supported by the Ministry of Education, or a local school or community center (Matnas), or are initiated by the Yemenite section of the Histadrut or a political party. Whatever the stimulus or the funding, they depend for their success upon the community's skilled performers and lecturers, and upon Yemenite audiences ready to attend and enthusiastically participate.[67]

Notes

1. See Elihu Katz and Awraham Zloczower, "Ethnic Continuity in an Israeli Town," *Human Relations* 14:293-327, 1961; Percy Cohen, "Alignments and Allegiances in the Community of Shaarayim in Israel," *Jewish Journal of Sociology* 4:14-38, 1962; Norman Berdichevsky, "The Impact of Urbanization on the Social Geography of Reḥovot" (doctoral dissertation, University of Wisconsin, Madison, 1974); Norman Berdichevsky, "The Persistence of the Yemeni Quarter in an Israeli Town," *Ethnicity* 4:287-309, 1977.

2. Yael Katzir, "The Effects of Resettlement on the Status and Role of Yemeni Jewish Women: The Case of Ramat Oranim, Israel" (doctoral dissertation, University of California, Berkeley, 1976).

3. Lisa Gilad, "Changing Notions of Proper Conduct: The Case of Jewish Unmarried Yemeni Women in an Israeli New Town," *Cambridge Anthropology* 7:44-56, 1982; "Contrasting Notions of Proper Conduct: Yemeni Jewish Mothers and Daughters in an Israeli Town," *Jewish Social Studies*, 45(1): 73-86, 1983; *Ginger and Salt: Yemeni Women in an Israeli Town* (Boulder, Colo.: Westview, 1989).

4. Jean-Jacques Berreby, "De l'Intégration des Juifs Yéménites en Israel," *L'Année Sociologique*, 3rd series: 69-163; Raphael Patai, *Israel Between East and West: A Study in Human Relations* (Philadelphia: The Jewish Publication Society of America, 1953). Eliezer Ben-Rafael's book, *The Emergence of Ethnicity*, (Westport, Ct.: Greenwood Press, 1982), is built partly around the results of an attitudinal survey of 139 "upwardly mobile" Yemenites. Although there is considerable disagreement between us regarding the attitudes of the upwardly mobile, Ben-Rafael's findings with respect to the Yemenite community in general tend to agree with those presented here. This is true especially of such key matters as ethnic pride and cohesion, endogamy, religiosity and the role of the synagogue. See, especially, pp. 141-143.

5. See *Social Profile of Cities and Towns in Israel*, Part 2 (Jerusalem: Ministry of Social Welfare, Division of Planning, 1977). [Hebrew] This publication indicates, for example, that in Kiryat Eliahu 2.6 percent of the population receive welfare, which is precisely the overall Israel figure, and puts Kiryat Eliahu in a tie for 36-38 place out of sixty-three cities and local councils (p. 48). As for "families receiving 1-5 types of financial help from the Ministry of Social Welfare" Kiryat Eliahu stands in 35th place, with 9.3 percent vs. the Israeli average of 8.1 percent (p. 55). And it ranks 46-49 in "dependency ratio" (p. 29).

6. Central Bureau of Statistics, Government of Israel, Census of Population and Housing 1974: *List of Localities* (Geographical Information and Population), No. 3. For an overview of Yemenite settlement see Raziel Mamet, "The Geography of Yemenite Settlement in Israel," in Shalom Seri, ed., *Se'i Yona: Yemenite Jews in Israel* (Tel Aviv: Am Oved, 1983), pp. 163-194. [Hebrew]

7. Berreby, "De l'Intégration," p. 138.

8. See Vivian Z. Klaff, "Residence and Integration in Israel: A Mosaic of Segregated Peoples," *Ethnicity* 4:103-121, 1977.

9. Cf. Berreby, "De l'Intégration," p. 140. It is often assumed that ethnic residential concentration in Israel is the result of "short-sighted absorption policies of the bureaucracy" or of labor market forces. While there is clearly some validity to this, a subtler and fuller understanding of the situation calls for attention to the specific histories of places and interests, the attitudes and motivations of the people themselves. Cf. Harvey Goldberg, "Historical and Cultural Dimensions of Ethnic Phenomena in Israel," in Alex Weingrod, ed., *Studies in Israeli Ethnicity: After the Ingathering* (New York: Gordon and Breach, 1985), pp. 185-186.

10. *Encyclopaedia Judaica*, Vol. 16 (Jerusalem: Keter, 1972), p. 754.

11. Cf. Berdichevsky, "The Impact of Urbanization," p. 294; Berdichevsky, "The Persistence of the Yemeni Quarter," p. 297.

12. Harold I. Greenberg, "Rosh Haayin—Neglect and Tradition," *Plural Societies* 11:71, 1980. My family and I once went in search of a Yemenite family in Arad, a new and modern development town. As we passed one high-rise building after another on their street I feared for my hypothesis. Abruptly the apartment buildings left off and we found the family we had come to visit in a neighborhood of *vilot*. A number of other Yemenites live in this same section, which is newer, more fashionable, and more mixed than the typical Yemenite *shkhuna*. Yemenites have only just started to move to this city, however.

13. Yosef Tobi lists thirty-seven such settlements established before the state. Many are still primarily Yemenite communities. See Tobi, *I Will Ascend in Tamar: One Hundred Years of Aliyah and Settlement* (Jerusalem: Ben-Zvi Institute and E'eleh B'tamar Association, 1982). [Hebrew]

14. Katz and Zloczower, "Ethnic Continuity," p. 313.

15. *Ibid*, p. 304.

16. Berdichevsky, "The Persistence of the Yemeni Quarter," p. 302. He discusses the reasons and feelings of those who have left, as well.

17. *Social Profile of Cities and Towns in Israel*, 1977.

18. Israelis use the expression *seder adifut*, "order of preference" or "priorities." The following may serve to indicate the strength of these priorities for Yemenites. Two couples from Kiryat Eliahu currently live in a small city in the Tel Aviv area. All four are well-educated and have high-status occupations: one engineer, two teachers, and a teacher of teachers. We must assume that their status and salaries permit them to live almost anywhere and in almost any kind of housing, yet the two couples live in adjacent two-story houses, exactly like those they grew up in, in an unprepossessing Yemenite neighborhood. Whatver their reason for living in that town, presumably for their work, their choice of neighborhood and type of house fits perfectly with our expectations.

19. The Ben-Tsion quarter of Netanya is composed of several sections. Some contain one-story *vilot*, but one consists of the same kind of two-story, four-apartment buildings as those in Kiryat Eliahu. This is called "the Romanian *shkhuna*" because it once housed Romanian Jews who have since moved away, leaving it to Yemenites.

20. This is supported by data from a survey of Israeli men born in 1954 which indicate that, even if they are less observant than their fathers and mothers, they are still more observant than their contemporaries of other groups. I am grateful to Drs. Judah Matras and Yossi Shavit for access to this information from the study. See also Ben-Rafael, *Emergence of Ethnicity*, pp. 87, 141.

21. Cf. Gilad, "Changing Notions," p. 45. It has been claimed that some young men turn to crime. I have no way to assess the extent to which this is true.

22. See Dov Weintraub et al., *Immigration and Social Change: Agricultural Settlements of New Immigrants of Israel* (Manchester: Manchester University Press, 1971), p. 1ff.

23. Central Bureau of Statistics, State of Israel, Census of Population and Housing 1972: *Demographic Characteristics of the Population*, Part II, No. 10 (Jerusalem, 1976).

24. For discussions of Tripolitanian, Moroccan, and Yemenite *moshavim*, see Harvey E. Goldberg, *Cave Dwellers and Citrus Growers: A Jewish Community in Libya and Israel* (Cambridge: Cambridge University Press, 1972); Moshe Shokeid, *The Dual Heritage: Immigrants from the Atlas Mountains in an Israeli Village* (Manchester: Manchester University Press, 1971); Yael Katzir, "The Effects of Resettlement." For a survey of Yemenite settlement in agricultural villages see Yisrael Kessar, "Yemenite Agricultural Settlement after the Creation of the State," in Shalom Seri, ed., *Se'i Yona: Yemenite Jews in Israel* (Tel Aviv: Am Oved, 1983), pp. 231–342. [Hebrew]

25. For accounts of the early periods in several Moroccan *moshavim*, see Alex Weingrod, *Reluctant Pioneers: Village Development in Israel* (Ithaca, N. Y.: Cornell University Press, 1966); Dorothy Willner, *Nation-Building and Community in Israel* (Princeton, N. J.: Princeton University Press, 1969).

26. Katzir, "The Effects of Resettlement," pp. 217-222.

27. Gilbert Kushner, *Immigrants from India in Israel* (Tucson: University of Arizona Press, 1973).

28. See Naomi Nevo, "A Problematic Moshav in the Central District" (Jerusalem: Settlement Department of the Jewish Agency, 1976). [Hebrew] Unfortunately the *moshavim* encountered economic difficulties in the late seventies and early eighties apparently as a result of government economic policies.

29. Emanuel Marx, "Rehabilitation of Slums? The Case of Hatikva Quarter," *The Jerusalem Quarterly* 22:38-44, 1982.

30. See Pinhas Kapara, *From Yemen to Shaarayim, Rehovot* (Rehovot, 1978). [Hebrew]

31. See Katz and Zloczower, "Ethnic Continuity," p. 295.

32. P. Cohen, "Alignments and Allegiances," p. 19.

33. Berdichevsky, "The Persistence of the Yemeni Quarter," pp. 291-292.

34. Berdichevsky, "The Impact of Urbanization," pp. 167-168.

35. *Ibid*, p. 174.

36. *Ibid*, pp. 174-175.

37. *Ibid*, p. 180.

38. Marx, "Rehabilitation," p. 38ff.

39. *Ibid*, p. 42.

40. Greenberg, "Rosh Haayin," p. 69.

41. Fanny Raphael, "Rosh Ha'Ayin: The Development of an Immigrant Settlement," in C. Frankenstein, ed., *Between Past and Future* (Jerusalem: Henrietta Szold Foundation, 1953), p. 209. Carol F. Zimbrolt's study of family planning in Rosh Ha'Ayin lends impressionistic support to this conclusion. The people she portrays seem to be more isolated than the Yemenites of Kiryat Eliahu and the large heterogeneous communities around Tel Aviv, as might be expected. *Ideology, Policy and Identity: Family Planning in a Yemenite Community in Israel* (doctoral dissertation, University of Minnesota, 1984).

42. Greenberg, "Rosh Haayin," p. 59.

43. *Ibid*, p. 60.

44. *Ibid*, p. 71.

45. *Ibid*, p. 71.

46. *Ibid*, p. 72. Cf. Raphael, "Rosh Ha'Ayin," pp. 206-207; *Encyclopaedia Judaica*, Vol. 16 (1972), p. 754.

47. Greenberg, "Rosh Haayin," p. 63.

48. *Ibid*, p. 66.

49. *Ibid*, p. 66.

50. In 1986 I was told that the local school had been so successfully improved that parents now send their children to it in preference to boarding schools.

51. I obtained this information from a close friend, a Yemenite, who worked in this community for several years in an administrative capacity.

52. Yisrael Yeshayahu, a longtime Labor Party activist within the Yemenite community, served for many years in the Knesset and held the position of Speaker for some time. Yisrael Kessar, as head of the powerful General Federation of Labor, the Histadrut, is one of the key figures in Israeli political and economic life in the 1980s.

53. See Theodore Herzl, *Old-New Land* (New York: Bloch, 1941).

54. *Encyclopaedia Judaica*, Vol. 16, p. 755.

55. *Ibid*, Vol. 14, pp. 945-946.

56. See Robert Shereshevsky, ed., *One Hundred Years and Another Twenty*, Vol. 1 (Jerusalem: Ma'ariv, 1967), pp. 198-199. [Hebrew]

57. *Encyclopaedia Judaica*, Vol. 16, p. 758.

58. *Ibid*, Vol. 16, p. 967.

59. See Judith Brin Ingber, "The Russian Ballerina and the Yemenites," *Israel Dance 1975* (Tel Aviv, 1976).

60. See Judith Brin Ingber, *Shorashim: The Roots of Israeli Folk Dance*, Dance Perspectives No. 59 (New York: Dance Perspectives Foundation, 1974). Also G. Manor, "'Inbal' and Yemenite Dance in Israel," in Shalom Seri, ed., *Se'i Yona: Yemenite Jews in Israel* (Tel Aviv: Am Oved, 1983), pp. 399-414. [Hebrew]

61. The prominence of the more popular syncretic material does not mean that the more traditional arts were neglected. From the 1920s, Yehiel Adaqi and many others worked to foster and create musical performance. Choruses were formed and the radio broadcast their music. They were often supported by the Histadrut's cultural department.

62. See Uri Sharvit, "On the Role of the Arts and Artistic Concepts in the Tradition of Yemenite Jewry," *Pe'amim* 10:119-130, 1981.

63. *Ibid*, p. 122; Mishael Maswari Caspi, *Daughters of Yemen* (Berkeley: University of California Press, 1985).

64. Musicologists Naomi and Avner Bahat discuss the influence of Yemenite music in Israeli popular music (old and new), the concert hall, ballet, and folk dance, as well as the continuing innovativeness of Yemenite artists within the context of their traditions. In Shalom Seri, ed., *Se'i Yona: Yemenite Jews in Israel* (Tel Aviv: Am Oved, 1983), pp. 415-438. [Hebrew]

65. On modern Yemenite authors and their works see Yosef HaLevi, "Some Examples of Modern Hebrew Literature by Yemenite Authors," in Shalom Seri, ed., *Se'i Yona: Yemenite Jews in Israel* (Tel Aviv: Am Oved, 1983), pp. 349-386. [Hebrew]

66. These "weekends" are by no means unique to the Yemenites. Judith L. Goldstein presents a discussion of this phenomenon among Iranian Jews in Israel. See "Iranian Ethnicity in Israel: The Performance of Identity," in Alex Weingrod, ed., *Studies in Israeli Ethnicity* (New York: Gordon and Breach, 1985), pp. 246-249.

67. For a fuller discussion of Yemenite identity and the organization of ethnicity in the context of Israeli ideology and politics see Herbert S. Lewis, "Yemenite Ethnicity in Israel," *Jewish Journal of Sociology* 26:5-24, 1984.

9

Conclusions and Implications

In 1949 and 1950 more than 48,000 Jews were flown from Yemen to Israel. They left one of the most isolated, tradition-bound Muslim societies in the world and entered a rapidly changing, experimenting, modern economy and society. The Yemenite Jews moved within a few months from isolated mountain villages and the Jewish quarters of traditional cities to the growing cities and new farming villages of Israel. They went from a static occupational structure to a dynamic, developing industrial economy in which they had to find new ways of earning their livings. Artisans who had made jewelry, embroidery, and window tracery found that their skills were no longer needed or sufficient. Women who had never dreamed of working outside their homes now commuted by bus to work in other cities. Disenfranchised "protected" subjects moved to a state in which they were citizens expected to join the military and urged to join unions and political parties and to participate in local and national party politics. From a "theocratic" society in which they were supposed to practice their own religion faithfully they were transported to a Jewish state which was largely secular, partly socialist, and somewhat discouraging of the very Jewish practices the imams protected. How have they fared in the thirty-five years since making this striking change in their lives?

If we take the Yemenites of Kiryat Eliahu as a representative case, the answer must be that they are doing very well. By their own hard labor, and by taking advantage of the opportunities offered by Israel's modern economy and welfare state, they have attained a considerable measure of well-being and educational and occupational mobility over the past three decades. By any objective standards they are succeeding both in comparison to their own situation when they arrived thirty years earlier, and in comparison to the rest of the Israeli population. They own their own housing, have rapidly increased their educational attainment, and have moved into occupations that bring increased prestige and higher financial rewards. They are now moving more rapidly into positions of influence and importance in the political and administrative system of the city and state.

There is no sense in which these Yemenites are a problem population, "culturally deprived," or "in need of fostering" (*t'unei tipuaḥ* is the current term for a troubled, poor, unsuccessful population). They contribute very little to the city's crime, delinquency, and welfare rolls, or to the case loads of the truant officer and the social workers. They have successfully adapted to the new world they came to in 1950, without retreat or breakdown.

Subjectively, they are proud to be Jews and Israelis. Just as everyone else in Israel, they have their complaints (and these have undoubtedly increased over the past few years as complaining has become even more popular as an Israeli pastime). Many are critical of trends in their country and the world, but they have the perspective of full citizens and loyal Israelis.

All of this contrasts with the stereotype which automatically classifies them as "Orientals," members of "the Other Israel" or "the Second Israel" and thus leads us to expect them to be poor, troubled, dependent, and disaffected.[1] Their objective situation does not conform to the expectations of either side in the debate about the ethnic gap. They do not appear to be hampered by "traditionalism," by fatalism, patriarchalism, or "superstition," or by a culture of poverty, cultural deprivation, or disorientation due to the traumas of rapid change. On the other hand, neither are they suffering from neglect, discrimination, enforced cultural divestiture, or permanent relegation to an underclass.

If Kiryat Eliahu's Yemenites are becoming very much like other Israelis with respect to their occupations, education, and political life, they do, however, have another side, shared with other Israeli Yemenites but not with their non-Yemenite neighbors. They have a distinctive identity and a social and cultural life, Yemenite in origin, that they have retained and adapted for life in Israel.

The Nature of Yemenite Ethnicity

As we noted in the Introduction, there is a school of thought in current social science that "tends to reduce all ethnic awareness and action ultimately to instrumental political and economic interests and strategies."[2] According to this view, the roots of ethnicity do not lie deep in sentiment, or in history and tradition, or in a need or desire to affiliate with "the same kind of people," but in competition for scarce resources and in the "conscious efforts of individuals and groups *mobilizing* ethnic symbols in order to obtain access to social, political, and material resources."[3] Stephen Steinberg, very much an opponent of "the ethnic myth," grants at most that "The ethnic community also functions...as a refuge against the alienation that pervades modern society," which "helps to explain why people cling to remnants of the ethnic past, why they crave ritual and a sense of belonging."[4] Or, as an Israeli social scientist said to me, "You have to understand the economic and political context that makes the Yemenites want to stress this identity and heritage." Without for a moment denying the actual and potential political/instrumental significance of Yemenite ethnicity, I contend that the phenomenon involves much more than this.

Yemenite ethnicity in Kiryat Eliahu and elsewhere in Israel is a multidimensional complex that is at base inner-directed and not primarily in reaction to economic and political problems or alienation in modern society. Yemenites regularly base their ethnicity on common residence, on the maintenance of synagogues and local institutions, and on the continuity of their traditions of religious practice and teaching. In so doing they are constantly involved with kin, ethnic friends, and fellows in joint activity. There is a core of shared understandings, important values, and group-specific art forms and celebration. In addition to the conscious positive evaluation of religious practice there is also the sharing of fun and beauty in the music, poetry, dance, and costumes. To reduce all of this to a seeking for economic advantage, or clustering together in the face of alienation, is to trivialize and misunderstand the nature of culture itself.[5]

There are powerful elements of emotion, loyalty, and moral obligation in being Yemenite, though it might be overstating the case to think of it as having an "apparently imperative and involuntary character."[6] Israel is a multiethnic society; Yemenites are exposed to other subcultures, and individuals may decide to lessen their involvement with their fellow ethnics and increase their interactions with others, modifying their behavior accordingly. But many Yemenites are drawn to interact with other Yemenites because of the positive attraction, the ease of interaction, the common understandings, and the valued activities and behavior associated with Yemenite ethnicity. Conversely, there are costs to leaving the community, above all the loss of the esteem and support of one's "significant others"—or a portion of them. Yemenite ethnicity cannot be understood primarily or exclusively as a situational, instrumental, reactive phenomenon.[7]

The Origins of Yemenite Ethnicity

In contrast to the traditional emphasis on the transplanted cultural heritage as the principal antecedent and defining characteristic of ethnic groups, we suggest that the development and persistence of ethnicity is dependent upon structural conditions characterizing American cities and position of groups in American social structure. Attention is focused on the question: under what conditions does ethnic culture emerge? Specifically, what social forces promote the crystallization and development of ethnic solidarity and identification?[8]

W. L. Yancey and his colleagues wrote about ethnicity in the United States, but their arguments could apply to the study of ethnicity in any immigrant society. Shlomo Swirski and Sara Katzir made use of this idea in their paper trying to demonstrate the reality of a newly emerging "Oriental" ethnic group in Israel.[9] In conversation a number of Israeli social scientists have implicitly taken a similar stand regarding Yemenite identity and ethnicity, preferring explanation in terms of conditions in Israel and rejecting the idea of a "transplanted cultural heritage."[10]

It is unfortunate that in this case as in so many others, social scientists insist on a dichotomous polarity, an either/or situation. Much of what Yancey and his colleagues say about the importance of economic and structural factors in the receiving country makes perfect sense, but their argument becomes forced and unnatural when they insist that "The assumption of a common heritage as the essential aspect of ethnicity is erroneous."[11] Surely when dealing with such a complex, worldwide, variable phenomenon it is self-defeating to insist on the primacy, in all cases, of one type of cause over another. Their otherwise suggestive article suffers from the strain to discount "the old world" at all costs.

In the case of the Jews of Yemen there can be no question whatever that they arrived with a distinct ethnic identity, for it was in Yemen, over two millennia, that their identity and heritage were formed. As Yael Katzir has pointed out, "Jewish ethnic identity in Yemen over the centuries was dependent upon the interplay between segregation and integration boundary maintenance mechanisms, both external and internal."[12] If this identity was fostered by the peculiarities of *dhimmi* status and isolation, it also had a content at its core to sustain it: the Torah and the religion of Israel with its laws, practices, and beliefs. Even in Yemen two thousand years ago there was an interplay between structural, ecological, economic, and political exigencies and a tradition imported from another "old world"—Palestine. By 1880 the Yemenites had lived as "a people apart" for centuries and thus had a clear sense of themselves in relation to all others. And there is no sign that one hundred years later in Israel they are on the verge of merging their own identity in any generalized "Oriental" ethnicity, despite Swirski and S. Katzir's claims to this effect.

If the basis of the Yemenites' ethnicity has obvious origins in Yemen, it is not so simple a matter to dismiss the question of the origins of their cultural characteristics, those things which have come to be associated with them in Israel today, and which I have singled out for discussion. On the one hand, it hardly needs saying that the Yemenites of Kiryat Eliahu have been deeply influenced by Israeli culture; indeed they have in many respects been made over by it. On the other hand, they maintain an important set of behaviors, ideas, and values that distinguish them from others in the Israeli population. Rather than think in terms of their behavior as being either imported *or* created in the new country, it is reasonable to expect an interplay between the two, and not automatically assume that one or the other must be the *real* basis.

Richard Ehrlich expresses an alternative view of American ethnicity, one which represents neither the earlier assimilationist and "melting pot" approach, nor the new revisionist one of Yancey. It is an approach which is evident in recent writing on immigrants to industrializing America in the nineteenth century. As Ehrlich observes,

> . . . the behavior of immigrants in America was very much a function of their respective ethnic backgrounds rather than being exclusively a reflection of external circumstances, such as class membership . . . Rejecting the proposition that the encounter with industrial America was overwhelmingly disorienting and destructive of traditional life-styles the authors [of the papers in this volume] assert that the immigrant peoples who flocked to the United States in such great numbers brought with them highly resilient cultures that were able to survive in their new environment. Because of this resilience, the immigrants are seen not as passive agents upon whom a new and alien culture was quickly imposed, but rather as individuals able to maintain their customs and, to some extent, to influence the institutional forms they encountered in the United States.[13]

I believe that the Israeli evidence also suggests that this is a sensible approach, and not mere romanticism or fileopietism. In the following pages we shall consider a few of the prominent elements of Yemenite behavior in the light of the interplay between imported elements and conditions in the new country.

Residential Segregation and the Building
of Yemenite Communities

Ethnically based residential clustering is a very common phenomenon in all kinds of societies, modern and traditional, and is well known in Israel.[14] Nevertheless Yemenite clustering is quite striking and is probably matched in Israel only by that of various Hasidic groups. It would be all too easy for an observer to assume that this must be the result of segregation by the non-Yemenite neighbors and authorities, or the "ecological structure of cities," or the "processes of industrialization"[15] and the Yemenites' position in the occupational structure of Israel. But such assumptions would be misleading.

We know that in Yemen the Jews were almost invariably settled in their own quarters or villages, away from the non-Jews. The historical record further tells us that from the 1880s, when they built their own quarters in Jerusalem, through the 1910s, when they established their own communities on the periphery of the new Jewish towns, through the 1920s and 1930s, when they developed the urban quarters in Tel Aviv and Netanya, the Yemenites chose such settlements. They also established their own agricultural settlements, both before and after 1948. The best explanation for this consistent and persistent pattern, despite differences of time, place, or occupation, must be preference. As we suggested earlier, many Yemenites today have the money and the mobility needed to move to non-Yemenite areas, but relatively few do. Berdichevsky found this in Sha'arayim as well.[16] On the contrary, many young people specifically choose to move *to* Yemenite *shkhunot*. They have consistently demonstrated loyalty to these communities over the decades.[17]

It would be pointless to deny that relations with the Ashkenazim in the old days may have been so unpleasant, and that Yemenites may have felt so unwanted, that part of the motivation may have been to avoid unpleasant encounters with outsiders. Perhaps here and there Yemenites were, or would have been, rejected. Certainly this could play a reinforcing role. But the reasons for positively selecting the company of coethnics outweigh this element. (In this connection it is appropriate to point out that Israel has a number of prosperous, middle-class sections maintained by particularly orthodox Jews. These are places to observe *shabbat* according to the law. Yemenite communities have some of the same atmosphere.)

The Yemenite neighborhood in Israel is more than an automatic carry-over from Yemen. It is not just a matter of "custom." It establishes the demographic and residential basis for the social, religious, and cultural life which means so much to the inhabitants of these communities.

The Yemenites and Work

Most Yemenite immigrants, regardless of which wave of immigration they came with, began their work careers at or near the bottom of the occupational ladder. In each case they soon established their reputations as desirable workers to hire: (1) they accepted any sort of work, no matter how menial and degrading others might consider it; (2) they gained the reputation for working diligently and responsibly; and (3) they appeared content with their lot and are invariably described as "cheerful."

Some social scientists have suggested to me that these characteristics (if they really exist) must surely have been created in Israel, under conditions of capitalism, expanding industrialization, and the building of the state's infrastructure. Aren't they exactly the traits one would hope for in a pliable, reliable, undemanding labor force? Perhaps they are, but the evidence again suggests that the roots of these attitudes were there in Yemen, although they may have been strengthened in Israel.

A study of the literature of the first and second waves of immigration, from the 1880s to the early 1900s, shows that even then, before the development of Palestine's economy and industry, the Yemenites were seen as lovers of work, the exemplars of "Jewish labor," capable of the "conquest of labor."[18] "As early as the 1880s they had made a name for themselves as highly skilled, reliable, and competent workers. Their industry, cleanliness, modesty, and reliability soon made them a respected and welcome element in the pioneering laboring class."[19] This reputation intensified after the coming of the agricultural workers in 1907 and was to continue after the "Wings of Eagles" *olim* arrived in 1949-50. As each wave of immigrants arrived it proved itself in these terms. It stretches the credulity to argue that there was an instantaneous transformation as the immigrants looked around upon arrival, saw what was needed, and immediately adapted their behavior and attitudes accordingly.

We have seen in Chapter 7 that the Yemenites already had distinctive values related to the importance of work. (Yehuda Nini quotes excerpts from letters sent by Jews from Yemen to the Zionist authorities in the 1920s, stressing their ability to work well and to contribute to the building of the land.)[20] And it is particularly relevant that they did not object to menial work, of which many had done their share in Yemen. Their *amour-propre* was not associated with the nature of their work, but with their religiosity, *derekh erets*, their care of their families, and their homes. Many other immigrants came to Israel from scores of other countries, but none established the particular reputation of the Yemenites.[21] Surely this suggests the significance of a foreign heritage rather than the transformative power of the Palestinian/Israeli society and economy.

On the other hand, we must assume that these attitudes were reinforced in the Land of Israel. Such workers would be welcome, and, in times of unemployment or competition for jobs, being known as a Yemenite might give a worker a clear advantage. As the first Yemenite I ever met told me, "It is important to work hard. A good, serious worker can get on. People want honest, good workers above all." (This man was a university graduate who had been a teacher and was, in 1969, working in a government office in Jerusalem.) It is reasonable to see the propagation of this image as a useful tactic, especially for people with few other options. But it could only be effective if there were enough truth to it to continue to give it credence. In accepting apparently undesirable work, and doing it uncomplainingly, Yemenites were not simply accepting their lesser status in life but were "casting their bread upon the water"—in the words of a favorite proverb.

Yochanan Peres has suggested that Yemenites got their good reputation partly because they are the least troublesome of ethnic groups. He writes that their "preparedness to identify with Israeli society without demanding a full portion of its resources is without doubt one of the reasons for the sympathy that the Yemenites received from the veteran Europeans."[22] This idea is plausible on the face of it, but as we have seen, it does not seem to conform to the realities of Yemenite political activity. Individuals may have worked hard and cheerfully, but no other ethnic group has the history of ethnic organizations and pressure groups that the Yemenites do. They started working for recognition and resources in the 1880s in Jerusalem; they campaigned for funds and for land from the second decade of the twentieth century; they formed their own sections of the labor movement and organized their own central committee; and they enrolled in the movements to fight for independence, both socialist and Revisionist. In the light of all this Peres's suggestion fails to do justice either to the Yemenites or to the Ashkenazim who had sympathy for them. They enjoyed their reputation *despite* their efforts to improve their situation.

Histapkut B'mu'at, Thrift, and Display

Once again we have a complex of traits which critics might regard as the product of economic and political conditions in Israel. Wouldn't this "satisfaction with little" be consistent with the Yemenites' place in the ethnic division of labor as menials, unskilled laborers, and those who have been thrust into a subordinate position with little chance for escape? Is their "thrift" anything other than the fruits of poverty? Obviously I think it is.

There is ample testimony to the proposition that the Jews of Yemen were forced to control the display of their wealth for fear that they would incur the jealousy and wrath of their non-Jewish neighbors, against whom they had little protection. They had no protection against the envy of their protectors, the *sayyids* and others. There were limits on the grandeur of their houses, the colors and fineness of their clothes, and the ownership and use of riding animals. They did not want to invite confiscation and other punishments by flaunting what wealth they had.

Although the rooms of their houses in Yemen might be quite large, and the windows nicely decorated, the walls were usually white-washed and simple. Their interior space was generally uncluttered and open, the major furnishings being pillows and cushions lining the walls. There were rugs, trays, and water-pipes, but not sofas, chairs, tables, and buffets.

To some extent the esthetics, the tastes, and the negative attitude toward display seem to have been transplanted to the Israeli context, where they may still have useful functions. Material display is considered somewhat vulgar, fellow ethnics appreciate the esthetics of the spare furnishings, and the money that is saved can be used for other purposes. High on the list of uses for this money is the purchase of housing, the expansion of current apartments, education, the purchase of automobiles, and aiding children and near kin with their purchases and plans.

Thrift and "contentment with little" are not the product of naivete or a simple adaptation to poverty. As a group Yemenites are obviously very successful accumulators of wealth, despite their relatively low-paying jobs. On a number of occasions I was surprised to learn of considerable sums that simple, apparently poor older parents had given or lent to their children. (Fanny Raphael was impressed by the amount of savings which were in evidence when the Yemenites of the Rosh Ha'Ayin *ma'abara* moved into their first homes and began to furnish them in 1951. After one or two years of irregular and low paid work many families had saved hundreds of pounds—when the pound was worth more than $2!)[23]

We might consider both the work ethic and the Yemenite propensity to limit their consumption as "preadaptations" from Yemen, whose value has led to their retention. Beyond mere continuity, they have been raised to the level of conscious principles. They continue to be useful in Israel, and are supported both by the success, the pay-offs, of these strategies and by the values of the members of the reference group. One's peers understand and appreciate the results.

Yemenite Arts and Traditions in the Israeli Setting

There is no doubt that the nurturance and efflorescence of Yemenite art forms owe a great deal to their reception in Erets Yisrael. It is most likely that the Yemenite community would still be holding to many of these forms even if they had not had the acceptance they enjoyed in the wider Jewish community during the past fifty years, but the support and esteem they received must be credited with strengthening them.

As we have seen, from the 1920s their music and dance have been appreciated, at least in modified form, by the rest of the *yishuv*. Yemenite performers, composers, choreographers, and artists have made important contributions to general Palestinian Jewish and Israeli culture and show business. On the other hand, the Yemenite artists have received the cooperation of non-Yemenites in the adaptation of their works, and preparation for performance in modern settings and media. This enthusiastic reception has continued to provide inspiration, motivation, and rewards, so that the traditions have been reinforced and are flowering today. There is economic opportunity and a chance for fame for successful artists, which serves as a source of pride for the whole ethnic group. Thus, once again, we see a propitious convergence of imported tradition and reward and reinforcement in the new context.

Conclusions

An Israeli social scientist once said to me, "It is easy to play the game of 'what they brought with them from the old country,'" implying, of course, that it is a naive pastime. But if it is "easy," perhaps it is because it is parsimonious. It is simple, logical, and may accord with the facts. If a particular people seems to have been characterized by certain practices, behaviors, and attitudes at time A, and if those same traits can be seen among the same people in a new setting at time B, it is surely a waste of effort and ingenuity to attempt to explain these phenomena primarily as the result of creative forces in the new society.

In the present case this seems all the more true since the same complex of traits does not seem to apply to any other group in the society. The Yemenite combination of residence, local organization, religious practice, involvement with heritage, and attitudes toward work, expenditure, and display is quite distinctive. Is it conceivable that this cultural complex could have been created *de novo* in Israel, as a response to economic and political conditions, yet not be found among some other groups similarly placed in the economic and political structure?

The Yemenite way, the "style"[24] that we have described, is not a "working-class culture." Alex Weingrod has suggested that there is an emerging "Israeli working-class culture," a culture based on a stratum "composed primarily of persons of Middle Eastern origin . . . ."[25] I have doubts about this hypothesis in general (I doubt very much that the majority of Moroccan, Iranian, Iraqi, Egyptian, Kurdish, Turkish, Tunisian, Tripolitanian, and Indian Jews are blending into one "working-class culture"), but I am sure that the traits Weingrod selects as typifying this class are inadequate to capture the Yemenite cultural reality. (This is not to deny that there are some Yemenites who do some of the things that Weingrod says characterize this class. There are, indeed, Yemenites who exhibit passionate support for their local soccer teams.)

Furthermore, Yemenite ethnicity is not just for the working class. Religious learning and practice, ceremonial and the carrying out of *mitsvot*, residence with fellow Yemenites, hard work, and thrift can be for anyone. As Berreby noted almost thirty years ago, "The most developed (*évolué*) Yemenites don't want to renounce their sociocultural characteristics, which they consider as the precious and authentic heritage of Judaism."[26]

Nor is Yemenite ethnicity in any sense typical of a general "Oriental" ethnic group. Swirski and Katzir claim that the "collective experience of life in Israel" is providing Asian and African immigrants "the major components of the 'cultural package'" to become a genuine (composite) ethnic group.[27] As evidence they offer what they believe are similarities in voting behavior, crime and delinquency rates, and interethnic marriage. Both their premises and their data are very questionable, but in any case the Yemenites offer no support for the idea.[28]

Yemenite ethnicity today, in all of its aspects, is obviously the result of a combination of causes and factors, involving both the culture and expectations they brought with them and conditions in Israel at various times and places. It is manifest and undeniable that today's Yemenites do many things that they first learned about in 1948, or earlier in Palestine. Today they are nurses, lawyers, metallurgists, teachers, military officers, bureaucrats, labor organizers, party officials, Knesset members, deputy ministers, and voters. All these are new roles with new behaviors.

Similarly, much behavior common in Yemen has been modified or extinguished in Israel. Young Yemenites are controlling their fertility and the size of their families; the role of women and sexual segregation have been greatly changed, as have courting and mate selection.[29] Family organization and authority have apparently been changed considerably as well.[30] There are, however, other realms of behavior that continue very much as in Yemen (such as synagogue life), and still others that, I believe, have been *reinforced* in the new country. And these are some of the very practices and traits that give the Yemenites their distinctive reputation and visibility.

The Transmission and Maintenance of Yemenite Israeli Culture

Culture

I contend that Yemenite ethnicity has a definite cultural component in addition to boundaries, symbolic aspects, and an actual or potential political dimension. This culture has behavioral implications and is not merely symbolic or emblematic. But I should make it clear what I do and do not mean by "culture."

To begin with the negative, culture is not an actual system, internally consistent, something with a life of its own, capable of action. Culture should not be reified, although it so often is, along with such ideas as "society," "the state," and "capitalism." Cultures are not clearly defined entities with fixed personnel, boundaries, and characteristics. Culture does not operate through a set of conditioned responses, nor does it consist of a definite collection of customs and institutions.

My concept of culture is an "ideational" one and has elements in common with Keesing's, building upon those of Goodenough and Geertz. In Goodenough's words,

> A society's culture consists of whatever it is one has to know or believe in order to operate in a manner acceptable to its members.[31]

> Culture . . . consists of standards for deciding what is . . . for deciding what can be . . . for deciding how one feels about it . . . for deciding what to do about it, and . . . for deciding how to go about doing it.[32]

As Keesing adds, "So reconceived, cultures are epistemologically in the same realm as language...as inferred ideational codes lying behind the realm of observable events."[33] But these codes, these general patterns available to individuals who share a culture, are not fixed or determinative in a direct and simple manner. While these codes must be shared in general outline, behavioral outcomes are variable. The code is differentially shared among individuals and subgroups. No one person can, or has to, know "the whole code," even if there were such a thing. And just as there is a constant production of argots and dialects in language, so there are subgroupings of cultural understandings in regions, villages and towns, and within occupational and ethnic groups.

Keesing writes,

> [Culture is a person's] *theory of what his fellows know, believe, and mean*, his theory of the code being followed, the game being played, in the society into which he was born. It is this theory to which a native actor *refers* in interpreting the unfamiliar or the ambiguous, in interacting with strangers . . . and with which he creates the stage on which the games of life are played . . .
>
> We can recognize that not every individual shares precisely the same theory of the cultural code, that not every individual knows about all sectors of the culture. Thus a cultural description is always an abstracted composite.[34]

This conception of culture recognizes variation, only partial sharing and choice, in *any* society. All of these sources of uncertainty and unpredictability are multiplied in complex societies such as Israel, with its many ethnic groups, its veterans and newcomers, and its differences in religiosity and socioeconomic status. There are many variations, and the individual may be presented with many choices among alternative cultural models. "Culture can be employed strategically and should not be conceptualized as a conditioned response. Usage of culture requires motivation and, in particular, identification with those who use the cultural items."[35]

On the other hand, it is also true that much of a person's culture lies below the level of awareness and thus may guide behavior without his being conscious of alternatives. To add to our picture of complexity, then, we have *both* conscious choices among alternative styles and identification with different groups in the society and unconscious conformity to the behavior one thinks is expected by the significant others with whom one is in regular interaction.

It is my contention that a great many Israelis of Yemenite origin continue, both consciously and unconsciously, to act in terms of a *Yemenite Israeli* cultural code, *along with other choices*. In the next sections we shall consider how the Yemenite cultural component is being maintained and transmitted.

Transmission

Kiryat Eliahu's Yemenite high school students of the mid-1970s had gone to school in ethnically mixed classes since they were five or six years old, if not younger. Most of their teachers were not Yemenites; often they were Ashkenazi. They grew up with radio and television, media which normally reflect prevailing "general Israeli" standards, attitudes, and ideology—again usually Ashkenazi-influenced. (The other influences reflected in Israeli television are American and British.) There is no denying the impact and significance of these influences. The ten Yemenite students in our survey all consider themselves "Israeli in every respect" and project the very clear attitude that ethnicity plays little role in their friendships, their thoughts about marriage, or their evaluation of others. In this they agree with their classmates of other ethnic backgrounds. (Eight of them also claim that they have never personally felt any discrimination.)

The socialization of Yemenite youth by non-Yemenites does not end with graduation. The men will spend three years in the army, and men and women will enter fields which have their own professional characteristics and demands: industry, teaching, bureaucracy, and the military. Some will continue studying in teachers' seminaries and universities. All of these will lead them to new colleagues, friendships, influences, and attitudes. None of these is trivial.

On the other hand, their mothers and fathers, their aunts and uncles, and their grandparents also embody the Yemenite heritage, with *its* attitudes, values, sentiments, and expectations. These are the people they knew *before* they went off to the first grade, and the people to whom they return after school. Most of their neighbors—or at least the ones they interact with—are also Yemenites. Every *shabbat*, for most men, is first spent in the synagogue; afterward men and women visit with other Yemenites. Some of their most enjoyable celebrations, involving the most emotion, are with their fellow ethnics, as is much of the traveling they have done outside of school and youth movements. For many, their after-school and off-the-job social relations are primarily with other Yemenites.[36]

Kiryat Eliahu's Yemenite youth may have their own youth culture, but they are still very close to their elders. Their parents are generally in their forties and fifties, were born in Yemen, and lived there long enough to have been socialized in that culture. Their older uncles, aunts, and grandparents were already mature adults before their emigration. The heritage from Yemen is not at all remote.

In a few years these former high school students will be faced with the prospect of choosing mates, finding places to live, deciding how many children to have, and when and how to raise these children. They will be pressured by their families and their peers. Free choice in marriage is the rule, but others besides the couple have an interest in these choices and may exercise influence. Relatives and friends are also concerned with where the young couple settles and how they bring up their children. The influence of parents and family may be more powerful, more real, more filled with emotion as well as immediate rewards and punishments, than is that which comes from fellow-workers and from society in general. These familial and neighborhood significant others have a great deal to bestow emotionally, socially, and materially. They can also punish by withholding support.

The cultural elements of ethnicity are maintained in part through the social relations of the family, the peer group, the community, and the ethnic network, reinforced by emotion, sentiment, and familiarity. Other things being equal, it is with fellow Yemenites that they feel most comfortable; they have the most in common (*safa mshutefet*, a "common language") and can be most at ease. Ward Goodenough discusses the theoretical basis for this phenomenon in the "perception of shared competence,"[37] and A. L. Epstein remarks on its presence among Africans on the "Copperbelt" in Zambia and among American Jews.[38] But Edwin O'Connor, in his novel *The Edge of Sadness*, captures the notion beautifully in the following assertion of one Irish-American priest to another:

> We all know what a real parish is. A real parish is an old-time parish. One with a fine, big old-fashioned, well-kept church with— and here's the important things—lots of Irish to put inside it! People like ourselves, Hugh. The kind of people you grew up with; the kind of people you like; the kind of people you *understand*: comic, picturesque, a little sharp in the tongue at times, maybe, but decent, God-fearing, generous, and devout. The kind of people who can sing "Ave Maria" inside the church, but can give you a chorus of "There's a Little Devil Dancing in Your Laughing Irish Eyes" on the way home.[39]

Yemenites are certainly not the only people in Israel whose ethnic background plays an important, multidimensional role. But the Yemenites are one of the most distinctive for several reasons. Their devotion to ethnic neighborhoods guarantees that most Yemenites grow up in the midst of a pool of fellow ethnics. Secondly, there is great stress on loyalty to the group, and acute awareness of their heritage and traditions, bolstered by the religiosity, which was not undercut by any trends toward secularization at the time of the exodus from Yemen. The music, poetry, and other arts that mean so much both within and beyond the community also play a unique role. In these ways the Yemenites are unusual in the degree to which ethnicity influences their lives.

Ethnicity, however, comprises only a portion of the complex cultural competences which Yemenites carry around with them. As with any other element, its impact is variable from place to place, group to group, and individual to individual. The ethnic element is cross-cut by education, occupation, social status, and community. There are many available reference groups; influences flood in from all sides. There may be rebellion and attempted escape, or change throughout the life cycle from rebellion to return. There is no automatic conformity to a set of absolute norms. The effects of ethnicity are not equally strong for all members. In dealing with ethnicity in a complex society like Israel, as with cultural behavior in *any* society, we are dealing with tendencies and percentages, not with absolutes.

Prospects for Maintenance

Considering all of the changes which have occurred to the Yemenites of Kiryat Eliahu and the rest of Israel over the past three decades, what is the possibility that the cultural element of Yemenite ethnicity can be maintained in the future? If there is increasing education, and greater participation in higher-status occupations and in bureaucracy and politics, how can Yemenite ethnicity be maintained? Won't there soon remain *at most* only trace elements of symbolic ethnicity—some folklore, some foods, and possibly some terms and jokes, much as American Jews use Yiddish? (This is what Herbert Gans claims is the case with ethnicity in the United States today.)[40] Or, if political and economic conditions are bad enough, perhaps there will be some political uses for ethnicity. But what of the attitudes, the values, and the distinctive activities and social relations? I believe there are several reasons to think that, for many, these will continue to play significant roles.

In the first place, the same factors which account for the persistence of a distinctive Yemenite cultural style in Israel today—distinct from what it was a generation ago in Yemen—will continue to be significant in the future. Insofar as individuals and families remain within the same neighborhood, marry within the community, and attend the same synagogues, they will continue to be influenced by the same kinds of Yemenite reference groups. The content of this code may change to some extent, as it already has, but it can remain specific to the Yemenite-Israelis. As Kobrin and Goldscheider observe with respect to European ethnic patterns in Rhode Island, "The changing nature of ethnicity cannot be viewed simply as an indication of the diminishing importance of the ethnic factor or of the 'assimilation' of ethnic communities."[41]

Secondly, there may be no advantage in changing these values or behaviors in favor of other available choices. Yemenites may be aware of the cultural styles of others, and while some may emulate these, the remainder may reject the alternatives. This rejection can result both because of preference for traditional values and behavior and because their own represent quite successful adaptive strategies. They may believe in their particular family and religious values, in their version of *derekh erets*. They may think that hard work, thrift, and the maintenance of a good reputation are valuable for success.

Third, as time goes by, the older generation, against whom youth rebels, will no longer be so obviously "old-fashioned," even "primitive," in the eyes of their children. Instead of the unworldly-seeming old men, and illiterate, simple-seeming old ladies who were the parents of the first generation, the present and future parental generation consists of people who have succeeded within Israeli society. They are (and more will be) teachers (even principals), and soldiers (even officers), nurses, doctors, lawyers, engineers, social workers, bureaucrats, and elected officials, as well as technically competent electricians, metallurgists, musicians, and artists. There will be less reason to see the Yemenite tradition as incompatible with modern Israeli life.

Finally, there is a growing development of what Milton Gordon called *ethclass*.[42] Whereas most Yemenites began more or less equal in terms of wealth and educational background, there is a growing diversity of socioeconomic status. Although the differences are not very great, and the links between the top and the bottom of the social scale are many and close, growing education and occupational mobility will undoubtedly increase the degree of differentiation.

As some members of the community do better in the world, and especially as they gain more education and enter professions which offer a greater range of contacts in the wider Israeli world, their interests and ambitions will tend to diverge from those of their neighbors and kinsmen who are skilled workers. Rather than simply desert their ethnic fellows, however, it is most natural and normal for them to seek the company of other educated Yemenites. It is with *these* others whom they share the most: not only the education and the work experience, but the ethnic background as well. They have the greatest common understandings. They have come from the same origins, have faced the same struggles, and perhaps go home to the same situations.

At first it may be difficult for the upwardly mobile individuals because the pool of those they can draw upon for the most intimate friendship is small, especially in a community the size of Kiryat Eliahu. But with time this pool will grow, and we may expect that there will be new organizations established to cater to the interests and the needs of these better-educated, higher-status people. (There already are Yemenite organizations that draw their membership from among the young, but these encompass a relatively wide range of backgrounds and statuses.) In cities all over Israel new synagogues are being established as such young people come together. Ethclass is a most natural and important phenomenon in modern society, combining the elements of shared status and interest with the emotional, cultural, and sentimental one of shared ethnicity. Gordon's idea has not gotten the prominence it deserves.

There is no reason for the Yemenite elite to flee their people, their culture, or their heritage. The contrary is true. For one thing that tradition embodies significant values, ones which they have been brought up to believe, and which are, at the same time, core values in Judaism. They can be seen as part of the heritage of the whole Jewish people. Secondly, being Yemenite confers a certain distinction. On the basis of his work in 1954 Berreby wrote, "Indeed, the most westernized Yemenites deem their cultural heritage to be richer and more valuable, from the Judeo-National point of view, than the new culture" (i.e., the developing secular culture of Israel).[43] This is still largely the case today, thirty years later. Educated young people are likely to be quite eloquent and enthusiastic about the Yemenite tradition, while students, scholars, writers, and artists are hard at work studying and adding to the tradition. (See Postscript.) At least for the foreseeable future, Yemenite culture should continue to play an important role among the elite as well as among simpler folk.

Cultural Variation in Israel

Israel, like the United States, has a uniformitarian ideology, a powerful national culture, and very real and significant ethnic subcultures. Ethnically based social relations and cultural codes coexist with the expectation, in the Israeli case, that all Jews are, or soon will be, pretty much the same.[44] How is this contradiction possible?

In Israel, as in the United States, there is a developing pattern of behavioral conformity and mutual understandings in multiethnic public contexts, but the maintenance of ethnically specific behavior in more intimate contexts. What Milton Gordon describes as the situation in the United States is valid for Israel as well:

> The network of organizations, informal social relationships, and institutional activities which makes up the ethnic subsociety tends to pre-empt most or all primary group relationships, while secondary relationships across ethnic lines are carried out in the "larger society" principally in the spheres of economic and occupational life, civic

and political activity, public and private nonparochial education and mass entertainment. All of these relationships, primary and secondary, are contained within the boundaries of common political allegiance and responsibility to the politico- legal demands and expectations of American [substitute Israeli] nationality.[45]

Yemenite behavior and social life retain their "Yemenite" character above all in such settings as the home, the synagogue, the ethnic neighborhood, and in the context of the celebrations of the life-cycle rituals. In schools, on the job, in the army, and in the shops, Yemenites participate with others on a nonethnic basis. In public settings they behave for the most part like other Israelis. Non-Yemenites who serve in army units may be aware that some of their Yemenite buddies like to carry small jars of a hot sauce (*skhug*) to add to their food. Perhaps they have noticed that the Yemenites try to find ten men for a *minyan* for prayers each morning and evening, and use a variant pronunciation and melody when they pray. But these small differences may seem to be all that distinguishes them from others. (Of course any observant soldier would also want to participate in public prayer.) Otherwise they behave pretty much like everyone else: talking about favorite army subjects, especially about women, cars, and the cost of living. In the same way, those who go to school together and those who work together tend to interact according to the rules, norms, and expectations of those settings.

It is a standard Israeli belief, once common among social scientists as well, that the army is the setting where all of Israel's Jews become one. The military life and the shared dangers and experiences are said to be the crucible for forging this commonality. Perhaps it affects identity and sentiment, but it is doubtful that it has the same impact on more general cultural codes. A Yemenite friend, a former paratrooper, reports that in the army, on duty, everyone is governed by a special set of norms; everyone plays the role of soldier. Home and community are left behind. Nor, he claims, is it usual to discuss ethnic differences in mixed company.

The norms for behavior in public places and those which hold in more intimate settings may be quite different. More than that, when the soldiers go home, and when the school friends separate, they may return to neighborhoods, activities, and families which differ considerably from each other. (We certainly expect this to be true in the case of class differences. Why should it be surprising for ethnic ones?) Unless people of different ethnic backgrounds are intermarried, or have particularly close interethnic friendships or an unusual degree of curiosity, they may remain quite ignorant of each other's "backstage" life in the primary group sphere. And this ignorance is mutual.[46]

In Israel, as in the United States, the degree of mutual interethnic ignorance is striking. As a general rule outsiders haven't a clue as to what goes on in the private settings of others. If the surface differences are quite obvious, and the relations between groups are hostile, then we may get the classic "prejudiced" stereotypes which emphasize the supposed differences between groups. When, on the other hand, relations are not hostile, and the public behavior of the members of two or more groups is basically congruent, then we find that one assumes the others to be "just like us."

Mutual ignorance of ethnic difference is a prevalent and barely recognized phenomenon in modern complex societies. Children of different backgrounds can go to school with each other for twelve years, play ball together after school, and still have no knowledge of what happens to each other when they go home, when they attend religious services or go away for weekends to attend ethnic festivals. This may be even more the case with neighbors who live next door to each other but share far fewer common activities than do schoolmates.

In America, most non-Jews have little idea as to what Jewish life, belief, and culture are like. Nor do outsiders have any sense of the life of the Dutch Reformed farmers of Wisconsin,[47] or even of the existence of the "Russian-German" wheat farmers of the Great Plains. They are unlikely to be aware of the culture and sentiments of Armenian-Americans, or of the patterns of Italian-American life such as those described by Richard Gambino.[48]

The same is true in Israel. Few non-Yemenites have any idea of what Yemenites really do after school and off the job. Nor do Yemenites know much about the origins and culture of their Beni Israel neighbors from Bombay. There cannot be many Israelis who know that Kafkazim consider themselves different from Gruzinim, and it is doubtful whether many are aware of the significant Turkish Jewish population in their midst. But the members of these ethnic groups themselves know, although they, in their turn, may be as unaware of the differences among others.

The pattern of conformity in public settings, ethnic differentiation in private contexts, and mutual interethnic ignorance permits the perpetuation of cultural differences. To some extent it might be said to guarantee it, insofar as people are not even aware that what they do is different from what others do. What models can they emulate if the intimate behavior of others is hidden from them?[49]

Differences in values and attitudes, and in practice and behavioral style, are not merely symbolic. Nor are they of the same order as the conscious adoption and use of aspects of "heritage," or the politicization of ethnicity. These may or may not accompany the cultural differences. All of these elements of ethnicity can vary independently.[50]

In the case under consideration in this book I have argued that there are significant cultural differences associated with Yemenite ethnicity. The ethnic boundary does in fact contain cultural content as well as social identity. The Yemenites of Kiryat Eliahu, and of many other communities, seem to operate in terms of a distinctive cultural code, a set of ideas as to how a person is expected to behave.

While the Yemenites may be distinctive in the degree to which they maintain and adapt their traditions, they are by no means unique among Israel's Jewish ethnic groups in this respect. To a greater or lesser extent the members of many such country-of-origin groups have made similar adaptations, or are in the process of doing so. My experience with the Moroccan community convinces me that they, too, have distinctive values, attitudes, behavioral codes, although the picture is complicated by major differences among them in socioeconomic status and culture derived from their communities of origin. As Harvey Goldberg noted in a general statement about ethnicity in Israel in the late 1980s, "Immigrants and their children have been socialized into Israeli skills, roles, and styles, while preserving and reshaping significant elements of their particular traditions." While relatively little of the social science literature to date reflects this fact, the work of such anthropologists as Shlomo Deshen on South Tunisians, Moshe Shokied on Moroccans from the Atlas Mountains, Laurence Loeb on the Habbani Jews, Judith Goldstein on Iranain Jews, and Harvey Goldberg on Tripolitanians and other North African Jews, points toward this conclusion.[51]

Conclusions

Yemenite culture, as it appears today, is not a fossilized remnant of something imported from Yemen, nor was it created *de novo* in Israel by social and economic circumstances alone. It is neither unchanging and "pure" nor "deformed," "degraded," and about to suffer an inevitable decline. It represents a changing, but distinctive, set of guides for behavior and evaluation associated with a particular group of people. Many former customs and ideas have been abandoned and new ways adopted. Parts of old traditions have been elaborated, while in some cases new patterns have been adopted with a ready will and made the basis for further developments.

The Yemenites of Kiryat Eliahu are not downtrodden or passive; they do not stand trembling before the forces of modernization, nor are they being forced to, or choosing to, give up all of their ways in order to conform to some ideal "new Israeli." They are a self-aware, proud people who see no conflict between being Israeli and being Yemenite Jews.

Notes

1. This view, widely shared by social scientists, journalists, and some of the public, depends heavily and uncritically on aggregated statistics and impressions derived from "worst cases." The statistics are usually presented as "African- and Asian-born" versus "European- and American-born." We lack studies which distinguish between different country-of-origin groups or between different communities in Israel. The effect is to lose the meaningful variations and obfuscate causes and results. There is insufficient consideration of the middle range, of specific cases, of successes, and of variation.

2. See Judith Nagata, *Malaysian Mosaic* (Vancouver: University of British Columbia Press, 1979), p. 188.

3. See James McKay, "An Exploratory Synthesis of Primordial and Mobilizationist Approaches to Ethnic Phenomena," *Ethnic and Racial Studies* 5:399, 1982. Italics in original.

4. Stephen Steinberg, *The Ethnic Myth: Race, Ethnicity, and Class in America* (New York: Atheneum, 1981), p. 262.

5. Shlomo Swirski attempts to remove from ethnicity in Israel any meaning other than disenfranchisement: ethnics are people who have been prohibited from the expression of their humanity. Such an interpretation can only be the result of ideology and ignorance of the realities of life in communities other than his own. (See Shlomo Swirski, *Not Disadvantaged, But Disenfranchised: Oriental and Ashkenazim in Israel*, 1981. [Hebrew]) These findings also demonstrate just how wrong Joseph Ben-David was when he wrote, "The important point is that even groups hailing from the same country do not see, in their common origin or in the cultural traditions therein involved, any important or vital social value." Joseph Ben-David, "Ethnic Differences or

Social Change?" in C. Frankenstein, ed., *Between Past and Future*, (Jerusalem: Henrietta Szold Foundation, 1953.)

6. Nagata, *Malaysian Mosaic*, p. 190.

7. Max Weinreich has presented a similar argument with respect to the maintenance of distinctive Jewish culture in Europe. Taking exception to the "ghetto myth," he argues that "the basic causes for the rise and continuing existence of Ashkenaz must be sought not in curbs imposed from outside or in certain institutions but in the vitality of the society which, in spite of seemingly overwhelming odds, managed to keep its head above water . . . . It is the positive factor of striving for meaningful survival and not the negative one of exclusion or rejection, that is paramount in Jewish cultural history." (See Max Weinreich, "The Reality of Jewishness versus the Ghetto Myth: The Sociolinguistic Roots of Yiddish," in *To Honor Roman Jakobson: Essays on the Occasion of His Seventieth Birthday*, Vol. III, 1967, pp. 2204-2205.)

8. W. L. Yancey, E. P. Ericksen, and R. N. Juliani, "Emergent Ethnicity: A Review and Reformulation," *American Sociological Review* 41:391, 1976.

9. Shlomo Swirski and Sara Katzir, *Orientals and Ashkenazim in Israel: An Emerging Dependency Relationship* (Haifa: Research and Critique Series, 1978).

10. See Deborah Bernstein and Shlomo Swirski, "The Rapid Economic Development of Israel and the Emergence of the Ethnic Division of Labour," *British Journal of Sociology* 33:82, 1982.

11. Yancey et al., "Emergent Ethnicity," p. 400.

12. Yael Katzir, "Preservation of Jewish Ethnic Identity in Yemen: Segregation and Integration as Boundary Maintenance Mechanisms," *Comparative Studies in Society and History* 24:278, 1982.

13. Richard L. Ehrlich, ed., *Immigrants in Industrial America, 1850-1920* (Charlottesville: University Press of Virginia, 1977), pp. ix-x.

14. See Vivian Z. Klaff, "Residence and Integration in Israel: A Mosaic of Segregated Peoples," *Ethnicity* 4:103-121, 1977.

15. Yancey et al., "Emergent Ethnicity," p. 392.

16. Norman Berdichevsky, "The Persistence of the Yemeni Quarter in an Israeli Town," *Ethnicity* 4:306, 1977.

17. On the preference of European Jews to live in their own quarters, see Max Weinreich, "Reality of Jewishness," p. 2201.

18. See Yafah Berlovitz, "The Image of the Yemenite in the Literature of the First *Aliyot*," *Pe'amim* 10:100-101, 1981. [Hebrew]

19. *Encyclopaedia Judaica*, Vol. 5 (Jerusalem: Keter, 1972), p. 1099.

20. Yehuda Nini, "Immigration and Assimilation: The Yemenite Jews," *Jerusalem Quarterly* 21:94-95, 1981.

21. S. N. Eisenstadt quotes a Moroccan immigrant on the subject of work: "I do not want to do here all the things that only the Arab riff-raff did in Morocco. I did not come to Israel to become like one of them. We are better than they,

we are stronger—why should I perform all this manual labour? . . . At home they would laugh at us for it . . . ." Even more strongly, another North African immigrant said, "I have many friends here, but we do not want to meet and see one another because we are so ashamed of ourselves . . . we are no longer human beings." (See S. N. Eisenstadt, *The Absorption of Immigrants*, 1954, pp. 116, 120-121.) For some Moroccans, at least, such labor is definitely demeaning and contrary to their sense of honor. Their persona is distinctly different from that of the Yemenites. They wish to project a different image.

22. Yochanan Peres, *Ethnic Relations in Israel* (Tel Aviv: Tel Aviv University Press, 1976), p. 55. [Hebrew]

23. Cf. Fanny Raphael, "Rosh Ha'Ayin: The Development of an Immigrant Settlement," in C. Frankenstein, ed., *Between Past and Future* (Jerusalem: Henrietta Szold Foundation, 1953), p. 206.

24. See Anya Peterson Royce, *Ethnic Identity: Strategies of Diversity* (Bloomington: Indiana University Press, 1982), pp. 27-28.

25. Alex Weingrod, "Recent Trends in Israeli Ethnicity," *Ethnic and Racial Studies* 2:62, 1979.

26. Jean-Jacques Berreby, "De l'Intégration des Juifs Yéménites en Israel," *L'Année Sociologique*, 3rd series: 119, 1956.

27. Swirski and S. Katzir, *Orientals and Ashkehazim*, p. 38.

28. Laurence D. Loeb makes the same point regarding the Habbani. They have their own identity as Habbani, and can generally also see themselves as Yemenite, but "I have never met an informant who would characterize himself as 'oriental.'" See "Folk Models of Habbani Ethnic Identity," in A. Weingrod, ed., *Studies in Israeli Ethnicity* (New York: Gordon & Breach, 1985), p. 213.

29. See Judah Matras, "On Changing Matchmaking, Marriage, and Fertility in Israel: Some Findings, Problems, and Hypotheses," *American Journal of Sociology* 79:364-388, 1973; Lisa Gilad, "Changing Notions of Proper Conduct: The Case of Jewish Unmarried Yemeni Women in an Israeli New Town," *Cambridge Anthropology* 7:44-56, 1982.

30. See Yael Katzir, "The Effects of Resettlement on the Status and Role of Yemeni Jewish Women: The Case of Ramat Oranim, Israel" (doctoral dissertation, University of California, Berkeley, 1976).

31. Quoted in Roger M. Keesing, "Theories of Culture," *Annual Review of Anthropology* 3:77, 1974.

32. Ward H. Goodenough, *Cooperation in Change* (New York: Russell Sage Foundation, 1963), p. 259.

33. Keesing, "Theories," p. 77.

34. *Ibid*, p. 89.

35. Gary A. Fine and Sherryl Kleinman, "Rethinking Subculture: An Interactionist Analysis," *American Journal of Sociology* 85:13, 1979.

36. It should be remembered that Kiryat Eliahu's Yemenites represent a particularly well-integrated community in a very heterogeneous population.

There are other communities in which the Yemenites are more intensively and exclusively involved with each other in school and at work.

37. Ward H. Goodenough, *Culture, Language, and Society* (Reading, Mass.: Addison-Wesley, 1971), p. 38.

38. A. L. Epstein, *Ethos and Identity: Three Studies in Ethnicity* (London: Tavistock, 1978), pp. 105-106.

39. Edwin O'Connor, *The Edge of Sadness* (Boston: Little, Brown, 1961), p. 418.

40. Herbert J. Gans, "Symbolic Ethnicity: The Future of Ethnic Groups and Cultures in America," *Ethnic and Racial Studies* 2:1-20, 1979.

41. Frances E. Kobrin and Calvin Goldscheider, *The Ethnic Factor in Family Structure and Mobility* (Cambridge, Mass.: Ballinger, 1978), p. 226.

42. Milton M. Gordon, *Assimilation in American Life: The Role of Race, Religion, and National Origins* (New York: Oxford University Press, 1964), p. 51.

43. Berreby, "De l'Intégration," p. 160.

44. It is accepted that Jews and Arabs are different peoples, and there is no expectation that these cultural and national differences will disappear. In the United States it is expected that all those of European origin, at least, will more or less conform to the same "American" model.

45. Gordon, *Assimilation*, p. 37.

46. A. L. Epstein comes to similar conclusions about "intimate culture" and "public culture" and notes that expressions of "intimate" culture may even "escape the sociologist's net." Epstein, *Ethos and Identity*, pp. 111-112; also Goodenough, *Culture, Language*, p. 40.

47. See A. W. van den Ban, "Locality Group Differences in the Adoption of New Farm Practices," *Rural Sociology* 25:308-320, 1960.

48. Richard Gambino, *Blood of My Blood: The Dilemma of the Italian-Americans* (Garden City, N. Y.: Doubleday/Anchor, 1975).

49. Harvey Goldberg demonstrates this point in his study of Tripolitanian Jewish immigrants living on a *moshav*. He found that "most of the adult villagers ignored the cultural differences between themselves and the 'outside world' and for the most part were content in this ignorance." As for the children and youth, "they were exposed to a relative homogeneous cultural environment in which the main values and role models that they encountered were those of their parents and other villagers." Harvey E. Goldberg, *Cave Dwellers and Citrus Growers: A Jewish Community in Libya and Israel* (Cambridge: Cambridge University Press, 1972), p. 2.

50. See Andrew M. Greeley, *That Most Distressful Nation: The Taming of the American Irish* (Chicago: Quadrangle, 1972), pp. 7-8.

51. Harvey Goldberg, "The Changing Meaning of Ethnic Affiliation," *The Jerusalem Quarterly*, # 44, Fall 1987, p. 50. See also: "Historical and Cultural Dimensions of Ethnic Phenomena in Israel," in A. Weingrod, ed., *Studies in*

Israeli Ethnicity: After the Ingathering (New York: Gordon and Breach, 1985); J. Goldstein, "Iranian Ethnicity in Israel: The Performance of Identity," in A. Weingrod, ed., *Studies*: L. Loeb, "Folk Models of Habbani Ethnic Studies," in A. Weingrod, ed., *Studies*; M. Shokied, *The Dual Heritage: Immigrants from the Atlas Mountains in an Israeli Village* (Manchester: Manchester University Press, 1971); H. Goldberg, *Cave Dwellers and Citrus Growers; Shlomo Deshen*, *"Political Ethnicity and Cultural Ethnicity in Israel During the 1960s," in Abner Cohen, ed., Urban Ethnicty* (London: Tavistock, 1974); Shlomo Deshen and Moshe Shokied, *The Predicament of Homecoming: Cultural and Social Life of North African Immigrants in Israel* (Ithaca: Cornell University Press, 1974).

10

Postscript—1987

In 1987, ten years after I had left Kiryat Eliahu, I returned for three more months of intensive fieldwork. I wanted to find out what had happened to the young people who were still in school, or were just beginning their careers and the formation of their families in 1977. I intended to investigate (a) their educational and occupational attainments; and (b) the effects of social mobility on their choices in marriage and residence, as well as on their attitudes to and involvement with religion and with Yemenite ethnicity.

A man or woman who was above the age of forty in 1975, in mid-career and with teenage children, would have been at least fourteen years old at the time of emigration from Yemen. Much of his or her socialization took place in South Arabia. Those who were twenty-five to thirty years old in 1975, were born to parents who had just come from abroad, without "modern" education or training. Times were difficult and resources very limited in the 1950s. Those who were fifteen to twenty, however, had parents who were better established in Israel, with more education and knowledge of the country, and they grew up in a more affluent world. It was these younger *sabras* that I proposed to study.

In 1987 I devoted almost all my time to finding out about those Yemenites who were then in their late teens to their early forties. Part of the work involved the acquisition of information for as many individuals as possible regarding education, occupation, place of residence, marriage status, ethnicity and occupation of spouse, and religiosity. The other part was devoted to open-ended interviews of couples and individuals, both men and women in about equal numbers. These discussions, which sometimes went on for three to five hours, dealt primarily with their attitudes towards marriage, friendships, religion, Yemenite identity, values, traditions, etc., in short, with ethnicity in its various aspects. Since I was already familiar to many of these people from my earlier visit, and knew a great deal about their parents, siblings, and culture, it was usually very easy to gain access to them. Even people who didn't know me and were hesitant at first to talk to a stranger usually soon warmed to the subject of their own lives and feelings. This was some of the most enjoyable fieldwork I have ever conducted, with people who understood what I was after and were happy to discuss it. They were articulate, aware, and thoughtful, and I am very appreciative of their help and interest.

The Problem

Eliezer Ben-Rafael, Hannah Ayalon, and Stephen Sharot have argued that, as people of African and Asian origin ("ethnics") advance in social and economic status in Israeli society they tend to leave their ethnic group behind, with the effect that the ethnics remain lower class, while the middle class individuals pass into the general population as just plain "Israeli." According to this view, given socioeconomic success and the opportunity to join those from other ethnic backgrounds in the middle class, the costs of maintaining ethnic identification are not offset by the advantages, such as solidarity and ethnic mobilization, that are useful for those at the lower end of of the socioeconomic scale. The upwardly mobile will therefore choose to divorce themselves from their fellow ethnics.[1]

As is evident from my discussion in Chapter 9, I place more importance on the positive benefits and attractions of ethnicity, on the "natural," "unconscious," culturally-derived elements of ethnicity, as well as on the significance of pride in one's people and traditions. In contrast to Ben-Rafael and his colleagues, I expected the development of *ethclasses* so as to produce middle class as well as working class Yemenite, Moroccan, Turkish, Iraqi Jewish Israelis. In my 1987 research I intended to compare my findings against these views of class and ethnicity.

Education and Occupation

As predicted in Chapter 5, there has been a continuing rapid upward curve of educational attainment and occupational status since 1977. Many students are continuing to study after they complete the twelve grades of secondary school. Some take two year courses as teachers and nursery school teachers, or at the Technion and other technical institutes in order to achieve the rank of "technologist" (*handesa'i*) with specialities in electronics, computers, metallurgy, etc. And an increasing number are going to four year academic institutions, studying a variety of subjects, gaining the background for such careers as teaching, engineering, social work, business, law, and medicine (one doctor to date). This was not a completely new development in 1987, but the increase in the numbers is striking.

Of 233 men and women born from 1946 through 1967 (thus from forty-one to twenty years old in 1987, when these data were collected) a total of 121, 51.9 percent, had continued for at least one year or more of post-secondary education, with 48 percent completing at least two years of study. Fifty-three of these, or 22.8 percent, opted for four-year degrees in universities. For those born since the mid-1950s the percentage of those who are studying beyond secondary school rises to over 60 percent. These figures are striking not merely in comparison to the educational attainments of their parents, but also when we compare them to the Israeli population at large.

Table 1 Years of Post-Secondary Education

(a) All Israel (x)

Age	13-15 years	16+ years	Total Post-Secondary
35-44	18%	19.2%	37.2%
25-34	20.8%	16.9%	37.7%

(b) Kiryat Eliahu Yemenites (n = 233; absolute numbers in parentheses)

35-41 (58)	25.9% (15)	10.3% (6)	36.2%
25-34 (134)	29.1% (39)	26.9% (36)	56%
20-24 (41)	34.1% (14)	26.8% (11)	60.9% (y)

(x) Source: *Statistical Abstract of Israel*, 1987, #38, p. 572.[2]
(y) These figures include a few individuals who are still in school.

In 1986 over 37 percent of the Jewish population of Israel aged twenty-five to forty-four had from thirteen to sixteen or more years of schooling.[2] Of these, approximately 19 percent had thirteen to fifteen years and about 18 percent had sixteen years or more. It is clear that the Yemenites of Kiryat Eliahu are attending university with greater frequency than do Jews within the population generally, and are continuing to study for at least two years of post-secondary education half again as often as the Israeli population generally. This is true for both men and women.

It is clear, as we predicted earlier, that these people are increasingly availing themselves of general and technical training beyond the post-secondary level to improve their positions and status in society. In this younger cohort there are, among the women, more than twenty-five teachers, nine bookkeepers, an accountant, an assistant bank manager, two computer technologists, a doctor, nine clerks of various sorts, a social worker, and one university graduate working in an investment firm. Among the men are a half dozen engineers, nine technologists, several technicians (a status generally requiring one year of post-secondary training), several teachers, non-commissioned military officers and a major in the air force, men teaching and studying in *yeshivot* (religious academies), bureaucrats and administrators (including the assistant director of a boarding school for Ethiopian Jews and the head of the payroll office of a large firm), a bank worker with ambitions to move to an investment firm, a law clerk, as well as university students, drivers, workers in industry, a nurse, welders, electricians, a carpenter, etc.

There is also a songwriter (living in the U. S.), a calligrapher writing *ktuvot* (marriage contracts), and a photo-journalist. In addition, the spouses of these people, some of whom are not Yemenite, or come from other communities, have a similar range of occupations. It is noteworthy that hardly any of these people are engaged in independent businesses. Continuing the pattern evident a decade earlier, almost all work for large firms, the government, or educational institutions. Several Yemenite women are married to non-Yemenites who own businesses, but the Yemenites themselves do not.[3]

In 1987 I found evidence of a new and unexpected development: at least seven young men had opted to study in religious institutions rather than in universities or other secular schools. This trend seems to be related to the religiosity of the Yemenites and their growing ability to indulge such interests. Most of those Yemenites from Kiryat Eliahu who are teachers work in the religious schools and have a continuing connection with religious education, but now, with increasing well-being, young men who might otherwise go to university or the Technion apparently feel they can afford to continue with their own religious studies, as their elders could not. Some have quit other jobs to return to *yeshivot*. One such man was an aeronautical engineer with a good job in industry. A recent secondary school graduate had a choice between a scholarship for the study of chemical engineering at the Technion, or entry into the pilot's course in the air force, but chose instead to go to a leading yeshiva in Jerusalem.

Another factor in this development is undoubtedly the changing ideological climate in Israel, since about 1980. Recently, ultra-orthodoxy has been much more prominent in the life of the nation. These young men are influenced by the widespread growth of religious activity, the political and intellectual aggressiveness of orthodox groups, and the increased public acceptance of orthodoxy. There is a developing movement to create distinctive Yemenite religious institutions [see below] but these students are attending Ashkenazi-dominated *yeshivot*, some of them connected to extreme orthodox (*haredi*) movements.

Residence

The Yemenite *shkhuna* had changed little physically since my earlier stay. There were three more synagogues, formed as the result of schisms in existing ones. The three tiny grocery stores were no longer in business, but an additional *felafel* stand had opened up, run by a retired air force officer. Otherwise there were no more Yemenite businesses than there had been before. But there was another change underway.

For several reasons, an increasing number of young people were moving out of the *shkhuna*, to other parts of Kiryat Eliahu, to surrounding towns, or even to cities some distance away. Some left in order to live with spouses who came from other towns; others, to pursue educational or occupational opportunities elsewhere, nearer to or in the major cities. But others were leaving for better housing or to get away from a section of town that they believed was no longer the quiet and safe place it once was. In their perception, the old neighborhood had been taken over by rough, crooked, unpleasant and irreligious people of other ethnic backgrounds. They claimed that the crime rate had risen enormously and that it was no longer a nice place to live. They would have liked to stay with their parents and kin and community, but for them the balance was tipped in favor of moving out.

As predicted in Chapter 5, more young couples have moved to the other side of Kiryat Eliahu, where a nucleus of half a dozen yemenite families were living in the 1970s. Today there are more than thirty Yemenite (or half-Yemenite) families there, a 15-20 minute walk from the old center. They have organized a new Yemenite synagogue, which meets in a school, and they are looking for funds to build their own building and furnish it with Torah scrolls and the necessary accoutrements. Most weeks throughout the year they worship at this synagogue, but the walk is not so great, especially in good weather, that they can't attend their families' synagogues in the old *shkhuna* when there is a special occasion, or on the high holidays. (One man walks with son throughout the year in order to maintain his late father's synagogue.) They are also close enough to visit their parents on *shabbat* during the drier and warmer months. And some men have developed the tradition of visiting their mothers' homes on Friday afternoon, perhaps eating a meal there, before returning to their own homes for *shabbat* evening. It is, of course, no problem for them to return for rituals, ceremonies, and holidays. And they have started to reproduce the same kinds of *shabbat* visiting patterns, including *ja'ale*, in their neighborhood.

Some of those who have moved further away have moved to Yemenite sections of such cities as Herzliya, Kiryat Ono, and Jerusalem where they join established Yemenite communities. One thirty-five year old teacher and his wife have joined a new ultra-orthodox all-Yemenite community, recently established on the West Bank, where they can be "truly" Yemenite. Interestingly, as a university student in the 1970s he had seen himself as much more modern and secular than his parents, and just plain "Israeli."

Still others have moved to relatively prestigious communities, such as those surrounding Kiryat Eliahu, which have no Yemenite *shkhuna*, and where, until recently, few Yemenites lived. If they remain religious, as so many of them do, the men will have to attend a nearby non-Yemenite synagogue, often a "Sephardi" one (i. e. Moroccan, Iraqi, etc.). But often, little by little, the Yemenite men in such places find each other, and eventually establish their own synagogue in a central location to which they can all walk. They no longer live in the midst of a Yemenite quarter, but they create a new Yemenite synagogue in a mixed area, as the men did in the new section of Kiryat Eliahu. Thus they and their sons can carry on their distinctive tradition. This has occurred, for example, in Arad and in Eilat, two cities with relatively few Yemenites, and it is evidently happening in the residential districts of other cities, such as Netanya, as young Yemenites move out of the *shkhunot* and into mixed middle class areas.

Marriage

The most striking change has occurred in marriage choices. The trend toward marrying out of the Yemenite group that we saw developing in 1975-77 continued, so that by 1987, for the people in my sample, that figure had risen to 56 percent marrying outside of the group. A total of 22 percent had chosen Jews of European or American background while 34 percent married people from other Asian or African origins. Exactly 50 percent of the men married within the group, but only 38 percent of the women did.

Table 2 Marriages: The Ethnicity of Spouses

Yem.	Yem.				Other			
			Eur/Am		Afr/Asia		Total	
sex	#	%	#	%	#	%	#	%
male n = 76	38	50	13	17	25	33	38	50
female n = 89	34	38	23	26	32	36	55	62
Total n = 165	72	44	36	22	57	34	93	56

Based on my earlier work I did not expect so rapid a change, so I questioned many men and women from the age of eighteen to forty-five, both married and unmarried, about their attitudes to marriage partners. Their reactions throw some light on a few of the considerations that lie behind the business of mate selection.

Above all, these people insisted on the rightness of marriage between Jews of different origins. Over and over I received responses to the effect that, "We are all Jews and Israelis—all one people—and these differences shouldn't matter among us." Or, "It is time for a change, time to reach out and learn from others. Why should we always be among ourselves?" And, "Love, marriage, is a question of luck, chance. It could be (could have been) someone of any background." Both the ideology of Jewish unity and *mizug galuyot*, as well as the values of romantic love and free choice, support marriage out of the *eyda*.[4] They express confidence in their ability to adapt and get along with others. But actual choices may be affected by a variety of perceptions and beliefs about ethnic characteristics.

After voicing support for marrying out, many people would also say that, other things being equal, it is easier to marry another Yemenite. As one young woman put it, "I would know his behavior, his customs, and the food he likes. I wouldn't have to learn another way of cooking. We would have a *safa mshutefet* ("shared language") and I could be more relaxed with his family than I could with those of a different *eyda*." As one man expressed it, "Marriage is a gamble. If I marry a Teymania it is less of a gamble." And all recognized that their parents and families would probably prefer that they marry within the *eyda*.

There were, however, a number of women who said they did not want to marry Yemenite men, or that their mothers had advised them not to. They believed that Yemenite men expect too much and are not willing to accept their share of the family and household burdens. A mother counselled her daughter, "Don't marry a Yemenite because they are demanding and don't marry a Moroccan because he will beat you. Marry a Polani (Polish Jew). He will take out the garbage in the morning." (She did; but I don't know if he does.) One well-educated woman, describing herself as *feministit*, said she had married a recent immigrant from Europe in the hope of finding someone "who would see me as an equal. This is important to me because I want to work, to read, and to be in the world."

On the other hand, thinking of her sons, a fifty year old teacher said, "It seems that marriage between a Yemenite woman and an Ashkenazi husband is OK, but not vice versa. The Yemenite wife works hard, keeps the house, and is a good wife and the husband accepts it and all goes well. But the Ashkenazi wife is too spoiled and doesn't keep the house as it should be." Still others thought that Ashkenazim were too cold, too closed, too snobbish, whereas "Sephardim" (their generic term for most African-Asian Jews other than themselves) were warmer, easier to feel at home with.[5] However, over and over again I heard that it was not a good idea to marry someone of Moroccan background. Despite these perceptions, 19 percent of the marriages in this group were, in fact, with Moroccan Jews. At the time of my research, however, 19 percent of the Yemenite-Moroccan marriages had ended in divorce.

Although I believe the testimony of my informants who say that they would marry any Jewish Israeli (or even Jew from abroad, as a number have), demographic factors and socioeconomic status also play a significant role. The high incidence of out-marriage among Kiryat Eliahu's Yemenites may be atypical and the result of special circumstances. As suggested in Chapter 7, the Yemenites of Kiryat Eliahu may be caught in a demographic and socioeconomic "marriage squeeze." They are faced with a shortage of eligible Yemenite mates in the appropriate age and status categories because there are only a handful of Yemenite men and women in each year's cohort, and Kiryat Eliahu is atypically isolated from the major Yemenite population centers.[6] They do not have the pool of eligible Yemenite mates that exists in the center of the country. They must either seek a Yemenite spouse from far away, and perhaps move there after marriage, or marry someone from another ethnic group if they remain in and around Kiryat Eliahu. It is my suspicion, supported by the impressions of informants from several communities around Tel Aviv, that such a high proportion of ethnic exogamy is *not* the general rule for Yemenites there. But this can only be determined after similar surveys are done in other Yemenite communities.

As of August 1987 there had been eleven divorces in this sample of 165 marriages—a far higher incidence than among their elders. Ten of these eleven were from *non-Yemenite spouses*, only one from a Yemenite spouse. The sample is small, but it certainly suggests much greater stability for Yemenite-Yemenite marriages. On the other hand, six of the divorces were from Moroccans, and this represents 18.75 percent of the thirty-two marriages between Yemenites and Moroccans, while only one was from among the thirty-six marriages to people of Euro-American background.

In any case it is clear, at least for the Yemenites of Kiryat Eliahu, the Israeli "pressure cooker" seems to be having an effect.[7] Their ideology supports the "fusion of the exiles," and more than half of these young people have put their lives where their ideology is: they have fused themselves and their families with members of other ethnic communities.[8]

Intermarriage and Ethnicity

As suggested in Chapter 7, intermarriage does not necessarily portend the end of ethnicity through a simple blending and mixture. Perhaps the result is somewhat more like that of Gregor Mendel's pea plants with mixed genetic inheritance. Some resemble one parent's side, some the other, and others combine elements of both that may emerge in unpredictable ways in the following generation. Informants and my own observations point to the significance of the family's place of residence, its relations to the spouses' parents, the degree of religiosity and the personalities of each parent, etc., in influencing the identities, loyalties, and activities of the children. And when a tradition is as rich and colorful as that of the Yemenites, it exerts a strong pull. The community life, the music, the dance, the history, and the distinctive foods, all combine to make them feel special, as does the Yemenites' positive reputation. Yemenite women, in particular, may appreciate the aura of romance and elegance that this identification tends to bestow in the estimation of many Israelis. (See the romantic image of *The Yemenite Girl* in Curt Leviant's book of that name.)[9] All of these may play a role in the identity, interests and loyalties of the children of mixed marriages.

Children from the same family may differ in their preferences. In several mixed families, one or more children expressed a closeness to the Yemenite side, while others said they favor the non-Yemenite side. There is a dynamic here which depends upon many factors, but the outcomes are not automatic and are not predictable. The result for the individual is certainly an added appreciation of Israel's ethnic mixture, but it does not necessarily lead to a blending and loss of identification and ethnic culture.

Ethnic Attitudes and Loyalties

The people I interviewed in 1987 were generally quite well educated and "middle class" in occupation, material situation[10] and style. Most had at least two years post-secondary education, quite a few had four and several had post-graduate education. They were articulate and alert to questions of social relations and cultural life. (To some extent this is typically Israeli. Aided and abetted by television and radio talk shows, newspapers, university and extension courses, Israelis tend to engage in a lot of analytical discussion.) All of these people had grown up in Israel, and all of them live with a balance between the ethnically specific world of their families of orientation, their religious community, and their neighborhood on the one hand, and the heterogeneous world of school, the city, work, shopping, bureaucratic agencies, and the army on the other. None works in an ethnically homogeneous setting. And their attitudes and concerns display the varying results of this combination.[11]

No one admits to embarrassment at being Yemenite. All assert pride in their identity and belief in the value and importance of their heritage. (Some claim to be *Teymani giz'i*, meaning, in this context, "pure Yemenite" or "proud Yemenite.") But individuals vary in the degree of their involvement with and concern about Yemenites and the Yemenite tradition. It is important, however, to remember that this can change over time throughout the life of an individual. Many are still quite young, and their attitudes may vary greatly as they rear children, grow older, and react to influences in the Israeli environment. Enthusiasms and fashions come and go. These are dynamic processes, and ones not susceptible to simple categorization or to analysis in terms of straight-line trends.

It seems clear that the respect for the religious tradition is largely unabated. I heard from many young men that they or their kin and friends had turned their backs on religious observance when they were teenagers but returned to it as they grew older and got married. Although I heard several complaints about people who went to the beach, rode in cars, smoked, or played stereos or television on *shabbat*, I saw very little evidence of it. Certainly there are some who do (and more who admit that they did before "returning"), but it is clearly not the norm among Kiryat Eliahu's young Yemenites. Insofar as it exists it is covert and unacceptable. I can vouch for regular synagogue attendance on *shabbat* on the part of almost all the married men of the community. And for all but a half dozen or so this means attendance at one of the ten Yemenite congregations, while the others attend the integrated synagogue.

After synagogue, *shabbat* is observed by a meal at home with the family, quiet visiting and *ja'ale*, and perhaps a return to the synagogue for religious study and afternoon prayers. Although I have only limited information about the religiosity of those who have moved away, what I know indicates that the majority of them, too, remain observant and associated, where possible, with Yemenite congregations. It is frequently the best educated and those with the highest status who are the most observant and involved with Yemenite congregations. [12]

In Israel, in the 1980s, Yemenite "culture" is very much in vogue. The number of singers and musical and dance groups continues to grow, as do nightclubs that feature Yemenite entertainers and *ḥafli Teymani* ("Yemenite parties"). There are special "Yemenite evenings" put on by schools, community centers, and other organizations. And new little Yemenite restaurants are springing up all over the country, featuring baked goods such as *m'lawaḥ* and *jeḥnun*, as well as the distinctive Yemenite soups. These are becoming popular with others besides Yemenites, of course, and serve to spread the legitimacy of ethnic practices.

Beyond these popular manifestations, there is a growing trend for the young and well-educated, to want to become more deeply involved and more knowledgeable about the tradition. Far from fleeing their heritage, they are seeking to get beyond what they consider the superficialities of music, dance and food. [13] ("Folklore" is sometimes considered frivolous, compared to the deeper values of religion, history, and other learning.) They are writing, publishing and buying new religious works, editions of texts edited or analyzed by Yemenite scholars, as well as works of secular scholarship. They are seeking cassette tapes containing authentic prayer traditions, or cantillated readings of the Passover story (*haggada*) and the Book of Esther (*megillah*) for reading on Purim, and other Yemenite renderings of Jewish religious works. There is an increased awareness of regional differences in Jewish customs and pronunciation in Yemen, and there are more students interested in pursuing scholarly study of these traditions. I know of at least five such students from Kiryat Eliahu alone.

Lisa Gilad claims, contrary to my contention in earlier articles, that this "is a State supported movement more so than a grassroots one," and considers it to be "state-controlled (and largely generated) ethnicity." [14] I could not disagree more completely. It is one thing for members of various political parties, the Histadrut, branches of the Ministry of Education or of Religion, or the Bezalel art school to feel, for one reason or another that it is worthwhile supporting such activities. It is quite another to convince people to be interested, to participate, to spend money. It is not "the state" or the Histradut or the Labor Party that produces and buys the music cassettes, opens the nightclubs and the restaurants and supplies them with clientele. "The state" doesn't create singers and bands, and young scholars and artists in search of authenticity. At most these agencies can provide some budgets and advertising and encouragement. And to the extent that outsiders are doing this it is in response to the positive reception they know it will receive.

Gilad is right in pointing out that politicians try to use ethnic celebrations for self-aggrandizement, but that does not give them control, or put them in a position to "generate" the whole complex of Yemeniteness. As she notes, Yemenites (and members of other ethnic groups) are very much aware of, and quite cynical about, attempts to exploit their activities for partisan political ends. Nor can the popularity of Yemenite traditions be accounted for merely because "their *male* folklore and ritual dramas are based on *Jewish* religious themes" as she claims (p. 223). Women are very much involved with formal dance groups. They perform at *hinna* celebrations, frequently take the lead in group singing, and are among the most prominent and popular singers and dancers. The delight that so many Yemenites take in these activities is absolutely clear.

Finally, there is a new movement to develop Yemenite *yeshivot* and associated religious institutions in order offer to talented and interested young Yemenite men the opportunity to learn and to develop authentic Yemenite religious learning and practice. To date they have had little choice but to go to schools dominated by European traditions, and those who learn in these institutions are limited in their knowledge of their own ancestors' ways. A dynamic young rabbi, educated in university as well as *yeshivot*, and influenced by the traditions of the *Dor-de'ah* movement of San'a, recently established an academy (a *koylel*) and supporting research institutions and is attracting students. He intends to develop a center of religious thought and education based on the principles of Jewish worship and learning in Yemen. He aims to demonstrate to these students that the Jewish religious learning and traditions of Yemen, based on the principles of Maimonides, are as valid as those from Europe, and deserve similar serious consideration.

In 1987 as in 1977 it is precisely among the young, many quite well educated, that Yemenite ethnicity takes on increasingly self-conscious importance. Most of those whom I know are not doing this to get back at anybody; they are not rebelling, nor do most of them support ethnic political parties. These traditions and their ethnic identity have special importance to them and they seek to intensify their connections and involvement. Indeed, it is not uncommon to find, anywhere in the world, that it is precisely those who are at some distance from the ethnic center who feel most strongly the need to search for their roots.

It seems clear that in Israel, as in many parts of the world, the intellectual elite plays a leading role in ethnic continuity and revival. As Harvey Goldberg points out, "While much attention has been paid to the fact that ethnic symbols can be used to mobilize political power or organize economic action, only recently has it been explicitly noted that the side of ethnicity based upon individual choice not only can help maximize a person's social position, but can be an *expression of individuality* . . . Ethnic related symbols are becoming common signs of the individual in 'post-industrial' society."[15] Contrary to Yochanan Peres's contention that, "Israeli Jewish ethnicities are more concerned about reaping a fair share in the present and future than with revealing the roots of the past," I would argue that these two are in no sense in conflict, and when the former is secure, the latter may become quite important.[16]

Conclusions

Forty years after the arrival of the Yemenites to Kiryat Eliahu, there is no question that much of the integration and acculturation that the founders of Israel envisaged has indeed occurred. Much of the time of the members of the younger generation is spent with Jews of all backgrounds, in school, at work, in the army, in the neighborhood—in almost all settings. They insist that they feel at home with everyone and they believe that they belong to *am ekhad*, one people. And to some extent their marriage choices, their residence patterns, and their friendships are consistent with this. And yet, they also have a special connection to other Yemenites. They partake of the general political, social, and the intellectual life of the country in every way. They testify, again and again, that their friends are drawn from their fellow students, fellow workers, and those who share common interests, such as folk-dancing or sports.

Even some of those who were most vocal about being equally at home with all, would admit, in the course of conversation, to feeling something special when they are with other Yemenites. For example, when they encounter strangers who turn out to be Yemenites they feel a particular affinity that they do not share with those who are not. As one man in his thirties said, "When I am in the home of another Yemenite I can tell within five minutes if I can look in the refrigerator." He did not say that he *could* look in the refrigerator, but that he might understand the situation well enough to know whether he could take such liberties. He was faced with less uncertainty; he knew the rules better. Many others spoke of the sense of something special, a *safa mshutefet* ("shared language"), "a chemistry," "a click" (their words) that they felt. (A few used the Arabic expression, *minh'ageneh*, "ours" or "our way.")

These people live and operate well in a largely heterogeneous world, and they believe in the rightness of this integration. But it is quite natural to feel at home with "one's own," those who share the most common understandings. Some of these come from the old school tie, from the army experience, from shared interests at work and similar social status. But despite their social and geographical mobility, significant shared understanding is still associated with ethnic experiences, those derived from family and community life, the synagogue and shared ceremonial, music, and dance. Everything we know about social life should lead us to expect this.

In contrast to Ben-Rafael's expectation that the upwardly mobile "ethnics" will desert their brethren, I suggest that we are dealing with complex, variable, dynamic, and highly individual and indeterminate processes. The contending forces are not just those of "modernization," "secularization," "westernization," "Ashkenazation," "social mobility," "materialism," but include, as well, powerful sentiments, peer evaluations, values, and religiosity, inculcated by parents, siblings, grandparents, and community. To some extent these people are self-consciously choosing among the many conflicting values in their wider social and cultural world. As a young father put it, "I expect my son to be a lawyer or an engineer, but also to be Jewish and to know how to pray and read from the Torah in the Yemenite way. The Yemenite diaspora culture was the most authentically Jewish one, and it is not just for the museum but should exist now—among good Israelis." There is not just

one standard of evaluation in Israel—or any modern complex country—
and the current climate in Israel with respect to ethnicity, religion, and
other values is one which permits considerable variety. Indeed, in 1989,
in view of events all around the world, including Canada, Yugoslavia,
the Soviet Union, the United States, it would be foolhearty for anyone
to prophecy the end of ethnicity.

Notes

1. Eliezer Ben-Rafael, *The Emergence of Ethnicity: Cultural Groups and
Social Conflict in Israel*. (Westport, Ct.: Greenwood, 1982.) pp. 176-
177, 222ff.; and Ben-Rafael, "Social Mobility and Ethnic Awareness: The
Israeli Case," in A. Weingrod (ed.), *Studies in Israeli Ethnicity: After the
Ingathering*. (New York: Gordon and Breach, 1985), pp. 76-78. See also
Hannah Ayalon, Eliezer Ben-Rafael, and Stephen Sharot, "Variations in Ethnic
Identification among Israeli Jews," *Ethnic and Racial Studies*, 8 (3): 389-407,
1985; and "The Costs and Benefits of Ethnic Identification," *The British Journal
of Sociology*, 37 (4): 550-568, 1986.

2. *Statistical Abstract*, #38, 1987 (Jerusalem: Central Statistical Bureau),
p. 572. Although the *Statistical Abstract* contains tables that distinguish
between the schooling of people of African-Asian and Euro-American origin,
none of these are presented in ways that permit exact comparison with our
figures from Kiryat Eliahu. The indications are, however, that our figures for
Yemenite post-secondary education are far higher than those for people born
in Israel to fathers born in Africa and Asia, roughly comparable to those with
fathers born in Europe or America for university attendance, and somewhat
higher for study in two-year programs. These figures are high in worldwide
perspective as well.

3. Interestingly, a number of young people who have gone to live in the
United States *do* work in stores, as, indeed, do some people in the older,
established Yemenite community of New York City. See Dina Dahbany
Miraglia, "An Analysis of Ethnic Identity among Yemenite Jews in the Greater
New York Area." Ph.D. dissertation, Columbia University, 1983. A dozen or so
have left Israel, at least temporarily, and are living primarily in the Northeastern
United States.

4. Cf. Gilad, *Ginger and Salt: Yemeni Jewish Women in an Israeli Town*,
(Boulder, Co.: Westview, 1989), p. 171.

5. It is also the case that people from San'a are said to be cold, closed,
and snobs. They consider themselves better educated, more polite, more
serious. While some young people claim to see no differences, others have
strong feelings on the subject of the differences between San'anim, Dhamayrim,

Shar'abim, Bladim ("country folk"), and other such categories from the old country.

6. Young men are in particularly short supply, as boys are more often sent away to boarding schools during secondary school years, and then go to the army for three years. The women complain of a lack of Yemenite men, and, while 50 percent of these men have married Yemenite women, only 38 percent of the women have married Yemenite men.

7. The "pressure cooker" metaphor has been adopted in Israel because it implies a speedier version of the "melting pot," more appropriate to the intensity and pace of change there.

8. A university student, admitting a number of advantages to marrying another Yemenite, and speaking of the importance to him of the transmission of the Yemenite heritage, said the following:

> I know that—in time—intermarriage means that part of the folklore will be fit only for the museums. The children will have two identities. I will have to work on the problem of transmitting the heritage to them. But I believe in ending the separation of ethnic groups, *eydot*, and the ethnic stereotypes. We are all Jews. I am ready to pay the price of giving up some of the folklore for the cause of oneness (*ahdut*).

9. Curt Leviant, *The Yemenite Girl* (New York: Bobbs-Merrill, 1977).

10. If they are middle-class, what has happened to *histapkut b'mu'at* and the Yemenite style of "less is more" decoration? Most of these people will insist that they are like all young Israelis, that they want good homes, the necessary appliances, a car, etc., but many will add, "but not at *any* price." (By 1987 *video* [videocassette recorder] had replaced *tapetim* as the metonym for the material externals of modernity.) As Yisrael Yeshayahu claimed (see Chapter 7), it is not that Yemenites don't want or need, but that they know how to get along without when necessary. As to furnishings, it is still generally the case that Yemenite homes in Kiryat Eliahu feature open spaces and relatively simple furnishing and decoration. Of course there are exceptions.

11. Lisa Gilad, *Ginger and Salt*, does not believe that "a Yemeni Jewish culture, with any community strength, has a hope of surviving several generations in Israel, at least not in such a culturally diverse place as Gadot," (p. 238), the pseudonymous community that she studied. Unfortunately her book appeared just as I was completing this Postscript so there is no time for an extended consideration of her arguments. In making her case, however, she refers to earlier articles of mine, from which she got the impression that Kiryat Eliahu's Yemenites comprised an "introspective and 'closed' ethnic neighborhood" (p. 226). I hope that the figures on education, occupation, and current residential mobility will serve to correct this misapprehension. The Israeli-born generation which I am discussing in this Postscript is very much part of Israeli society. They are aware, articulate, and see themselves as "Yisraeli

b'khol davar"—"Israeli in everything." I chose Kiryat Eliahu precisely because it was heterogeneous and integrated in so many ways. In addition, I have had comparative experience with the Yemenite communities of a number of larger cities, and have good reason to believe that the picture is fundamentally the same in those as well.

12. It remains the responsibility of the devout to see to the training of their sons in Torah. In addition, in Kiryat Eliahu and in some other communities they have reinstituted the Yemenite practice of having older men, called *mori* (teacher), give lessons to the boys.

13. Some young men are joining their elders in the practice of chewing *gat* in social settings, as was the custom in Yemen. *Gat* is normally consumed in small gatherings of friends, who sit on the floor on cushions, or on benches in specially constructed sheds, chewing, drinking tea, smoking, and talking. (Older people often smoke the *narghila*, water pipe.) This practice is increasing in popularity in part because it is seen as an authentic Yemenite custom. It is more common in the Tel Aviv area than in Kiryat Eliahu.

14. Gilad, *Ginger and Salt*, pp. 210; 223

15. Harvey Goldberg, "The Changing Meaning of Ethnic Affiliation," *The Jerusalem Quarterly*, #44, Fall, 1987, pp. 47-48.

16. Yochanan Peres, "Horizontal Integration and Vertical Differentiation among Jewish Ethnicities in Israel," in A. Weingrod (ed.), *Studies in Israeli Ethnicity*. (New York: Gordon & Breach, 1985), p. 54.

Glossary

'arak. Distilled liquor.

aliya. Immigration to Palestine/Israel, lit. "going up"; or, to be called up to read from the Torah.

Ashkenazi. Jews from or derived from Europe.

baladi. One of two Jewish prayer traditions in Yemen; cf. *shami*.

bar mitsvah. "Coming of age" ceremony for Jewish boys, at age 13.

beit knesset. Synagogue.

bid'. Celebration for the groom-to-be in Yemenite tradition; cf. *ḥinna*.

brit mila. Ritual circumcision of Jewish boys.

dati. "Orthodox," rigorously observant of Jewish religious traditions.

derekh erets. Right conduct, lit. "the way of the country."

dhimmi. Status of Jews in Muslim countries, as tolerated and protected minority, but second-class subjects.

divrei torah. Discussion of "Torah," a "sermon."

diwan. Compendium of Jewish poetry from Yemen.

Dor-De'ah/Darda'im. Twentieth century Jewish religious reform movement in Yemen.

evel. Seven day period of mourning for the dead.

eyda. (Pl. eydot) generic term for Jewish ethnic groups in Israel, lit. "community."

felafel. Popular food, made of ground chick peas, usually sold at stands.

gabbai. Synagogue official, often a treasurer, perhaps general director of services.

galut. Diaspora, "exile" from the Holy Land.

gat/qat. Plant with stimulant properties, *Catha edulis*, whose leaves are chewed.

ghane. Songs, with lyrics in Arabic, composed and sung by Yemenite Jewish women.

hazan. Leader in religious services, a reader, etc.

hevra. A group of friends, a clique, lit. "society."

ḥinna. Red dye (henna) used in ritual; by extension, the celebration for a bride-to-be.

hinukh. Education, upbringing.

haftara. Readings from the prophets, associated with weekly Torah readings.

halakha. Jewish religious law, codes for right practice, lit. "the way."

haskala. Learning, enlightenment.

Histadrut. General Federation of Labor, a central Israeli institution, as union, owner of industries, etc.

histapkut b'mu'at. "Contentment with little."

imam. Title of ruler of Yemen; also an important Muslim religious leader more generally.

ja'ale. Lit. nuts, fruits, etc.; by extension an important social gathering at which these are served.

jeḥnun. Baked goods, served primarily on sabbath morning; cf. *kubane*.

jizya. Tax levied on Jews of Yemen and other Muslim states.

Kabbalah. The esoteric teachings of Jewish mysticism.

kaddish. Memorial prayer recited for the dead.

kibbuts. Communal farm community.

kibbuts galuyot. "The ingathering of the exiles"; "return" of Jews from all over the world to the land of Israel.

kibbutsnikim. Members of kibbuts communities.

kiddush. "Sanctification." A term used, among other things, for a prayer said over wine.

kin'a. Envy.

kipa. Skull cap (*yarmulke* in Yiddish).

kolel. Charitable institutions, especially in Jerusalem, supporting students and others.

kosher. Proper according to Jewish dietary laws.

kubane/kubano. Baked goods, served on shabbat morning, especially (cf. *jeḥnun*).

landslayt. Yiddish term for people from the same district in a country of origin.

ma'abara. (Pl. ma'abarot) temporary camps for immigrants to Israel in the 1950s.

Matnas. Acronym for Center for Culture, Youth and Sport: community centers.

mezuza. Parchment scroll attached to doorposts of Jewish houses.

minyan. The quorum of ten men needed for public worship.

mitsva. (Pl. mitsvot) lit. "commandment(s)": good deed(s); religiously mandated proper behavior and celebrations.

mizug galuyot. "Fusion of the exiles," after ingathering in Land of Israel. Cf. *kibbuts galuyot*.

mlawaḥ. Yemenite baked goods now being sold at restaurants, a variant of *pita*.

mori. Teacher of Torah and prayer to young boys.

narghila. Water pipe.

nashid. Songs sung by men to poetry of the diwan.

olim. Immigrants to Palestine and Israel.

Onkelos (Targum). Aramaic translation of the Torah, read in Yemenite synagogues.

pakid. (Pl. p'kidim) clerk, bureaucrat.

parasha. One of the fifty-four weekly sections into which the Torah is divided for reading each *shabbat*.

pe'ot. Side-locks worn by strictly orthodox Jewish men.

pita. Middle Eastern flat, round bread.

safa m'shutefet. Lit. "shared language"; common (cultural) understandings.

sayyid. (sg.) Privileged elite Muslims in Yemen.

seder adifut. "Order of preference," priorities.

Sephardi. Jews who trace their origins to Spain before the expulsion in the late 15th century.

shabbat. Sabbath, Saturday.

shami. A prayer tradition of the Jews of Yemen; cf. *baladi*.

shashlik/shishlik. Skewered meat, etc. (cf. shish-kebab) often sold from stands.

shkhuna. Residential quarter, neighborhood.

shul. Yiddish, synagogue.

simha. (Pl. smahot) celebration, happy occasion.

Talmud. Codified Jewish law, with rabbinic analyses and commentaries.

tapetim. Wallpaper, fashionable in the 1970s.

Teymani. Hebrew term for "Yemenite."

Torah. Five Books of Moses, the basis of Jewish learning and law.

vilot. (pl.) "Villas": single-family homes.

yeshiva. (Pl. yeshivot) academies for Jewish religious learning.

yishuv. The Jewish community of Palestine, before establishment of Israel in 1948.

zaf'a. Procession, accompanying people celebrating *smahot*.

Bibliography

Abir, Mordechai. "International Commerce and Yemenite Jewry; 15th to 19th Centuries," *Pe'amim* 5:4-28, 1980. [Hebrew]

Adaqi, Yehiel and Uri Sharvit. *A Treasury of Jewish Yemenite Chants*. Jerusalem: The Israel Institute for Sacred Music, 1981. [Hebrew]

Ahroni, Reuben. *Yemenite Jewry: Origins, Culture and Literature*. Bloomington: Indiana University Press, 1986.

Ayalon, Hannah, Eliezer Ben-Rafael and Stephen Sharot. "Variations in Ethnic Identification among Israeli Jews," *Ethnic and Racial Studies*, 8 (3): 389-407, 1985.

————. "The Costs and Benefits of Ethnic Identification," *The British Journal of Sociology*, 37 (4): 550-568, 1986.

Bahat, Naomi and Avner. "Music and Dance of the Yemenite Jews in Israel—the First Hundred Years of Research." In Shalom Seri, ed., *Se'i Yona: Yemenite Jews in Israel*, pp. 415-438. Tel Aviv: Am Oved, 1983. [Hebrew]

Barer, Shlomo. *The Magic Carpet*. London: Secker & Warburg, 1952.

Barth, Fredrik. *Ethnic Groups and Boundaries*. Boston: Little, Brown, 1969.

Bat Ye'or. *The Dhimmi: Jews and Christians Under Islam*. Rutherford, N. J.: Fairleigh Dickinson University Press, 1985.

Bein, Alex. *The Return to the Soil: A History of Jewish Settlement in Israel*. Jerusalem: Youth and Hechalutz Department of the Zionist Organization, 1952.

Bell, Daniel. "Ethnicity and Social Change," in Nathan Glazer and Daniel P. Moynihan, eds., *Ethnicity: Theory and Experience*, pp. 141-174. Cambridge, Mass.: Harvard University Press, 1975.

Ben-David, Joseph. "Ethnic Differences or Social Change?" in C. Frankenstein, ed., *Between Past and Future*, pp. 33-52. Jerusalem: Henrietta Szold Foundation, 1953.

Ben-Rafael, Eliezer. *The Emergence of Ethnicity*. Westport, Ct.: Greenwood Press, 1982.

————. "Social Mobility and Ethnic Awareness: The Israeli Case," in A. Weingrod, ed., *Studies in Israeli Ethnicity: After the Ingathering*, pp. 57-79. New York: Gordon and Breach, 1985.

Ben-Yosef, Rivka W. "Desocialization and Resocialization: The Adjustment Process of Immigrants," *International Migration Review* 2:27-45, 1968.

Berdichevsky, Norman. "The Impact of Urbanization on the Social Geography of Rehovot." Ph. D. dissertation, University of Wisconsin, Madison, 1974.

————. "The Persistence of the Yemeni Quarter in an Israeli Town," *Ethnicity* 4:287-309, 1977.

Berlovitz, Yafa. "The Image of the Yemenite in the Literature of the First *Aliyot*," *Pe'amim* 10:76-108, 1981. [Hebrew]

Bernstein, Deborah. "Immigrant Transit Camps: The Formation of Dependent Relations in Israeli Society," *Ethnic and Racial Studies* 4:26-43, 1981.

Bernstein, Deborah and Shlomo Swirski. "The Rapid Economic Development of Israel and the Emergence of the Ethnic Division of Labour," *British Journal of Sociology* 33:65-85, 1982.

Bernstein, Judith and Aaron Antonovsky. "The Integration of Ethnic Groups in Israel," *Jewish Journal of Sociology* 23: 5-23, 1981.

Berreby, Jean-Jacques. "De l'Intégration des Juifs Yéménites en Israel," *L'Année Sociologique*, 3rd series: 69-163. 1956.

Brauer, Erich. "The Yemenite Jewish Woman," *The Jewish Review* 4:35-47, 1933.

————. *Ethnologie der Jemenitischen Juden*. Heidelberg: Carl Winters, 1934.

Brin Ingber, Judith. *Shorashim: The Roots of Israeli Folk Dance*. Dance Perspectives No. 59. New York: Dance Perspectives Foundation, 1974.

————. "The Russian Ballerina and the Yemenites," *Israel Dance 1975*:19. Tel Aviv, 1976.

Brown, Kenneth. "Words of an Other Israeli Poet: Erez Bitton," *MERA Forum* 5(4):13-17, 1982.

Burgess, Elaine. "The Resurgence of Ethnicity: Myth or Reality?" *Ethnic and Racial Studies* 1:265-285, 1978.

Bury, G. Wyman. *Arabia Infelix, or the Turks in Yamen*. London: Macmillan, 1915.

Caspi, Mishael Maswari. "Nahliel—Relations of Neighbors in Its Early Years," *Pe'amim* 10:70-75, 1981. [Hebrew]

————. *Daughters of Yemen*. Berkeley: University of California Press, 1985.

————. Manuscript of a paper "Dedicated to Professor Joseph Silverman" (n.d.).

Central Bureau of Statistics, Government of Israel. Census of Population and Housing 1974: *List of Localities* (Geographical Information and Population), No. 3.

Central Bureau of Statistics, State of Israel. Census of Population and Housing 1972: *Demographic Characteristics of the Population*, Part II, No. 10 Jerusalem, 1976.

Cohen, Hayyim. *The Jews of the Middle East, 1860-1972*. Jerusalem: Israel Universities Press, 1973.

Cohen, Percy. "Alignments and Allegiances in the Community of Shaarayim in Israel," *Jewish Journal of Sociology* 4:14-38, 1962.

Dahbany Miraglia, Dina. "An Analysis of Ethnic Identity among Yemenite Jews in the Greater New York Area." Ph. D. dissertation, Columbia University, 1983.

Dashefsky, Arnold and Howard Shapiro. *Ethnic Identification Among American Jews*. Lexington, Mass.: D. C. Heath, 1974.

Deshen, Shlomo A. *Immigrant Voters in Israel: Parties and Congregations in a Local Election Campaign.* Manchester: Manchester University Press, 1970.

————. "Political Ethnicity and Cultural Ethnicity in Israel During the 1960s," in Abner Cohen, ed., *Urban Ethnicity*, pp. 281-309. London: Tavistock, 1974.

Deshen, Shlomo and Moshe Shokied. *The Predicament of Homecoming: Cultural and Social Life of North African Immigrants in Israel*. Ithaca: Cornell University Press, 1974.

DeVos, George and Lola Romanucci-Ross. *Ethnic Identity*. Chicago: University of Chicago Press, 1983.

Druyan, Nitza. *Without a Magic Carpet: Yemenite Settlement in Eretz Israel* (1881-1914). Jerusalem: Ben-Zvi Institute, 1981. [Hebrew]

————. "'Workers Born and Bred'—Yemenite Immigrants in Agricultural Settlement," in Shalom Seri, ed., *Se'i Yona: Yemenite Jews in Israel*, pp. 195-210. Tel Aviv: Am Oved, 1983.

Ehrlich, Richard L., ed. *Immigrants in Industrial America, 1850-1920*. Charlottesville: University Press of Virginia, 1977.

Eisenstadt, S. N. "The Process of Absorption of Immigrants in Israel," in C. Frankenstein, ed., *Between Past and Future*, pp. 53-81. Jerusalem: Henrietta Szold Foundation, 1953.

————. *The Absorption of Immigrants*. London: Routledge & Kegan Paul, 1954.

Encyclopaedia Judaica. Jerusalem: Keter, 1972. 16 Volumes.

Epstein, A. L. *Ethos and Identity: Three Studies in Ethnicity*. London: Tavistock, 1978.

Fine, Gary A. and Sherryl Kleinman. "Rethinking Subculture: An Interactionist Analysis," *American Journal of Sociology* 85:1-20, 1979.

Gambino, Richard. *Blood of My Blood: The Dilemma of the Italian-Americans*. Garden City, N. Y.: Doubleday/Anchor, 1975.

Gamliel, Shalom ben Sa'adya. *The Jizya Poll Tax in Yemen*. Ed. M. M. Caspi. Jerusalem: The Shalom Research Center, 1982.

Gamlieli, Nissim B. "The Arabs Amongst Whom the Yemenite Jews Lived: Islamic Sects, Their Inter-Relationships and Relations with the Jews," in Y. Yeshayahu and Y. Tobi, eds., *The Jews of Yemen*, pp. 165-192. Jerusalem: Ben-Zvi Institute, 1975.

Gans, Herbert J. "Symbolic Ethnicity: The Future of Ethnic Groups and Cultures in America," *Ethnic and Racial Studies* 2:1-20, 1979.

Geertz, Clifford. "The Integrative Revolution," in *Old Societies and New States*. New York: The Free Press, 1963.

———. "The Impact of the Concept of Culture on the Concept of Man," in E. Hammel and W. Simmons, eds., *Man Makes Sense*. Boston: Little, Brown, 1970.

Gerholm, Tomas. *Market, Mosque and Mafraj: Social Inequality in a Yemeni Town*. Stockholm: University of Stockholm, 1977.

Gilad, Lisa. "Changing Notions of Proper Conduct: The Case of Jewish Unmarried Yemeni Women in an Israeli New Town," *Cambridge Anthropology* 7:44-56, 1982.

———. "Contrasting Notions of Proper Conduct: Yemeni Jewish Mothers and Daughters in an Israeli Town," *Jewish Social Studies*, 45:73-86, 1983.

———. *Ginger and Salt: Yemeni Jewish Women in an Israeli Town*. Boulder, Colorado: Westview, 1989.

Glazer, Nathan and Daniel P. Moynihan, eds. *Ethnicity: Theory and Experience*. Cambridge, Mass.: Harvard University Press, 1975.

Gluska, Zekharya. *On Behalf of Yemenite Jews*. Jerusalem: Y. Ben-David Gluska, 1974. [Hebrew]

Goffman, Erving. *The Presentation of Self in Everyday Life*. Garden City, N. Y.: Doubleday/Anchor Books, 1959.

Goitein, S. D. "The Transplantation of the Yemenites: The Old Life They Led," *Commentary* 12:24-29, 1951.

———. "The Community Life of the Jews in the Land of Yemen," in *Jubilee Volume to Honor Mordechai Menahem Kaplan*, pp. 43-61. Philadelphia: Jewish Theological Seminary of America, 1953. [Hebrew]

———. "Jewish Education in Yemen as an Archetype of Traditional Jewish Education," in C. Frankenstein, ed., *Between Past and Future*, pp. 109-146. Jerusalem: Henrietta Szold Foundation, 1953.

———. "Portrait of a Yemenite Weavers' Village," *Jewish Social Studies* 17:3-26, 1955.

———. *Jews and Arabs: Their Contacts Through the Ages*. New York: Schocken Books, 1964.

———. *A Mediterranean Society*, Vol. I. *Economic Foundations*. Berkeley: University of California Press, 1967.

———. "The Jews of Yemen," in A. J. Arberry, ed., *Religion in the Middle East*, pp. 226-235. Cambridge: Cambridge University Press, 1969.

———. *From the Land of Sheba: Tales of the Jews of Yemen*. New York: Schocken Books, 1973.

Goldberg, Harvey. *Cave Dwellers and Citrus Growers: A Jewish Community in Libya and Israel*. Cambridge: Cambridge University Press, 1972.

———. "Historical and Cultural Dimensions of Ethnic Phenomena in Israel," in Alex Weingrod, ed., *Studies in Israeli Ethnicity: After the Ingathering*, pp. 179-200. New York: Gordon and Breach, 1985.

———. "The Changing Meaning of Ethnic Affiliation," *The Jerusalem Quarterly* 44:39-50, Fall 1987.

Goldstein Judith L. "The Rise of Iranian Ethnicity in Israel," *The Jerusalem Quarterly* 29:38-53, Fall 1983.

———. "Iranian Ethnicity in Israel: The Performance of Identity," in Alex Weingrod, ed., *Studies in Israeli Ethnicity*, pp. 237-257. New York: Gordon and Breach, 1985.

Goodenough, Ward H. *Cooperation in Change*. New York: Russell Sage Foundation, 1963.

———. *Culture, Language, and Society*. Reading, Mass.: Addison-Wesley, 1971.

Gordon, Milton M. *Assimilation in American Life: The Role of Race, Religion, and National Origins*. New York: Oxford University Press, 1964.

Greeley, Andrew M. *That Most Distressful Nation: The Taming of the American Irish*. Chicago: Quadrangle, 1972.

Greenberg, Harold I. "Rosh Haayin—Neglect and Tradition," *Plural Societies* 11:59-73, 1980.

Greitzer, Dina. "The Settlement of Yemenite Immigrants at Kefar Marmorak—Between Separatism and Integration," *Cathedra* 14:121-151, 1980. [Hebrew]

Grunebaum, Gustave E. *Medieval Islam*. Chicago: University of Chicago Press, 1946.

Habib, Jack, Meir Kohn, and Robert Lerman. "The Effect on Poverty Status in Israel of Considering Wealth and Variability of Income," *Review of Income and Wealth* (series 23) 1:17-38, 1977.

HaLevi, Yosef. "Some Examples of Modern Hebrew Literature by Yemenite Authors," in Shalom Seri, ed., *Se'i Yona: Yemenite Jews in Israel* pp. 349-386. Tel Aviv: Am Oved, 1983. [Hebrew]

Halpern, Ben. *The Idea of the Jewish State*. Cambridge, Mass.: Harvard University Press, 1969.

Halpern, Ben and Shalom Wurm, eds., *The Life and Opinions of Giora Yosephthal*. New York: Schocken Books, 1966.

Heilman, Samuel C. *Synagogue Life: A Study in Symbolic Interaction*. Chicago: University of Chicago Press, 1973.

Herzl, Theodore. *Old-New Land*. New York: Bloch, 1941.

Herzog, Hanna. "Ethnicity as a Negotiated Issue in the Israeli Political Order: the 'Ethnic Lists' to the Delegates' Assembly and the Knesset (1920-1977)," in A. Weingrod, ed., *Studies in Israeli Ethnicity: After the Ingathering*, pp. 159-178. New York: Gordon and Breach, 1985.

———. *Political Ethnicity: The Image and the Reality*. Tel Aviv: Yad Tabenkin, 1986. [Hebrew]

Hoffman, Haya. "'Kfar HaShiloah,' a Saga of Yemenite Immigration by Israel Zarhi," in Shalom Seri, ed., *Se'i Yona: Yemenite Jews in Israel*, pp. 113-127. Tel Aviv: Am Oved, 1983. [Hebrew]

Howard, Alan. *Ain't No Big Thing: Coping Strategies in a Hawaiian-American Community*. Honolulu: University of Hawaii Press, 1974.

Inbar, Michael and Chaim Adler, *Ethnic Integration in Israel*. New Brunswick, N. J.: Transaction Books, 1977.

Isaac, J. "Israel: A New Melting Pot?" in W. D. Borrie, ed., *Cultural Integration of Immigrants*, pp. 234-265. Paris: UNESCO, 1959.

Isaacs, Harold R. "Basic Group Identity: The Idols of the Tribe," in Nathan Glazer and Daniel P. Moynihan, eds., *Ethnicity: Theory and Experience*, pp. 29-52. Cambridge, Mass.: Harvard University Press, 1975.

Izraeli, Dafna N. "Ethnicity and Industrial Relations: An Israeli Factory Case Study," *Ethnic and Racial Studies* 2:80-89, 1979.

Kafih, Yosef. *Jewish Life in Sanà*. Jerusalem: Ben-Zvi Institute, 1969. [Hebrew]

————. "The Ties of Yemenite Jews with the Jewish Centers," in Y. Yeshayahu and Y. Tobi, eds., *The Jews of Yemen*, pp. 29-46. Jerusalem: Ben-Zvi Institute, 1975. [Hebrew]

————. "What is the Eating of Ja'ale?" in Y. Tobi, ed., *Legacy of the Jews of Yemen: Studies and Researches*, pp. 53-64. Jerusalem: Bo'i Teman, 1976. [Hebrew]

Kapara, Pinhas. *From Yemen to Shaarayim, Rehovot*. Rehovot, 1978. [Hebrew]

Katz, Elihu and Awraham Zloczower. "Ethnic Continuity in an Israeli Town," *Human Relations* 14:293-327, 1961.

Katzenstein, Mary Fainsod. *Ethnicity and Inequality: The Shiv Sena Party and Preferential Policies in Bombay*. Ithaca, N. Y.: Cornell University Press, 1979.

Katzir, Yael. "The Effects of Resettlement on the Status and Role of Yemeni Jewish Women: The Case of Ramat Oranim, Israel." Ph. D. dissertation, University of California, Berkeley, 1976.

————. "Preservation of Jewish Ethnic Identity in Yemen: Segregation and Intregation as Boundary Maintenance Mechanisms," *Comparative Studies in Society and History* 24:264-279, 1982.

Keesing, Roger M. "Theories of Culture," *Annual Review of Anthropology* 3:73-97, 1974.

Kessar, Yisrael. "Yemenite Agricultural Settlement after the Creation of the State," in Shalom Seri, ed., *Se'i Yona: Yemenite Jews in Israel*, pp. 231-342. Tel Aviv: Am Oved, 1983. [Hebrew]

Klaff, Vivian Z. "Residence and Integration in Israel: A Mosaic of Segregated Peoples," *Ethnicity* 4:103-121, 1977.

Kleinberger, Aharon F. *Society, Schools and Progress in Israel*. Oxford: Pergamon Press, 1969.

Klorman-Eraqi, Bat-Zion. "Messianism in the Jewish Community of Yemen in the Nineteenth Century." Ph. D. dissertation, University of California, Los Angeles, 1981.

Kobrin, Frances E. and Calvin Goldscheider. *The Ethnic Factor in Family Structure and Mobility*. Cambridge, Mass.: Ballinger, 1978.

Korah, Amram. *Whirlwind of the South: History of the Jews of Yemen*. Jerusalem: Rav Kook Institute, 1954. [Hebrew]

Kosmin, Barry. "Exclusion and Opportunity: Traditions of Work Amongst British Jews," in Sandra Wallman, ed., *Ethnicity at Work*, pp. 37-68. London: Macmillan, 1979.

Kraus, Vered. "Occupational Perceptions in Israel," *Megamot* 26: 283-294, 1981. [Hebrew]

Kushner, Gilbert. *Immigrants from India in Israel* Tucson: University of Arizona Press, 1973.

Laumann, E. O. *The Bonds of Pluralism*. New York: John Wiley, 1973.

Leach, E. R., ed. *Aspects of Caste in South India, Ceylon and North-West Pakistan*. Cambridge, 1960.

Lee, Chang Soo and George DeVos. *Koreans in Japan*. Berkeley: University of California Press, 1981.

Leviant, Curt. *The Yemenite Girl*. New York: Bobbs-Merrill, 1977.

Lewis, Arnold. *Power, Poverty and Education*. Ramat Gan: Turtledove, 1979.

Lewis, Herbert S. "Historical Problems in Ethiopia and the Horn of Africa," *Annals of the New York Academy of Sciences* 96:504-511, 1962.

————. "European Ethnicity in Wisconsin: An Exploratory Formulation," *Ethnicity* 5:174-188, 1978.

————. "Yemenite Ethnicity in Israel," *Jewish Journal of Sociology* 26:5-24, 1984.

Lewis, Oscar. "The Culture of Poverty," *Scientific American* 215(4):19-25, 1966.

Lissak, Moshe. *Social Mobility in Israeli Society*. Jerusalem: Israel Universities Press, 1969.

Loeb, Laurence D. *Outcaste: Jewish Life in Southern Iran*. New York: Gordon & Breach, 1977.

————. "Folk Models of Habbani Ethnic Identity," in Alex Weingrod, ed., *Studies in Israeli Ethnicity*, pp. 201-215. New York: Gordon and Breach, 1985.

Macro, Eric. *Yemen and the Western World*. London: C. Hurst, 1968.

Mamet, Raziel. "The Geography of Yemenite Settlement in Israel," in Shalom Seri, ed., *Se'i Yona: Yemenite Jews in Israel*, pp. 163-194. Tel Aviv: Am Oved, 1983. [Hebrew]

Manor, G. "'Inbal' and Yemenite Dance in Israel," in Shalom Seri, ed., *Se'i Yona: Yemenite Jews in Israel*, pp. 399-414. Tel Aviv: Am Oved, 1983. [Hebrew]

Marx, Emanuel. "Rehabilitation of Slums? The Case of Hatikva Quarter," *The Jerusalem Quarterly* 22:38-44, 1982.

Matras, Judah. "On Changing Matchmaking, Marriage, and Fertility in Israel: Some Findings, Problems, and Hypotheses," *American Journal of Sociology* 79:364-388, 1973.

———. "Ethnic and Social Origin 'Dominance' in Occupational Attainment in Israel." Discussion paper for Brookdale Institute of Gerontology and Adult Human Development in Israel, Jerusalem, 1977.

———. "Sociology and Its Own Society: Israel," Departmental Working Paper 82-3, Department of Sociology and Anthropology, Carlton University, Ottawa, 1982.

Matras, Judah and Dov Weintraub. "Ethnic and Other Primordial Differentials in Intergenerational Mobility in Israel." Discussion paper for Brookdale Institute, Jerusalem, 1977.

McKay, James. "An Exploratory Synthesis of Primordial and Mobilizationist Approaches to Ethnic Phenomena," *Ethnic and Racial Studies* 5:395-420, 1982.

Medina, Shalom. *The Messiah from Yemen*. Tel Aviv: Aviner, 1977. [Hebrew]

Mintz, Jerome R. *Legends of the Hasidim*. Chicago: University of Chicago Press, 1968.

Nagata, Judith. *Malaysian Mosaic*. Vancouver: University of British Columbia Press, 1979.

Nahshon, Yeḥiel. "Jewish Leadership in Yemen," in Y. Yeshayahu and Y. Tobi, eds., *The Jews of Yemen*, pp. 73-94. Jerusalem: Ben-Zvi Institute, 1975).

Nahum, Y. L. and Y. Tobi. "R. Yosef Shemen's Pamphlet *Hayei haTemanim* (On the Distress of Yemenite Jews in the Twentieth Century)," in Y. Yeshayahu and Y. Tobi, *The Jews of Yemen*, pp. 115-143. Jerusalem: Ben-Zvi Institute, 1975.

Nevo, Naomi. "A Problematic Moshav in the Central District." Jerusalem: Settlement Department of the Jewish Agency, 1976. [Hebrew]

Niebuhr, C. *Travels Through Arabia and Other Countries in the East*. Edinburgh, 1792; repr. Librairie du Liban, Beirut, 1969.

Nini, Yehuda. "From Joseph Halevy till the '*IQSHIM* and *DARDA'IM* Dispute in 1914" in Y. Yeshayahu and Y. Tobi, eds., *The Jews of Yemen*, pp.95-113. Jerusalem: Ben-Zvi Institute, 1975.

———. "Immigration and Assimilation: The Yemenite Jews," *Jerusalem Quarterly* 21:85-98, 1981.

———. *Yemen and Zion: The Jews of Yemen, 1800-1914*. Jerusalem: Hassifriya Haziyonit, 1982. [Hebrew]

O'Connor, Edwin. *The Edge of Sadness*. Boston: Little, Brown, 1961.

Olneck, Michael R. and Marvin Lazerson. "The School Achievement of Immigrant Children, 1900-1930," *History of Education Quarterly* 14:453-482, 1974.

Ozeri, Zion Mansour. *Yemenite Jews: A Photographic Essay*. New York: Schocken, 1985.

Palgi, Phyllis. *Socio-Cultural Trends and Mental Health Problems in Israel*. Jerusalem: Ministry of Health, 1969.

————. "Discontinuity in the Female Role Within the Traditional Family in Modern Society: A Case of Infantcide," in E. J. Anthony and C. Koupernik, eds., *The Child in His Family*, pp. 453-463. New York: John Wiley, 1973.

————. "Mental Health, Traditional Beliefs, and the Moral Order among Yemenite Jews in Israel," in L. Romanucci-Ross, D. E. Moerman, and L. Tancredi, eds., *The Anthropology of Medicine: From Culture to Method*, pp.319-335. New York: Praeger, 1982.

Patai, Raphael. *Israel Between East and West: A Study in Human Relations*. Philadelphia: The Jewish Publication Society of America, 1953.

————. *Tents of Jacob: The Diaspora—Yesterday and Today*. Englewood Cliffs, N. J.: Prentice-Hall, 1971.

Patterson, Orlando. *Ethnic Chauvinism*. Briarcliff Manor, N. Y.: Stein & Day, 1977.

Peres, Yochanan. *Ethnic Relations in Israel*. Tel Aviv: Tel Aviv University Press, 1976. [Hebrew]

————. "Horizontal Integration and Vertical Differentiation among Jewish Ethnicities in Israel," in A. Weingrod, ed., *Studies in Israeli Ethnicity*, pp. 39-56. New York: Gordon & Breach, 1985.

Peres, Yochanan and Ruth Schrift. "Intermarriage and Ethnic Relations: A Comparative Study," *Ethnic and Racial Studies* 1:428-451, 1978.

Peterson Royce, Anya. *Ethnic Identity: Strategies of Diversity*. Bloomington: Indiana University Press, 1982.

Poulos, Constantine. "The Transplantation of the Yemenites: In the New Land," *Commentary* 12:29-33, 1951.

Raphael, Fanny. "Rosh Ha'Ayin: The Development of an Immigrant Settlement," in C. Frankenstein, ed., *Between Past and Future*, pp. 194-214. Jerusalem: Henrietta Szold Foundation, 1953.

Rathjens, Carl. *Jewish Domestic Architecture in San'a, Yemen*, Oriental Notes and Studies 7. Jerusalem: Israel Oriental Society, 1957.

Ratzaby, Yehuda. *Yemenite Jewry*. Tel Aviv: Education Office, Israel Defense Forces, 1958. [Hebrew]

Rosen, Sherry. "Intermarriage and the 'Blending of Exiles' in Israel," *Research in Race and Ethnic Relations* 3:79-101, 1982.

Rosner, Jakob. *A Palestine Picture Book*. New York: Schocken, 1947.

Rothschild, Joseph. *Ethnopolitics: A Conceptual Framework*. New York: Columbia University Press, 1981.

Rubenstein, Shimon. "'Gibeonites'?" in Shalom Seri, ed., *Se'i Yona: Yemenite Jews in Israel*, pp. 211-230. Tel Aviv: Am Oved, 1983.

Ryan, William. *Blaming the Victim*. New York: Vintage, 1976.

Schechtman, Joseph B. *On Wings of Eagles: The Plight, Exodus, and Homecoming of Oriental Jewry*. New York: Thomas Yoseloff, 1961.

Schwarz Perelman, Leslie. "Something Old, Something New: The Domestic Side of Moroccan-Israeli Ethnicity." Ph. D. dissertation, University of Wisconsin, Madison, 1983.

Serjeant, R. B. "The Zaydis," in A. J. Arberry, ed., *Religion in the Middle East*, pp. 285-301. Cambridge: Cambridge University Press, 1969.

Shama, Avraham and Mark Iris. *Immigration Without Integration: Third World Jews in Israel*. Cambridge, Mass.: Schenkman, 1977.

Sharvit, Uri. "On the Role of the Arts and Artistic Concepts in the Tradition of Yemenite Jewry," *Pe'amim* 10:119-130, 1981.

Shenhar, A. "Fraternity in the Folktales of Yemenite Jewry," in Y. Yeshayahu and Y. Tobi, eds., *The Jews of Yemen*, pp. 395-403. Jerusalem: Ben-Zvi Institute, 1975. [Hebrew]

Shereshevsky, Robert., ed., *One Hundred Years and Another Twenty*, Vol. 1. Jerusalem: Ma'ariv, 1967, pp. 198-199. [Hebrew]

Shokeid, Moshe. *The Dual Heritage: Immigrants from the Atlas Mountains in an Israeli Village*. Manchester: Manchester University Press, 1971.

Smooha, Sammy. *Israel: Pluralism and Conflict*. Berkeley: University of California Press, 1978.

———. *Social Research on Jewish Ethnicity in Israel*. Haifa: Haifa University Press, 1987.

Smooha, Sammy and Yochanan Peres. "The Dynamics of Ethnic Inequalities: The Case of Israel," *Social Dynamic* 1:63-79, 1975.

Social Profile of Cities and Towns in Israel. Part 2. Jerusalem: Ministry of Social Welfare, 1977. [Hebrew]

Statistical Abstract of Israel. No. 38, 1987. Jerusalem: Central Bureau of Statistics.

Staub, Shalom. *A Folkloristic Study of Ethnic Boundaries: The Case of Yemeni Muslims in New York City*. Ph. D. dissertation, University of Pennsylvania, 1985.

Stein Howard F. and Robert F. Hill. *The Ethnic Imperative: Examining the New White Ethnic Movement*. University Park, Pa.: Pennsylvania State University Press, 1977.

Steinberg, Stephen. *The Ethnic Myth: Race, Ethnicity, and Class in America*. New York: Atheneum, 1981.

Strickon, Arnold and Robert A. Ibarra. "The Changing Dynamics of Ethnicity: Norwegians and Tobacco in Wisconsin," *Ethnic and Racial Studies* 6:174-197, 1983.

Swirski, Shlomo. *Not Disadvantaged, But Disenfranchised: Oriental and Ashkenazim in Israel*. Haifa: Research and Critique Series, 1981. [Hebrew]

Swirski, Shlomo and Sara Katzir. *Orientals and Ashkenazim in Israel: An Emerging Dependency Relationship*. Haifa: Research and Critique Series, 1978.

Tabib, Mordechai. *As the Grass in the Field*. See the English excerpt, "1917," in M. Z. Frank, ed., *Sound the Great Trumpet*. New York: Whittier Books, 1955.

Tamarin, George R. "Three Decades of Ethnic Coexistence in Israel," *Plural Societies* 2:3-46, 1980.

Tobi, Yosef. *The Jews of Yemen in the Nineteenth Century*. Tel Aviv: Afikim, 1976. [Hebrew]

————. *The Legacy of the Jews of Yemen: Studies and Researches*. Jerusalem: Bo'i Teman, 1976. [Hebrew]

————. "The Authority of the Community of San'aa in Yemenite Jewry," in S. Deshen and W. Zenner, eds., *Jewish Societies in the Middle East: Community, Culture and Authority*, pp. 235-250. Washington, D. C.: University Press of America, 1982.

————. *I Will Ascend in Tamar: One Hundred Years of Aliyah and Settlement*. Jerusalem: Ben-Zvi Institute and E'eleh B'tamar Association, 1982. [Hebrew]

Tsadok, Moshe. *History and Customs of the Jews in the Yemen*. Tel Aviv: Am Oved, 1967. [Hebrew]

————. "Jewish-Arab Relations in Yemen," in Y. Yeshayahu and Y. Tobi, eds., *The Jews of Yemen*, pp. 147-163. Jerusalem: Ben-Zvi Institute, 1975.

van den Ban, A. W. "Locality Group Differences in the Adoption of New Farm Practices," *Rural Sociology* 25:308-320, 1960.

Vester, Bertha Spafford. *Our Jerusalem: An American Family in the Holy City, 1881-1949*. Garden City, N. Y.: Doubleday, 1950.

Wallerstein, Immanuel. "Social Conflict in Post-Independence Black Africa: The Concepts of Race and Status-Group Reconsidered," in E. Q. Campbell, ed., *Racial Tensions and National Identity*. Nashville: Vanderbilt University Press, 1972.

Weingrod, Alex. *Reluctant Pioneers: Village Development in Israel*. Ithaca: Cornell University Press, 1966.

————. "Recent Trends in Israeli Ethnicity," *Ethnic and Racial Studies* 2:55-65, 1979.

————. ed. *Studies in Israeli Ethnicity: After the Ingathering*. New York: Gordon and Breach, 1985.

Weinreich, Max. "The Reality of Jewishness Versus the Ghetto Myth: The Sociolinguistic Roots of Yiddish," in *To Honor Roman Jakobson: Essays on the Occasion of His Seventieth Birthday*, Vol. III, pp. 2199-2211. The Hague: Mouton, 1967.

Weintraub, Dov, et al. *Immigration and Social Change: Agricultural Settlements of New Immigrants of Israel*. Manchester: Manchester University Press, 1971.

Wenner, Manfred. *Modern Yemen: 1918-1966*. Baltimore: Johns Hopkins University Press, 1967.

White, Naomi Rosh. "Ethnicity, Culture and Cultural Pluralism," *Ethnic and Racial Studies* 1:139-153, 1978.

Willner, Dorothy. *Nation-Building and Community in Israel*. Princeton, N. J.: Princeton University Press, 1969.

Yancey, W. L., E. P. Ericksen, and R. N. Juliani. "Emergent Ethnicity: A Review and Reformulation," *American Sociological Review* 41:391-403, 1976.

Yeshayahu, Yisrael and Yosef Tobi. *The Jews of Yemen*. Jerusalem: Ben-Zvi Institute, 1975. [Hebrew]

Yuchtman-Yaar, Ephraim and Moshe Semyenov. "Ethnic Inequality in Israeli Schools and Sports: An Expectation-States Approach," *American Journal of Sociology* 85:576-590, 1979.

Zimbrolt, Carol F. *Ideology, Policy and Identity: Family Planning in a Yemenite Community in Israel*. Ph. D. dissertation, University of Minnesota, 1984.

Zinger, Zvi (Yaron). "State of Israel (1948-72)," in *Immigration and Settlement*, pp. 50-74. Jerusalem: Keter, 1973.

Index